A Preferred Blur

(Reflections, Inspections, And Travel In All Directions 2007)

Henry Rollins

A Preferred Blur © 2009 Henry Rollins

Second Printing

Published by
2.13.61
7510 Sunset Blvd #602
Los Angeles, CA 90046
www.21361.com / www.henryrollins.com

Back cover photo: Charles Previtire
Design: Dave Chapple www.chappledesign.com

2.13.61

Thanks: Carol, Heidi, Road Manager Ward,
Mitch Bury of Adams Mass.

JOE COLE 04.10.61 – 12.19.91

00. How It Starts

10-27-06 LA CA: 2150 hrs. I have been off the road for several weeks. Besides a brief trip to Europe and Washington DC two weeks ago, I have been here in Los Angeles. I have been going to sleep early and waking up early. It's left over jet lag from the trip to France and I have kept it up so I am more effective at the office.

I go to the office every day and throw myself into whatever the task is as intently as I can so I can stay distracted from my thoughts. I come back here to the house and do the same thing until I am too tired to keep my eyes open.

It has been very difficult for me to adjust to the post-tour environment. I trained for the last band tour for four months straight and then toured for a solid month and then came back here to stillness and quiet. This is nothing new, this is always the situation. When I am on tour, I am living in a high-stress and result-oriented performance environment. I go from that to this without any half measure. It's always difficult but sometimes the transition is more trying than other times.

With no stage to be on, no obligation, no need for strictness and focus, I become depressed and unable to keep my self-contempt at a distance. There is no sense of duty here. It's Los Angeles, a place where adult men dress the same as twenty-somethings and dye their hair to look young. It's a filthy place full of violent, dangerous and vapid people. It has its share of good people, of course, but it's Los Angeles. It's very hard for me to be here after being out on the road.

The only thing that seems to keep me together, besides working out, is staying on my own as much as I can. When I am alone, it's a relief. There's no one here I want to spend time with or know more than I do already. The workouts are hard to draw inspiration from because they are without purpose. It is nothing more than maintenance.

I go to sleep depressed. I wake up early in the pre-dawn darkness feeling depressed and violent. I have been working on the notes for my radio show a bit too much. It's all I have at the moment so I over-work on them. I don't know what else to do with myself. I have been doing so many push ups I am starting to get the same pain in my right shoulder that I got nine years ago.

I have been wondering what the hell I will do next. The show I do on IFC will take up some time, writing the parts and researching guests and topics. The aggravation I go through with the producers of the show will take up some time too, as it always does. At this point, I can't see how we will be able to work with each other again after this season, I believe it's mutual. Two of the three are ok, it's just the one of them who wears me out. He's not a bad person, we just don't get along all that well. At the end of the day we get the work done and that's all that matters.

I need something to work towards, if I don't have that, it's very difficult to get through the days. As the last few weeks have passed, I have been getting more and more depressed and more and more angry. I have been reading as much as I can. I am stupid and working on getting some more knowledge. I have taken to reading while standing up as the books I have been reading are above my level and actually put me to sleep a few pages in. I started punching myself in the arm at one point because I was getting so mad at myself for shutting down. I know what it is, it's the truth of my below average intellect hitting its limits and crashing. I write things down as often as I can and read them over and over: JDAM is Joint Direct Attack Munitions, FISA is the Foreign Intelligence Surveillance Act. This is the stuff I want to know so I drill it into my head until it sticks.

Things started to look up the other day and I am starting to see the shape of what could be something worth living for. Management told me that some shows I had wanted to do had come through as well as some film work that I had been waiting to hear back about. For the last two days I have been looking at schedules and trying to figure out how to take it all and shape it into a mountain to climb. Basically, I am like Captain Willard in Saigon. I need a mission or there is noth-

Henry Rollins

ing for me. I don't miss anyone living. I don't want to go out on a fucking date with a female. I don't want the phone to ring. I don't want to know any more people than I already do and don't want to know any of them more than I know them now. I want days and nights that are hard to get through, where I will have to utilize all I know and have to force myself to be brave and reach for it. If I don't have that, then I am lazy and good for absolutely nothing. This may sound extreme or completely off the course but that's how it is for me. I'm tired of the bullshit. I'm not talking about anyone else's, just mine.

So, it looks like there might be some travel and some odd jobs coming up. I am starting to see the shape of the mountain.

For the last several days I have been thinking constantly about the Plain of Jars in Laos. I saw some shots of the area in a documentary recently and since then the place has been on my mind. Just the three words together sound at once surreal and primitive. This morning it occurred to me that I am going to Laos and am going to the Plain of Jars and so I better start learning about Laos and figuring out when I am going. Today, when I wasn't doing other things, I went online and dragged off a lot of pictures and information on Laos and the Plain of Jars. Over the weekend I am going to start learning what I can. 2231 hrs.

10-28-06 LA CA: 1639 hrs. I spent the day at the office working on the radio show and learning things online. I'm back home now and have fed myself and will workout in a couple of hours.

I was thinking this morning about a few things I saw on the news in the build up to the mid-term elections. It's easy to waste time on non-issues like the flap with Michael J. Fox's PSA on Parkinson's and Stem Cell Research getting mocked by conservative talk radio personality Rush Limbaugh, who also accused Fox of acting more symptomatic than he really is. Understandably, many people were offended. I hesitate to use the word "understandably" in that last sentence, to be offended by Rush Limbaugh is to take the guy way too seriously. What would anyone expect from him, hearts and flowers, a hug? The angry response to the things he says is like when the audience boos and hisses at the villain professional wrestler when he enters the ring. Even Katie Couric couldn't help digging into Fox when she interviewed him recently. These people seem to forget how they held up Terri Schiavo as a political ploy to advance their agenda. That's how it is. That's how the game is played. The left and right both demonize and attempt to paint the other side into a corner. I'm not saying they are the same, I know where my vote is going, too much attention is paid to the Rush Limbaughs and Ann Coulters of the airwaves. Recently, I had some layover time at an airport so I went to a store near my gate and read several pages of Bill O'Reilly's new book <u>Culture Warrior</u>. It's an easy read, there's not many words on the page, the type is big, and in the pages I read there was nothing of any great import. The only thing that's troubling to me is that it's a bestselling title. Anyone who buys the book and reads it can't really consider themselves a "reader" just as anyone walking out of a McDonald's can't say they've had a meal. The same may be said of any of my books but none of mine are bestsellers. Perhaps that's a good thing.

And another thing: When you read about all that's being done to disenfranchise certain people from voting and how suspect and sometimes out and out criminal some things appear concerning the run up to the elections, Americans should remember the Katrina disaster and see it for the lesson it is and the clear warning it sends. What's the lesson? The people running America Inc. don't care about poor people and would like it very much if they just disappeared. They will deny it and cite many examples of how they are working to make America a better place and doing all they can for the common good. They aren't actually and it's never been more glaringly apparent than now. Again, to those who think this is a bad thing, what were you expecting? Equality? That's a bit much to ask of those drunk on entitlement and insulated by wealth. It's the broke ass, meth lab making, below the poverty line, NASCAR watching, sub-literate, alcoholic, overweight, prone to crime element who boycott The Dixie Chicks and vote for people who send their jobs overseas that I feel bad for. Only kidding. They can go fuck themselves. Early this morning I was thinking about a sold out racetrack, thousands of people at a NASCAR event. There is a rumbling sound as an enormous sheet of metal covers the top of the massive oval shaped stadium. The entire structure starts to shake as metal seatbelts spring forth from either side of the spectator's seats and lock them securely in. The cars all come to a screeching burning rubber and metal on metal halt as everyone in the place is slammed by the increasing g-force as the rocket engines underneath the stadium roar. Over the public address system the new space explorers hear, "Welcome to the future. Yes, you're all Martians now. We finally figured out somewhere to put you. We were thinking of Canada but that's too close for comfort. Now you will be able to teach Intelligent Design and hold your God Hates Fags signs without getting teased by the cultural elite. Good luck and god speed." That would make a NASCAR fan out of me.

10-29-06 LA CA: 1510 hrs. I read a good chunk of Michel Gordon's Cobra II a little while ago. I am trying to make more sense of the initial invasion of Iraq and how one comes to the conclusion that it was the thing to do after getting attacked on September 11. I have learned a lot in just the first fifty pages. I got a lot from the book Fiasco, by Thomas Ricks, but I think I might learn more from this one.

In a couple of hours I am leaving for UCLA to check out Pere Ubu. Their new album, Why I Hate Women, is really great. I am listening to their previous album St. Arkansas right now as it's been awhile since I've checked it out.

I woke up after only a few hours of sleep. It occurred to me that I have a lot to get done and my heart was thudding in my chest and I felt out of breath for a second. That can't be good. I have to get learned up on the United Arab Emirates, I have to learn more about Israel and Lebanon as individual countries as well as territories in conflict. I have to learn more about Hezbollah and I have to drag more things off the internet about Laos. Laos is a slightly lower priority. I also have to learn about Djibouti, Africa. It looks like I will be in the UAE and Djibouti in December and in January I'll be in Israel for several days. I have been to some of these places before but don't know all that I should. I have my work cut out for me. I am out on a USO tour December 19-26. I end up in Dubai somehow and do a talking show there on the 27th and then have some days before three shows in Israel that will be filmed for an IFC special. I have a choice of staying out there somewhere or coming back to the USA for some days and then flying back out again. I reckon I should stay out there somewhere. I have been thinking that Israel might be the place to go. Perhaps spending some time there will let me get a feel of the place and make the shows better. It has to be better than coming all the way back here.

I read all the books I can but I know that there's nothing in any of those books that can teach me what I really need to know. I need experience. My common sense is almost non-existent. The only way I really learn anything is to get out there and force myself to deal with it as best I can. It's the only way I get anything of any real use. I need situations that force me to learn and, as usual, it's always the hard way for me. I have an almost uncanny ability to do precisely the wrong thing. The equation I have been using for many years means more and more to me as time goes on: knowledge without mileage equals bullshit. That's been the thing that gets me out the door more often than not. I can read all the books and do all the thinking I want but without getting out into it, what good is anything I know? I am therefore I go. That's it.

Tomorrow night I am going to be on the Tom Green show. I have no idea what that will entail. Apparently it tapes at his house. His people contacted me a few times asking if I wanted to be a guest. I passed and then it came up again and I decided to do it. I have seen the guy's show when he was on MTV and he was funny but I have no interest in being on the show. I'm doing it because I know what it's like to ask someone to be on a television show and how it feels when they say yes and when they say no. It's a relief when they say yes so I figured it's a good thing to say yes to someone's request. The shoot isn't all that far from here and it won't take long. It's after office hours so I can get all my day time stuff done.

There is no Tuesday night radio show because Engineer X wants to go to some party or something. I fully understand that so we taped the show last week. That means I will have Halloween night here without having to go to the station. I was thinking about it and perhaps I'll work here or at the office but I will try and write for as many hours as I can. Halloween night has a lot of sentimental resonance for me and will be the last night of my favorite month of the year so I better say goodbye to it as long as I can.

10-31-06 LA CA: 2121 hrs. I meant to get to this earlier but things took longer than I thought they would. I got a lot done at the office today and that makes me feel pretty good. I worked on upcoming broadcasts for the radio show. I am trying to get ahead of them. I am making good shows and am about a month ahead and am closing in on finishing the broadcast planning for the year. I am leaving spaces to mix in new arrivals. I am trying to get ahead enough to where I am into next year's shows because if all goes well, I will be on the road and need to have them prepared.

For the last several minutes, I was listening to Charley Patton but have switched to Generation X's 2nd album Valley Of The Dolls because I used to listen to this one a lot in DC and there's about 2.5 hours left in October and the record makes me think of DC.

This is the thing I wanted to write about tonight: There's a photo in the beginning of my book Get In The Van of a group of people gathered together on a sidewalk. I have the photo framed and it usually hangs on the wall here but at the moment it is propped up on the table on my right. It was taken by Jay Rabinowitz on 10-31-80. It was the last Halloween before I left town to be in Black Flag. It's an important photograph for me. I saw it very soon after it was taken and it struck me immediately. As the years go by the photograph takes on more meaning, the image resonates deeper within me. If the information on the flyer I have is correct, the photo was taken at a small club called The Chancery at 704 New Jersey Avenue. The Teen Idles were playing and the flyer says a band called The Voltags were the opening band. I don't remember The Voltags but I know for sure it was a Teen Idles show. Anyway, the photo at first glance is just a bunch of young people gathered together, very aware there's a camera in front of them, and acting up for it. A lot of the people are smiling and you can tell there is familiarity amongst them. No one looks like a stranger to anyone else in the group. No one looks like they just showed up and are trying to fit in. When I look at the photograph, my impression is that the group are trying to impress upon the photographer that they are close and are proud of the unity and very much want the photographer to know it and capture that fact with his camera. Dead center in the front there's a guy in a leather jacket with "The Teen Idles" written in duct tape on the back, that's Geordie Grindle, the guitar player in the Teen Idles. The next four people are in a staggered row. On the left is Eddie Janney, he's on some of the best records the Dischord label ever made like The Rites Of Spring and One Last Wish. On his left is me. My right hand is on his left arm as we are all shoving each other around. I am looking right down the barrel of the lens. Someone's hand is on my left shoulder, I don't know who it is. The person's face is obscured by two guys to my left. The first one is named Jay, he is grabbing a guy named Bill. Bill is looking a little glassy eyed because he's a bit drunk and he's already rebroken his nose again and his shirt has his blood all over it. Looking over Bill's left shoulder is Jeff Nelson and Ian MacKaye, the drummer and bass player of The Teen Idles. Other people in the group include Michael Hampton of S.O.A, Faith, and One Last Wish. I can see Kim Kane of the Slickee Boys behind Ian's left shoulder. Chris Edwards, who worked at the ice cream store with me, is in the picture and so is Nathan Strejcek, who was the singer in The Teen Idles. There's a lot of other people in the picture, some names I remember, several I don't. I do remember the smallness of the scene and how everything seemed to be full of meaning. 10-31-80 was a Friday night. It started off well enough but it didn't end all that great for me and the bass player of the band I was in. The poor bastard hit his head on something, perhaps someone else running around and I had to take him to the hospital. He had a pretty big knot on his head. It looked a lot worse than it was. I don't remember everything that happened that night. I know I took him to the ER and then I think his parents came and took it from there. I don't know if I went back to the show or not. I don't think I did. Like I said, the photo itself is good but if you didn't know anyone in it, you might not spend much time looking at it. For me, it's the end of some things. It's the last October I spent in DC. It was the end of my teenage years as I was to turn 20 fairly soon after. It was the end of a phase of music in our small scene. In a few weeks after the photo was taken, Minor Threat would play their first show. I was at that one. The idea of luck is foreign to me but I feel lucky to have been at that show. I look at this photograph on every Halloween night I can and remember those times. By 10-31-81, I was onstage with Black Flag and things were very different.

I was in DC for several months after that photo was taken. I left DC in the summer of 1981. I remember the autumn of 1980 being a very poignant one for me. I worked a lot of hours at the ice cream store on the night shift. The weather was cool and there were not many customers so I had a lot of time to myself. I remember feeling very frustrated with my life. I was lonely and where I was headed was unclear, actually, I had no real direction at all. I figured that this was my job and this was what life was like. You worked all the time and hung out with your friends when you could. That there was a world out there to be explored and things to be done was not clear to me. My world view was very small. I had a minimum wage job that was boring and I knew enough to know that I was going to be over the place sooner than later. I think of that place often and sometimes miss the simplicity of those times. It's a pizza place now and sometimes when I am in DC I will go in, get a bottle of water and just sit in there for a little while and think of those times. I try to avoid thinking about this stuff because I don't think it leads to anything but I still do it frequently. Sometimes it's something in the air, a smell, the temperature, a song, whatever, and I will be back in those thoughts, wandering around. Sometimes I retreat to those times when I am unhappy with the present, another thing I don't like doing but I do it a lot. I know one needs to live in the present and I try but sometimes it's extremely difficult for me.

So tonight I say goodbye to October. I am glad I got to see DC for a few days recently and I'm glad the weather was good for walking. I am waiting here, day after day, throwing myself into work to distract myself. I am having trouble figuring out what else to do. I am waiting for the schedule to firm up so I can see when I will be able to get to Laos and what the final deal on Israel is. Either I choke life or it chokes me. Right now it's bleeding me slowly. I get out of the car every day and walk into the office and it's a relief to be out of bed. A few hours later, I can't wait to get out of there and come here and then a few hours after that, all I want to do is shut myself off into a dreamless sleep. This conduct passes for fucked up and it makes me mad when I am this way.

11-11-06 LA CA: 2350 hrs. Hours ago, I watched a documentary that I had seen before about the Marines of Lima Company who suffered many casualties in Iraq. There were interviews with some of them after they had returned from war and they told the interviewer that things back home didn't seem real to them and that things moved too slow and they wanted to get back out there. I understand how they feel a lot more than I want to. Their wives and parents no longer understand them. They are different people. I know how that is. During the commercial breaks they had advertisements for the Army. There's a new line they're pushing where the soldier says that he weighed the risks and he still decided to go in. No doubt, this is to try and increase the ever decreasing number of people who are joining the Armed Forces. They will tell you that more people than ever are joining the AF but it's just statistical shuffling. These people are coming back with their heads all fucked up, disconnected from everything they knew. Some will re-adjust, a lot won't.

I stay to myself as much as I can. On the weekends I go out and get groceries and come back here or go to the office. That's what I did today. I just worked on trips to go on so I can get through more time. It's late on Saturday night. I have not spoken to anyone today. Alone in this house makes sense. It's all I need. Being non-reliant on people for contentment is a strength. Even when I feel like I want to be around people, I starve it out and make it die. I think it's the right thing to do. 0014 hrs.

Henry Rollins

01. American Landscape

12–02–06 LA CA: 2225 hrs. I spent a good part of the day at the office working on mail order. I usually go to the office on the weekends, even though I spend the week there. I try to be at the office more than I am here. It's one of the ways I get away from myself. I find something simple to do and do it. I clean the floors with a wet towel, clean flat surfaces, wash the car, work way too much on my radio show that no one listens to. I have many activities to keep myself away from myself. I only buy enough groceries for a couple of days so I have to go to the market a few times a week, besides the office and the radio station, it's one of the only places I go on a regular basis. Most of the time I am inside the house or the office, trying to keep busy. Distracting myself from myself takes up most of my waking hours. If I don't, I get mad at everything.

Sometimes I can figure out what it is that makes me so angry and sometimes I am just angry and I don't know why. The only way I have found to deal with it is to be alone as much as I can. Life for me is more bearable this way. It is not for me to judge anyone. Judgment just clouds my view and slows me down. I am no better or worse than a man who went from room to room and killed his family with a lead pipe. That's not to say that people can't be aggravating. Some of the things people say make me mad, politicians, pundits, there's a lot of bullshit and there's a lot to be angry at. All those men I visit in the hospitals who have lost limbs, it's all so extreme and sad and hopeless and stupid. I walk out of those experiences with an anger I don't know what to do with.

Expressing yourself with violence against another person inside the city limits is not advisable. When you appear in court, you will suffer the institutionalized and standardized consequences to your emotional and irrational loss of control. Imagine hauling off and punching someone in the face and then doing time for that five seconds of release. Not worth it, never worth it.

A little over two weeks from now will be the 15th anniversary of my friend Joe Cole's death. Besides leaving Washington DC for Los Angeles to join Black Flag, it is the most life altering experience I have had. The event changed me in ways that I am aware of and probably in many I am not. There are things I learned from the incident that can only be learned by going through something like that. What I learned, I cannot unlearn or forget. I cannot stop knowing what I know. That's the problem. Since that night almost 15 years ago, I have not forged any close relationships with anyone. The women who work at the company and Mike, who was my road manager for 8 years, they know me very well. A good part of that is due to proximity as much as anything else. They are very good people but we are very different from each other.

In the 15 years since Joe was killed, I have seen and done a lot but the event itself is still very vivid in my mind. It is with me always and as time goes on, continues to be a factor in my life.

I hold no anger at the shooter. That may strike some people as odd or not aggressive enough, what have you, but I really don't. I have come to the conclusion that the shooter was an assassin dispatched by America. He was selected from millions, trained and given everything needed to maximize his lethal potential. He was then sent into the urban American killing fields to make it a better place.

Make it a better place? How can shooting an unarmed man in California make America a better place? Here's how: when whites get shot by non-whites, it oils the gears of many profit-motivated American mechanisms. Crank up the levels of fear with real life homicide and profiling and stereotyping becomes rational behavior. Gun sales go up, property value in "safe" neighborhoods goes up, more parents pay more money to send their children to private schools, more gated communities, more separation, ignorance and resentment, racial tension thickens, more people bonded by fear, more arrests, more false arrests, more inmates means more prisons means more contracts and more money. More revenue has been made from Joe getting killed than had he not been. Joe's death helped profits

Henry Rollins

increase and as any board chairman will tell you, this is what it's all about. That the shooter was eventually going to shoot someone was almost an absolute. He had been in training from the day he was born. He was someone's investment and he paid off more than he'll ever know. That is why I don't want my five minutes armed with a hammer alone in a room with the shooter handcuffed to a chair. America is at war at all times: crime, drugs, terror, Christmas. Peace, it seems, would be our undoing. The belts would slip, the mighty engine would lose compression, it would be a mess. I have to go do something else now. 2251 hrs.

12-05-06 LA CA: 0836 hrs. It has been interesting to check the reactions to the Senator-elect James Webb/president Bush scrap. Webb has offended right wing pundits for being "rude" to the president. They seem so shocked and it was nothing really. At a recent White House reception, Bush asked the Senator, "How's your boy?" in reference to Webb's son, a Marine currently fighting in Iraq who recently had a close call in combat. Apparently, the president had been warned to be sensitive on the topic with Webb. Webb replied, "I'd like to get them out of Iraq, Mr. President." It is reported that Bush then said, "I didn't ask you that, I asked how he's doing." Webb replied, "That's between me and my boy." And that's about all there was to it. Webb said later that he had the urge to slug the president. James Webb, incidentally, is an ex-Marine and a Vietnam War vet and could probably put Bush on the carpet pretty quickly. Who cares? It's a non-event. Bush's question wasn't out of line to me and perhaps Webb was a little heated on the topic, being a father of a son in harm's way and all. Even though the event is days old and no one was killed, it still seems to be an issue. The press is so protective of Bush, it's hard to take. Less was made of Danny Devito's drunken teasing of the president during his appearance on <u>The View</u> recently, I guess because he's just one of those Hollywood elites and doesn't really count. I think Bush, Fox News, and their ever dwindling fan base should see these incidents as the start of a wave of highly visible dissent. The reaction of Fox News host Bill O'Reilly reminds me of a bully who gets shoved in the schoolyard. There is that momentary disbelief that anyone would dare and then there's the confusion as to what to do next. O'Reilly knows that Webb is a decorated Marine and was in his youth a Golden Gloves boxer, in other words, a real man. O'Reilly has to tread carefully. This is an administration that lies and kills, profits from blood and sacrifice and pillages the world in the name of Democracy. It cannot be surprising to any of them that some people are done being nice. Bush isn't man enough or smart enough to do the job and he and his supporters know it. Now all they can do is prolong, deny, evade, and wait for the indictments. They stand around, look at each other and ask, "Do you smell blood? I don't smell any blood." Everyone looks at the ground and then upwards as if it's going to rain and then looks at each other and says, "No. No blood here." But they can smell blood because they are covered in it. They are head to toe in American and Iraqi blood. The disenchanted and outraged are circling ever closer. Unafraid now, they take tentative nips at the fatted hind quarters because they smell the blood and their anger and hunger overrides their usual docile nature that a broken life of servitude has seared into their psyche. Have you ever seen a bully catch a couple of knuckles in the ear from a wildly thrown punch from someone who had finally had enough? Have you ever seen the expression on the bully's face? The expression says, "It's arrived, the end." It has. 0858 hrs.

12-09-06 LA CA: 0244 hrs. I can't sleep. A few hours ago I got my travel information for the upcoming journey and it made me charged up and mad. I don't know why I get mad. I guess it's because I'm not out there already. I get hyped up and feel so close to death I can taste it because I feel so alive. This is going to be a good one. I don't care if I make it out or not. I see the rest of my life inside the timeframe of the trip, never past it. Not at this stage at least. When I think of the trip, I get almost tunnel visioned on it to where it's all I think about even when I am doing other things. When I am here it feels like my blood gets thicker by the day and little by little I slip into a rut of regularity. My resolve weakens, the days pass unnoticed. The serrated blade turns scalpel smooth and I slice like veal. I like being in foreign lands, walking amongst strangers. When the setting is unfamiliar, then I use more of my brain. I have to pull myself from thought to thought like I'm climbing rope. When I am here, life shoves me around. When I am out there, I shove life around. It's the only time I feel like I am really living. I'd take a year of that over a decade of this any time. Nothing makes sense here. I don't understand why people do what they do here. I go to the grocery store and people just stand around, looking at food or into space. They talk on the phone and drive their carts into other people, sometimes me. They leave their carts in the middle of the aisle and just kind of stand near it and don't seem to be interested in actually getting any food. Last night, I was in line waiting to cash out and watched a woman get three calls on her phone, one after another. How do these people ever get a chance to define themselves when all they do is talk on the phone? I was walking into the grocery store a few weeks ago and saw a man parking a huge Hummer. I just stopped, looked at him through the windshield and started laughing like an idiot. I couldn't stop. I kept thinking, "Operation Grocery Store" and it made me laugh more. The guy wasn't out of the vehicle by the time I walked into the store so I don't know what he looked like. Marines get killed in those things, he gets errands done in his. What a bitch.

A guy wrote me a few hours ago. He's getting divorced. He gave the ex the house, all the stuff in it, and she still wants more. She won't let him see the kid and he's working an extra job to try and keep it all together. Not all divorces are this bad but I don't see why anyone would roll the dice on marriage to find out how it's going to go. I've never seen any proof that says being attached to someone is better than not. 0321 hrs.

12-10-06 LA CA: 0023 hrs. I am listening to one of the <u>Ethiopiques</u> series CDs at the moment. I didn't go to the office today except briefly to look some stuff up. I went to the grocery store and tripped on people. There's never any room there with the way people conduct themselves in that place. Just like the other day, people just standing around, time just flying by.

There is an organization called Operation Second Chance run by a really great woman named Cindy McGrew. OSC helps out veterans of Iraq and Afghanistan when they return to America. I met her at Walter Reed Hospital months ago. Several weeks ago, Cindy was out getting presents for soldiers and was mugged at the Lakeforest Mall in Gaithersburg, MD and beaten pretty badly. I wrote her yesterday, she's still a bit shook up but she's ok. I have been thinking about her the last few days. She wouldn't have to be getting presents for soldiers if Bush and his squad of pussies didn't start their fake war, would she? No, she wouldn't. Another thing that is Bush's fault.

I heard something on the news about a week ago that made me so mad that I nearly broke down. I heard that a flag draped coffin carrying an American soldier was loaded out of a Northwest Airlines plane onto a cart carrying luggage, so said Cynthia Hoag who witnessed it in Rochester, NY. I just looked up an article online about it. Here's a quote from her: "It looked awful, just awful. Maybe we made too much out of it, but it was very disturbing to us. If that had been my son, I would have been very upset." I went looking for things people were writing about the incident and there are people accusing Ms. Hoag of lying and that since she has no video or photographic documentation, she can't prove it and it probably didn't happen. Come on! She's a 56 year-old former fucking Army reservist, she and three other people, including her sister-in-law, saw what they saw, so don't try and call her a liar. Don't these people get tired of lying? Or do they tell so many that they're not even aware of it anymore? This example is all you need to know. This is what a soldier's sacrifice means to some people here. Something else that's the president's fault. He's the worst president ever. No other president comes close, none. There will be people who will stick up for him but they are idiots and no one is afraid of them and no one cares what they say. It's not even worth losing your temper over what these idiots say anymore, there's no point they can make that holds water and everyone knows it. All I can do at this point is perform custodial duties. I clean up in the wake of the Bush administration. That's why I do work for the USO, I am on clean up duty. Bush and his criminal sissy brigade make messes all over the world and I go in and help manage the situation. From now on, it will be the private sector that will be there for the Vets, Katrina survivors, etc. There's no use in asking the Government to do anything. They don't seem to want to work. Citizens below a certain pay grade are just a fucking annoyance to them.

The only people I spoke to today was a very young child who called my number for some reason, said hello after I said hello and then hung up and the guy at the grocery store. I call that a pretty good day. I am feeling better than last night, not as mad. The workout helped and knowing that I am leaving here soon has me focusing on the pack and what I have to do in the days coming up.

I work hard to feel better about myself. It is very difficult sometimes. If I can get the workout done, get some writing done that is true and hard to get out and get some hard reading done, then I feel a little better. The less I talk to people, the more I stay on my own, the better it is for me. It's a good feeling when I get lonely and I just stay to myself and let the loneliness starve to death. There's no one I would call anyway. When I really want to talk to someone, that's precisely the time not to. It's at those moments when I have the opportunity to learn something, to get a little stronger. I was born into an unstable environment. All my childhood memories are attached to nervousness, anxiety, instability, and weakness. I have been trying to strengthen myself ever since I realized that I wasn't going to get anything like that from the parental units. It's not a problem. I blame no one but myself. As soon as you're born you're on your own. I should have left home at the first possible opportunity and done four years in the Army. I would be better for it now. I didn't and now I grapple with myself and my contempt for life. Fuck life. Life isn't beautiful. Life isn't wonderful. It just isn't. An idiotic weak piece of shit person shot and killed Joe Cole for no reason. What's the good part of that? Mick Geyer gets cancer that eats up his spine and kills him. The upside of that is, what, that I had a chance to know him and I am the better for it? A young woman with two kids gets the phone call she has had nightmares about: Her husband has been killed in the Al Anbar Province in Iraq and his remains are hanging out with some fucking Samsonite luggage at an airport in upstate New York. PTL!

I am thankful for every piece of hate mail I get. All the misspelled, misguided, half thought out, xenophobic, douche bag, unsigned drivel I get from sub-literate products of poor education and intelligent design who tell me I am a communist just strengthens and emboldens me.

12-16-06 LA CA: 0024 hrs. I wish I could get to sleep and get up early but I am not tired. I am wired and very anxious. I have been this way all week. I am out of here in a few days and am wound up. I have been trying to work out of the slump I have been in lately. I have been too distracted by the upcoming month of travel to get my head clear to do anything. The week has been overwhelmingly underproductive and I am mad at myself. I was at the office all week and I got some things done but not enough. I have shows coming up and only this evening at a production meeting did I get my head around what I have to do. I get mad at myself all the time, I don't think I am doing enough most of the time and it makes me angry and leads me to further frustration. I have been waking up at all hours for the last several nights and on some nights only getting 3 to 4 hours of sleep and then falling asleep at my desk. This is a hard time of the year for me anyway but for some reason, this December has been harder to get through than past ones.

I have been reading a lot of articles online and greatly admire how some writers are able to put their thoughts across with such clarity, the ideas they express, so well rendered and presented. I try to learn from their writing in an attempt to make mine better.

There have been a few things that I saw in the news that have been bugging me. One of them happened a couple of days ago in Starke, FL at the Florida State Prison. Convicted killer Angel Diaz, 55, took 34 minutes to expire after receiving a lethal injection at 1800 hrs. At one point, a doctor administered a second dose of whatever it is they give the condemned to stop their heart. From what the articles I read said, it took him about three times longer than usual to die. It is difficult for me to explain why this disturbs me but I will try. I am against the Death Penalty™. On the other hand, I cannot argue with someone who is for it. I respect the reasons on the other side of the argument. A man abducts your daughter, kills her and leaves her in the woods and you are given the choice between the killer living for years in prison or being executed and you say, hell yes, kill the bastard. I see where you're coming from completely. I just think that nothing good comes of it. The girl doesn't come back, the desired closure never arrives and the pain stays for the rest of your life no matter what. Meanwhile, the Death Penalty™ doesn't seem to be much of a deterrent and it's always depressing when I see these "death chambers" and all these rituals like the prison guard saying, "Dead man walking!" The sanctioned death is as awful as the one that caused it. I'm not even going to waste time with the innocent man getting put to death scenario. Let's just stick to the repulsive and utterly obscene act of an execution carried out by men with their corny solemn face act. It is an act, too. It's so lame, like bad television acting. They attempt to portray some kind of decorum when all they do is amplify the overwhelming and pathetic obscenity of what they're doing. It is, in fact, complete bullshit posturing. You can call me anything you want if you don't agree and I will just take it because I see the other side of it too. I understand that kind of anger and hurt completely. But it's just too easy in my opinion. To act out from that impulse is to commit a kind of intellectual suicide. Again, if someone thinks that is just wrong, I understand. Since the Angel Diaz incident, Florida State Governor Jeb Bush has suspended further executions in the state. I am guessing that's only temporary. Starke is where Ted Bundy was executed by electrocution in 1989. That's as brutal as anything Bundy did to all those women. I am not so naïve to think that homicide will ever cease but I bet if we really wanted to, we could see it greatly decrease in our life time, but I also think there are mechanisms at work to make sure it never decreases. I am at the point in my life where I just want to take the harder road that leads to the higher ground. The Death Penalty™ and executions are a shortcut. Our public education system is a failure and a cop out. I really believe if we really wanted to, if it was truly a priority, we could, in a few generations, have the average IQ of America elevated to such a degree that crime, unwanted pregnancy and a lot of other things that keeps America from realizing all it could be would noticeably decrease. Why that isn't an alarming bullet point for any president his or her first day in office is beyond me. I think a president should fucking shock the entire nation during the inaugural speech. The new president should inform the American people that a lot of them are not as educated as they need to be and that it's time to get to work and the work will get done and that's that. What would you do? Rebel and stay stupid? If every person in America had a good education, we could save the world. Yes, we could. That's my story and I'm sticking to it. I failed to get to the other things that were bugging me but failure is a repeating event in my life and while I don't like it, I have grown accustomed to it. Good night.

12-18-06 LA CA: 2304 hrs. In about an hour, it will be 15 years since Joe Cole was killed. I have a lot on my mind. Joe is part of it and as well, some interesting things happened yesterday and today. I will write about it on the plane tomorrow. This night has become a strange anniversary. For the past 15 years I have sat alone on this night somewhere, re-living the event and all the things Joe and I said and did until he was killed. I never have any new thoughts about it, the story never has a different ending. I always wonder where the guy who shot at us is and if he's alive, what is he thinking? Does he know it's this night? Does he feel any different about what he did all these years later? It does no good to think these thoughts, nothing comes of it, it's just what I do every year on this night. I also wonder what Joe would be doing now and what things would be in his life. Again, it's not thoughts that do me any good. Joe is gone and everyone who knew him is left to deal with the empty space.

The event changed me in a lot of ways. I have written about it before. Getting put through all that ruined a lot of things for me, or perhaps took the filters off my senses so I see into things too much. The experience made me angry, very angry, to where it sometimes seems like a perpetual state of mad that I am in. It also made me not exactly brave but perhaps fearless and a bit reckless. Being alone helps. 2317 hrs.

02. Dubai To DC

In between the 20th and the 27th of December, I went on a USO tour that took me through the United Arab Emirates, Qatar, Djibouti and Bahrain. I will save those entries for another time. Onward!

12-28-06 Dubai UAE: 2130 hrs. Last night was the end of another USO tour that took me through the United Arab Emirates, Qatar, Djibouti and then to Bahrain, where I flew out of very early this morning. I arrived here at the massive, caterpillar-shaped Dubai Airport. The structure is a sight to behold. It looks like a massive insect larva. As we taxied in, I saw men on top of it working away as they are building, relentlessly adding onto the damn thing. I was met by the promoter reps for the show I am doing here tomorrow. We went immediately to the Iranian Consulate to see if my visa came through and it had. One of the promoter reps is Iranian and she was able to get around a lot of obstacles that would have stopped me cold or at least held me up for who knows how long. I am going to Tehran on new year's day for almost a week. I have wanted to go there for a long time and hopefully I get there and see some things I have never seen before. Anyway, we went from there to this massive shopping mall, The Mall of the Emirates, where I had to sign things at the Virgin record store there and do a phone interview with someone at a radio station. After that I was deposited at this completely over the top hotel and here I am.

There is much to note about Dubai. From the seemingly endless amount of cranes across the skyline and the already countless tall buildings, it's as if they wanted an entire modern city with cutting edge construction built virtually overnight. I have never seen so much construction in my life. Anything I write will sound like exaggeration but it's really amazing. From my window I can see the tops of the buildings along this highway and most of them have heliports.

Dubai, it is said, will be the home of the world's tallest building. I was told the number of floors is still a secret but the building is projected to be about a kilometer high. I am not exaggerating when I say it looks like a couple of Manhattan New York's strung together building wise when you go down the highway here. I was told that this will be the playground of the world at some point. I am not putting Dubai down but for the most part, it's not all that interesting a place to me so far. It's endless stores, most of which can be found in America and the roads are jam packed with high-end cars and SUVs. I did find that crazy shopping mall interesting though. So many different nationalities there. It reminded me of the same people I see in Beverly Hills. Many shoppers looked overfed and bored, idly walking down the mall's gleaming halls, looking with slight interest in store windows where they had probably already been in many times. Many were dressed in the overpriced finery they probably purchased at the mall. Many had a look that was a combination of boredom, sadness, and depression.

I like money because it protects me from having to live on the street and it allows me to go places and see things. One of the many downsides of money are places like the Mall of the Emirates and the debilitating degree of comfort it affords some people. It's not for me to go all tangential on the evils of money because I don't think it's evil, it's what you do with it that tells the tale. I am one of those "guns don't kill" types. You leave a gun on a shelf, it just sits there. You leave me on a shelf, I hop off and do what I want. It seems that the people I saw were reeling from some kind of toxic shock, the money had suffocated and poisoned them. It's that Beverly Hills thing where you see women driving around in their Jaguars with perfect hair, their faces so tight and strange, skinny noses, and not a damn thing to do with themselves all day.

I am happy to have done another USO tour and glad that I was able to bring a smile to some of the people I met. I am happy to spend Christmas day with the soldiers for as many years as the USO would like me to. At the end of the day, that's what it's all about, providing an opportunity for a soldier to do something else for a few minutes and also to show respect and support for their considerable efforts. There's nothing to take credit for, nothing to brag about and nothing really to be proud of. It's just something you do if you can. I saw some things on this last tour that were bad. I will write about them at some point.

2340 hrs. I don't know how I am still awake. I just got back from walking down the street that lines the highway I am living next to. I like walking alone in cities at night. For as many years as I have left, I will walk alone at night in cities all over the world.

12-29-06 Dubai UAE: 1311 hrs. In my ridiculously bodacious room. I saw something interesting a moment ago. Across the street from the hotel is a Mosque. They were having prayer and there were many men kneeling in rows outside, perhaps it was to capacity inside, what do that call that, kneeling room only? Hey! Below my left side is the hotel swimming pool full of people laid out on the deck chairs. I could see both pool and Mosque at once but couldn't get it all in my camera lens.

Dubai is all about the business. Nothing will get in the way of business. Whatever it takes to get a country where its leaders think it should be justifies any measures the leadership takes to get there. You see all those cars going down your street? That's business. You think you're going to change something with your fucking petition? Your protest march? This business will not stop until the last drop of oil is used up, the blood that is spilled on the way is just part of the price of doing business. That's all there is to it. If there is money to be made, someone will go after it. Another war will always start after the last one is done because it's good for business. I think it's a waste of time to wonder who knew what when. You know all you need to know at this very moment. It's business. It's always business. To think that any war in the last few centuries was started for any other reason is just being naïve.

On many of the bases I was at recently, I saw that KBR (Kellogg Brown and Root) just does shit to spend money. When they spend it, they get to keep some. When they spend our tax dollars, they make money. The more they spend the more they make so it's in their best interest to keep making things and spending money. They are one of the largest non-union companies in the world after all, they have to keep everyone there busy busy busy! At Camp Le Monier in Djibouti, where I spent Christmas, the dining facility was all decked out in Christmas stuff. I kept one of the KBR Christmas cards that was on the table I was sitting at as a souvenir. Here's what the card said:

Christmas is a time we gather with family and friends to celebrate our blessings and share gifts. This year, we celebrate with our extended family at Camp Lemonier as we provide for the security of our family and friends at home. It is an honor and privilege to serve our country and support the beliefs and values we all hold so deeply in our hearts. We are blessed to represent a nation that provides us with freedom and security. Your efforts in the Horn of Africa promoting peace and stability are making a significant impact by protecting our freedom and promoting freedom for this region.

As we celebrate this Christmas, reflect on the sacrifices that you and others are making to preserve our way of life. Especially remember those who have made the ultimate sacrifice in support of their nation. I personally want to take this opportunity to thank you for your hard work, commitment and devotion to duty while serving at Camp Lemonier. Special thanks as well to your families for their support as you sacrifice time away to defend the nation that we all love so dearly.

There's no signature so I don't know who the "I" is in the card's greeting. My favorite part is from the menu on the back of the card. Among the many delights the soldiers were served was "candid yamb." I thought they were great. So is that what these people are doing all the way out there? If that's what someone thinks, you have to wonder what else they could be talked into. It's such a trite and insulting load.

All the Christmas stuff will get pulled down eventually, if it's not down already. Now, do you think they will store all that stuff the way you put the ornaments back in the closet for next year, or do you think they will toss it all out and re-order it all next Christmas? The only bad thing that will happen to KBR is peace and they don't have to worry too much about that. It's a machine that seems to have no off switch. There is one but the people with access to it aren't making a move. Before they served up the feast, Road Manager Mike took me to a building next to the dining facility that had these ginger bread houses for decoration/dessert. They were soon going to be moved into the dining hall. They were covered with flies. We took a few pictures and moved out. The truth is that the KBR people are ghouls, fucking monsters.

12-30-06 Dubai UAE: 1310 hrs. Saddam was executed a few hours ago. A new low. I know someone would read that and think that I am soft or weak-willed, I don't care to think what else but it doesn't matter to me. It's just more pathetic, barbaric bullshit. Does anyone feel that much better about things now that Saddam Hussein is dead? How about that "trial"? That was a good one. When is Rumsfeld's fucking trial?

2137 hrs. I have been out for several hours but have been thinking about the Saddam thing on and off all day and at this late hour with the jet lag and my levels of nervousness and exhaustion, the whole thing just depresses me. I don't know why it's getting to me so much. Perhaps it's just that the whole thing is so obscene and brutal and idiotic. I work the argument in my head as I write this. "What Saddam did to all those people—now that was obscene and brutal." I know, I know. I just can't get past the idea that this would have been such a great opportunity for the Shia population of Iraq to show the Sunnis, Kurds, and the world that they really wanted peace and forward movement by just putting this piece of shit behind bars for the rest of his life. They had their number one enemy and oppressor in their grip and they could have spared his life and as hard as that would have been it would have been such a great step forward. As far as I'm concerned, the Shia are no better than Saddam now. I don't know for sure but isn't it possible that sparing Saddam could have perhaps kept some people from getting killed in the resulting fallout from the execution? Isn't it time for something else? That's all I'm saying. I have not seen any news but I imagine from his prop ranch, Bush said something about how the Iraqi people wanted justice and that Saddam was brought to justication and the justice was served and that the Iraqi people stood unified for justicization and the voice of freedom, not to mention the voice of justisciousness was heard on this day all over this post 9-11 world. Or something. Great.

2301 hrs. Just got off the phone from an interview from Tel Aviv. Today I did something out of the ordinary and it ended up being really cool. I spent some time with one of the people who put on the show last night. I needed to get some currency changed for Iran and she said she would help with that and she said that if I wanted to we could drive around some and see the sights. I said ok. She took me to the older part of the city and we walked all over. It's nothing remotely like where I am staying now. It is very beautiful, very old. There are boats that take you across the river to the other side. They go back and forth constantly, packed with people. You just hop aboard and hold on for dear life. When we pulled in, several boats arrived at the same time and they all slammed into each other and it was a miracle that no one fell in the water but everyone seemed used to it and just laughed about it. After that we went to an interesting neighborhood that seemed to be made up primarily of people from India and got the money sorted. Then we went to her friend's house who made us some great food and we stayed there for some time talking about Dubai and everything else. Her friend knew a lot about the history of the place. They were going to a Jazz club later and asked if I wanted to go but I started fading and wanted to be on my own so I passed. She just dropped me off here. It was a great afternoon and evening. She is very smart, strong and interesting. She is from Italy but has been living all over the world. She went to college in America and is now living out here. I love that kind of adventurous spirit. I am too attached to things to live like that. I think I am free until I hear a story like hers and then I realize how hooked up to the machine I really am.

It was great to spend time with a female. I don't do that very often. I spend time at the office with the gals there but thinking about it, I really don't spend time with any women at all. Very infrequently, I see a woman I went out with about 20 years ago, she brings her young boy over to the office when she's in the neighborhood and we hang out a little. The kid is fantastic and he and I have a good time. Past that though, I really don't have any contact with females except in passing. I like women but don't go out of my way to meet them. I don't have anything to say really. I did meet an amazing woman this year, Shirin Neshat, she is an Iranian photographer and activist. She is incredible and I am very glad to have met her. The woman I was with today, she was very generous with her time and it was good hanging out with her. I am definitely ready to get out of Dubai. I have nothing against the place but I have been here for enough days and am ready for the next destination, which I think is going to be quite interesting.

I am liking being alone in this room. I have some tunes going and some cold coffee and things are pretty good. I have a very large file of songs I put together on the iPod and it's playing away. I don't remember when I made the file so all the songs that are coming out are one surprise after another: Chicago, The Clash, Barry White, Alan Vega, it's great.

Have you ever seen that situation where a guy really wants to be with a female and he's trying to get it going and she only sees him as a friend and has no interest in him past that? It's painful to be the guy putting yourself through it because you know there's no chance as you're doing it but it's almost more painful to watch. I saw it recently. I really wanted to say out loud, "Pal, it's never going to happen! You know it, too. Stop doing this to yourself." Anything she said, he would use it as an opportunity to touch her arm, rub her back and act as if what she said was really important when she was just saying something trivial. I could tell that she was getting uncomfortable and the guy was just going for it anyway. I didn't know either of them but all the same, it was hard to watch. I remember doing shit like that years ago when I was alive and it makes me cringe just thinking about it. Things are much better now.

12-31-06 Dubai UAE: 0116 hrs. Night off over. Have to do better today. I want to be done with people early and be alone and on my own by the afternoon. Have to do some thinking. People cause me pain. Fuck it. Sick of sorrow and agony. Want silence.

Next week will be something, right? Basically, work hard next week and then cool out in Jordan for 48 hrs. I am almost there. I can do it. I saw a woman today, she looked beautiful in profile. I can't see myself with anyone though. I think about it now and then but it just strikes me as alien. Touch a stranger with a stranger's hands. Mine. Dead. 0120 hrs.

Late: A little after midnight. I went to a New Years Eve gathering with some people from the American Consulate here that I met the other day while on the USO tour. They have lived all over the world and have had amazing lives. Pretty cool to go from the hotel to the house in a bulletproof car. We talked about all kinds of things at dinner and at one point I asked them if there was one country they would not want to go back to and they all said Pakistan. That made me really interested in going there. They said that the place is very unstable and a dangerous situation is a definite possibility. I'll get there at some point. I have to get some sleep.

01-01-07 Dubai UAE: 0628 hrs. At the airport, which even at this hour is packed with people. The duty free area, which seems to stretch the entirety of the airport, is much like that Mall of the Emirates. Some people will wear anything. Those who can't fit into designer jeans don't allow that to stop them from pushing the denim, a remarkably strong fabric, to its very limits. Hey, it's fashion and seeing that all the clothing I have with me has a total worth of less than fifty bucks, I am not in a position to make comment.

In about 40 minutes I board a flight for Tehran, Iran. If everything goes to plan, I will be there for five days. Why Iran? A lot of reasons.

I became curious about Iran after going to school with some Iranian boarding students many years ago. When I met Shirin Neshat, the great Iranian artist, she told me that I would really like the city and that got me interested in going even more. The biggest reason is that Bush and all his cowards hate the place so much. Now I have to go. For Wolfowitz, Cheney, Kristol, Bolton and all those little bitches who work so hard to demonize Iran, this trip is for you. I know enough not to believe what they say and so I am going. I want to meet as many people there as I can. I want to ask them what they think of America, Bush, Ahmadinejad, Iraq, Saddam Hussein, Osama bin Laden, Israel and anything else that comes to mind. I never see anything on the news from an Iranian point of view. I wonder if there's a reason for that? So, all of the above is basically the reason I am going.

I have some shows coming up in about a week and half in Israel. Weeks ago, I looked at the calendar and wondered what I could do with the time between the Dubai show and the show in Jerusalem. I figured it was time to try and go to Iran. I use the word try because I had a feeling it wouldn't be easy and I was right. It was weeks of management and his very capable assistant going back and forth with the embassy and getting different stories that seemed to contradict each other at every turn. As my 12-19-06 evac came closer, the embassy said that there wasn't enough time and the only chance to get a visa now would be in Dubai. So, for several days my travel plans were hanging in the wind. I had no back up plan if the Iranian visa didn't come through. I guess I could have gone to Tel Aviv early and just waited it out. I am glad it all came together, even if it was at the last minute. For the last several days I have been going back and forth with Shirin and others, lining up some contacts in Tehran. Hopefully today I will be meeting up with a friend of Shirin's who will show me around.

This is interesting, for my stay in Iran, I am required to have a tour guide to show me around. I have to pay for his hotel, 50 Euros a day and I have to pay for his meals as well. This will be a costly trip but if this is the only way to see Iran, that's that. 0806 hrs.

1454 hrs. Now in Tehran, Iran. I made it. In my room. This hotel reminds me of the cheap hotels I've occupied in Russia. When I checked in a couple of hours ago, the man behind the counter asked if I would like the quiet side of the building that looks out on the park or the one that has a view of the mountains and the street. I took the street side and while I don't know what I'm missing as yet, I like the choice I have made. The view of the street is cool, the traffic is relentless. It's a never ending roar of car horns, engines and the occasional siren.

For the last couple of hours, I have been passed out on my small bed. I really needed it. I didn't get much sleep last night. I am supposed to get a call from a woman soon. I talked to her earlier today. She is a friend of Shirin's and called me when I arrived at the hotel and we agreed to talk around 1500 hrs. Hopefully, I can get together with her later on and hear what she has to say. If I can't, I will walk around here as long as I can and then come back to the room.

Something interesting happened when I arrived at the airport. After I had cleared immigration and was walking to the baggage carousel, a uniformed man asked to see my passport. He told me to have a seat and walked away. I started writing in my journal: 1035 hrs. Tehran Iran Khomeini Airport. Everyone gets to go to baggage claim but me. The nice men have taken my passport and politely asked me to have a seat. I have been here for awhile. Everyone is walking past me and staring. As the man in the glass booth checked out my passport, he would look up at me with an expression that seemed to say, "Why you're coming here is beyond me." This is an indicator that it's going to be an interesting trip if I can get past this next hurdle.

Then another man walked up, thanked me and gave me my passport back. I was about to leave and he asked to see it again. He took it for another minute and then gave it back and I was done. I went down the stairs to the baggage claim area which was largely empty now since everyone had gotten their belongings and departed. I looked through the glass partition to see if I could see any indication of someone waiting for me. A man caught my eye and waved. I nodded and then saw my bag on the belt. I got the bag and then went through the nothing to declare side and presented my passport to the guard. He took it in his hand and gave it back without opening it and waved me through.

I met up with the man who had waved at me. His name is Hamid, he was the one who finessed the visa. He seems like a good guy. We got in his car and took off towards the city.

Our conversation was interesting. He told me he had checked me out on the internet and that I was not to tell the tour guide, who would be with me for the duration of my stay, anything about what I did. I asked him what the problem was with what I did. He said that there would be a lot of static if the tour guide found out I had written books, done music, was on American television, etc. Hamid told me that the occupation he had assigned me on the visa was that of "manager" and if the tour guide asked me about that, I was to just make something up. Then he asked me if I knew anyone here and I told him that I had names and phone numbers that an Iranian person in America had given me and I was supposed to meet up with them during the week. He instructed me to not tell the tour guide anything of this and as far as the tour guide was concerned, I knew no one in Tehran. He went on to tell me that there was a good chance I could be followed to any of the addresses I went to and all the people there would be interviewed and he would also get hassled. It is clear to me that there's a lot of problems with doing what you want here. I asked Hamid what would happen if the tour guide decided to look me up on the internet and he said that he was hoping that wouldn't happen because if it did, it would be a very big hassle for the both of us.

We stopped for gas and Hamid filled his tank and showed me how cheap gasoline was in Iran. He said that gasoline has been subsidized by the government and was very cheap and this was going to deplete the country's supplies.

2200 hrs. Just got back to my room. I don't think I can capture with words all the things I saw, heard and felt today. I will try. Simin came to pick me up at the hotel at 1500 hrs. Simin is a friend of Shirin's who very generously offered to show me around. We got in a taxi and went to the north of the city to the neighborhood she grew up in. We went to the Tajrish neighborhood and went to the local Bazaar that resembled the souks I was in the day before in Dubai. We walked down a series of semi-open air hallways lined with small stalls selling everything from fish to gold. The merchants were waving their wares and the place was crowded and in constant motion. I don't think you could ever get bored walking through this place. Simin has been coming here since she was a child and says that most of it has changed and then pointed to an old marble floor of one of the stores and said that was part of the original construction. It was interesting to hear her speak of how so much of it had changed and how she missed the way it used to be because it reminded me of my old neighborhood and how it has changed over the years. I guess I also liked hearing someone talk about how they missed their old neighborhood because I miss mine although I don't like to allow myself to miss things because it gets in my way but all the same, I do miss my old neighborhood, sometimes even when I'm in it. It was nice to hear her speak about this place as being so familiar to her because to me it was so strange and exotic.

One of the things that made our walk interesting was that Simin is a very, I mean very, much loved actress here. People were parking their cars to get out and meet her. Every other minute people were saying hello to her and thanking her and taking her picture. At one point, we stood in line to get some bread that she wanted me to try. The people in line recognized her and put her at the front of the line and the baker brought out this large, flat piece of bread which he gave her and refused her money even though she tried to pay a few times. The bread resembles nan bread and is very good. I saw people folding it like a newspaper and putting it under their arm. It was obvious that she is very famous and I asked her about that and she gave me the aw shucks scenario. Then we passed a poster for a new film and there she was. I pointed to it and said, "That's you!" Again she was very self effacing about it while every third person who saw her was flipping out. I said, "You're like Ozzy Osbourne!" and she asked, "Who's that?" I am definitely not in Ohio.

We came back to the place where we had entered the market which is a convergence of streets ending up in a traffic circle that makes for complete vehicular chaos. The motorists seem to have some kind of system that looks like a series of orchestrated near-misses. As we walked up to the island in the middle, the sun was setting over the buildings and it was an incredible view that made us both stop simultaneously to take it in. This part of town is backed up against a wall of towering snow covered mountains. It was one hell of a view to take in. I live for these moments. I don't know how the rest of this trip will go but that walk with Simin and the sunset will make the whole trip worth it even if nothing else good comes of it. It's these moments that I travel the world for. When they happen, I know I am doing the right thing. This is what it's all about. These are the moments that make your life your own. There's a lot of servitude in life and a lot of it I don't mind but it takes a lot of time and if that's all you do, then that's all you are.

Simin made a phone call and her son Nariman came and picked us up and took us to Shirin's sister's house to visit. Shirin's sister is great. She welcomed us into her home and made us coffee and we sat at her table and talked for some time. Nariman and I talked about documentaries and film and music. He travels a lot so he is very knowledgeable about things happening outside Iran. At one point, Shirin called from America and she and I spoke briefly. She was very happy that I was at her sister's house and told me she hasn't been to Iran in 8 years and misses it very much.

From there, Simin, Nariman and I went to their place down the road. In their living room, I saw many awards given to Simin. She has three of the Iranian version of the Oscar, a life time achievement award and all kinds of awards from Europe. I met her husband who was really cool and we all sat around the table and talked for quite some time.

After awhile, Nariman asked me if I wanted to go out and see some of the city and get some food. We took off in his car. He asked me where I wanted to go and I asked him to take me to where all the youths hang out. We went to a small shopping mall and what a surprise, the young folks seem to do all the same things you see youngsters do anywhere else. They slouch and are so beautifully bored you can't stand it. I enjoyed that time of life when you had so much youth in such great supply you almost didn't know what to do with it. We went to a food court and ate some really mediocre chow that I knew was going to pummel me later but I was hungry so I went for it anyway. We talked a lot about music, Nariman is very curious about it and said that they don't get a great deal of new music in Iran and do a lot of file swapping. After awhile, we went down to the street and he fixed me up with a taxi and explained to the man where I was going and we went our separate ways. Now I am back in my small and ancient smelling room. It was a great first day. In the morning I meet up with my tour guide, not really looking forward to that but it will at least be interesting.

01-02-07 Tehran Iran: 2240 hrs. Today was long but really great. I met my tour guide. He's a very nice young man with confusing English and some of the worst breath ever. We went to one of the Shah's very boring palaces and checked it out. I can't help it, this kind of thing has always bored me. I am good in a museum for a little while and then I have to go. Same thing with a palace of any kind. Whenever I am in one, all I can think of is how it could be leveled and why any population allows someone to live in one on their dime.

The best part of the day started when I shook off tour guide boy, who from here on will be known as The Shadow, and went out on my own. We got back to the hotel around 1300 hrs. and I was able to convince The Shadow that I was really tired and had to go to my room for the next 21 hours until we met again. I don't know if he bought it or not. I waited in my room for awhile and then went to the lobby and looked for him there and in the parking lot. When I was sure he had left, I went walking all over the place. The sun was bright and it was cold as hell but I had a great time. I went into stores and talked to men. I didn't meet any women but I talked to men on the street and in shops, some gave me their card and asked me to come by their shop to check out their wares. I went into one shop and everyone just stared at me and finally I just said out loud, "I imagine I must appear to you as a rare import item!" and then a man came over very quickly as if he was apologizing for everyone in the shop staring and shook my hand and asked me where I was from. I told him my name and said I was American. He said, "Ah, you are England." I thought it was interesting that he thought I was a country but I repeated that I was American. Then he said, "You are from Canada!" I figured he was trying to give me an out and I told him that I appreciated that but I was going to stick to the whole I'm from America thing. He laughed and we shook hands again and he introduced me to a few of his friends. They asked me who I was here with and when I told them that I was here on my own and that the purpose of my visit was to meet as many Iranian people as possible and see as much of the city as I could, they seemed impressed and were all extremely friendly. Actually, that's the way everyone I have met has been to me so far.

Later on, I took a taxi to Shirin's sister's house and ate dinner and hung out with her friends and family. It was a great time. The food was really great and I ate caviar that I found to be very good. I have tried it before and never liked it. I told them that when it was offered to me but they insisted that this was Persian caviar and much better than all others so I checked it out. I liked it, perhaps it was because I was very hungry. We spent a good deal of the time talking at the dinner table and I asked them a lot of questions and the answers I got were fascinating. I asked them what was up with their boy Mahmoud Ahmadinejad and one of them shot back, "What's up with your boy?!" and they all roared with laughter. I asked them if any of them voted for him and they all said no and added that he was basically an idiot. Someone said that it was too bad that Bush and Ahmadinejad don't get along as they are so much alike and they all started laughing again. I asked them what they thought of America's invasion and occupation of Iraq. One of them said that they fought Iraq for 8 years and many of their friends were dead. Then I asked them what they thought of America and almost all of them started talking at once about how much they loved America and where they had visited or went to school and how much they loved Chicago and Seattle, etc. I asked them what they thought of Bush and they all got pretty quiet and serious and said they were afraid of what he might decide to do to Iran. If I was made to fear another country by their rhetoric or policies, my anger would be hard to contain and it would be hard for me to see around it to be calm enough to be rational or civil. You want to fuckin' kill me? I'll just kill you first. I would be first out the door for that. If I was in Iran and heard the bullshit John Bolton was spewing, he would be number one on my shit list. I bet it would be almost impossible for an Israeli to stand by when Ahmadinejad says he wants to wipe Israel off the map. I asked them if any of them wanted to wipe out Israel and they all looked at me like I was crazy and said all they want is peace. Basically, all this intimidation is just bullshit and goes nowhere good. All this stuff is coming from some true motivation. Ahmadinejad and his fans have a point of view they obviously believe in. I would rather take the time to understand it so I can disagree with a greater degree of understanding. All the information is there, you just have to want to know. I am sick of the denial and the lack of critical thinking in America. It makes us look so fucking stupid as the rest of the world laughs and prepares for battle. Look at Bush, you couldn't make that guy read no matter what you did. So far, this new century is a failure, or perhaps it hasn't started yet. Tonight was great and I am so glad I am here.

01-03-07 Tehran Iran: 2319 hrs. In my room, listening to Joy Division's BBC Recordings. It's perfect room music. I went out with Hamid and The Shadow earlier today. We went to the palace of one of the Shahs. It was very beautiful but thankfully the visit was over quickly. I don't have much stamina for the tour type stuff. I don't know what it is, I get bored really fast and can't tune in and listen to what is being said when in a gallery or wherever. I feel like I am 8 years old again and I just want to walk quickly through the place and get it over with. The Shadow is a nice enough guy. His English isn't very good and it is work getting through the hours with him. I won't be able to take this guy for longer than a couple of hours at a time.

What made today interesting is that The Shadow asked me a lot of questions. He was nonstop. He started by asking me what I did for a living. I told him I was a manager, which is really a lame thing to say. It's like saying, "I'm an employee." I was hoping The Shadow would not want to know more but he did. I told him I managed writers who are trying to get published and read their work and placed them at publishing houses. I told him I was always looking for the next Tom Clancy. I don't think he knew who that was and that shut him up for a few minutes but soon, he was back at me again. I wondered if he had looked me up on the internet and knew a few things. He never asked me any details about anything I did or anything of a political nature. After about ten minutes of this, I was starting to wonder if he was just asking me questions he already knew the answers to as all good inquisitors do but then he started asking me about how to get a permit to open a night club. One thing he seemed very curious about, or at least seemed interested in getting a satisfactory answer out of me, was about clubs in America. "Many men are members of special clubs in America, aren't they? Are you a member of one of these clubs?" Instead of asking him what the fuck he was talking about, which would be answering a question with a question, only leading to more questions, I replied with answers I hoped would tangle him up in useless information and strain the limits of his English. I went into a spiel about how there were many clubs in America for people who liked dogs and television shows and all kinds of other interests and while I wasn't a member of any clubs, I thought they were so very nice. That seemed to cool him out for awhile but then he came back around again to the club questions, basically asking them over again. I think he was trying to get me to say something, to admit to something, I can't be sure though. It did make me want to grab his trachea between my thumb and index finger though. Eventually, he stopped.

We got back to the hotel in the early afternoon and I made plans with The Shadow to see a couple of museums near the hotel in the morning. The Shadow and Hamid departed and I went to my room. A few minutes later, Hamid called me down to the lobby saying he needed to talk to me. I went down and he was sitting at a table and motioned for me to come over. He told me that The Shadow had called his boss and mentioned that Hamid had been coming along with us on the sightseeing and basically running a block between myself and him. The Shadow's boss called Hamid about it and Hamid explained that the Shadow's English wasn't up to par and he didn't want his client to not get all the proper information while seeing the sights. Hamid also explained that I would have to move carefully when I was on my own now because they were starting to check me out and do some research on me and it might make it a little tricky for us. That's when he explained that if I had listed that I was involved in film, writing or music on the visa that I might not have been given the go ahead to enter the country. He also added that The Shadow calling in about Hamid being along on the day trips prompted the visa people to shut down on permits for a 24 hour period thus forcing a group of Americans in Istanbul, Turkey waiting to get their visas approved to endure a minimum 24 hour delay. I single-handedly shut down immigration into Iran! Hamid said I was very lucky to get into Iran and urged me to be very low key when I came and went from the hotel as they were now making note of when I was coming and going. So, things are getting interesting. We'll see what The Shadow has to say for himself tomorrow when we meet at 1100 hrs. Now all I want to do is pound this fuckin' guy on sight. That would be so great. "Good morning, Mr. Henry, how was your..." Wham!

I went out for a walk tonight. I made a left out of the hotel and walked for quite some time. It was really cold out and that made it perfect. The traffic was down quite a bit and it was fairly quiet and there weren't many people out. I passed the Museum of Contemporary Art and noticed there was a park. I walked through it for awhile and sat near a fountain and watched people walk by. At the bottom of the park, near the fountain, there are stores and small coffee places. I walked around them and looked at the people inside. I saw a young man and woman seated in a corner. She had her mandatory scarf on and their heads were very close together. For a moment, I thought I was in France. The place was dimly lit with only a small neon sign over the door. I walked past the different kiosks and shops and back onto the street. I saw three men standing next to a small metal can with a fire burning in it. They were drinking from steaming cups of tea and listening to a small portable radio that one of them was holding in his hand. I saw two homeless men sitting amongst bags of garbage talking to each other and I wondered how they were going to get through the night.

It's at times like this that I am happy to be alive and alone. Walking streets in cities at night all over the world, that's what I do. It's one of the best things I have found to do with my remaining time.

In a way, it's nothing, just walking down a street somewhere but to me it's ultimate freedom and a state of perfection that is like nothing else I have ever experienced. I am alone on the streets of Tehran Iran walking around in the winter. It feels epic to me.

01-04-07 Tehran Iran: 1549 hrs. In my room. The Shadow and I went out to the Carpet Museum today and it was great. It is basically a building with a lot of rare carpets in it. The Shadow is actually a very nice guy and he did his best to tell me all he could about the carpets. I learned a lot about different kinds of carpets from different times, etc. It was cool but I only have so much time for the history of Iranian carpets dispensed from someone who struggles with the English language worse than the current American president. It was agonizing waiting for The Shadow to get through sentences. He is a professional tour guide but his English is by the book and it lacks context. Regardless, The Shadow is easy to like and he didn't ask any questions about what I do this time. He told me that his brother e-mailed him and told him to tell me Merry Christmas. It came out in Shadow speak, "My brother says to you Merry Christmas on earth to you and your blessed family but not in Iran." I asked him if he meant that in Iran, there is no Christmas holiday. He said, "Not to any extent, no." The Shadow also has this maddening habit of saying, "Really?" whenever I tell him of my plans. I told him that now that we had finished our daily sightseeing, I was going to back to my room. "Really? We will go have the lunch now. I am at your service." I tell him that I appreciate that but I am not hungry and am happy to go to my room now. "Really? After lunch, we can go see a handicraft shop where you can buy carpets and things of Iran." Finally I managed to convince him that we will get together again in the morning for the last of our sightseeing and that I will see him then. Then The Shadow said, "Then I will see you tomorrow morning." And then, his face brightening, he said, "Check you later!" and I said, "Check you later!" right back to him and got on the elevator. He seems like an alright guy besides being a spy motherfucker.

That part of the day finished, I settled into the lamer part of the day. I am battling against a pretty heavy dose of depression at the moment. I am not trying to be cosmic or spiritual in any way because I detest the concept of spirituality or anything having to do with the stars, the Zodiac, planets in houses, etc. but that being said, I notice that without fail, the worst bouts of depression hit me on the two days before the full moon. On those days, I want nothing more than lethal injection, sleep that kills, and any possible way not to be. As I sit here right now, I don't want to go anywhere. I have a bag of granola and some water and that is all the food I need. I have not eaten for about 24 hours now and have no appetite. I have been invited to dinner by Shirin's friend and of course I am going. I could never turn down such kindness, just out of respect alone, so I am going but it will be difficult. All I want to do now is wait for dark and go out walking for a very long time and then come back to this room and sit in it. I hate this aspect of my fucked up mind. I hate that feeling of torpitude. It overpowers me sometimes. There are times I can beat it and there are times I cannot. I disgust myself when I am like this. Sometimes when it hits me, all I can do is wait it out or walk it out, basically just endure it. The events of the last several days have stuck with me and compounded the effect. I feel like I am wading through mud. I don't know why but the Saddam execution is very depressing to me. Humans paint every available surface with so much fucking death and misery, it's amazing that humans survive humanity. Saddam was executed in a sanctioned and fairly orderly manner. The more orderly it is, the more obscene it is to me. I think that's the part of the Death Sentence™ that I hate the most. The fact that they build machines to kill with efficiency. Gas chambers, electric chairs, lethal injection rooms, etc. Someone has to sit there and come up with this stuff and run it by some other people who make comments and adjustments for optimum results. The art of hanging is an exercise in physics. Too much drop and the head can come off. Too little and the condemned can stay alive for quite awhile. Meanwhile, the number of deaths in Iraq just keeps increasing. As long as the American Forces are there, they will keep getting catastrophically injured and killed. The president says that American forces will stay there until the job is done and that American Forces will stand down when Iraqi forces stand up. Has anyone pointed out that all the American Forces members in Iraq completed their training in a matter of weeks? That you can take a young, able-bodied American male off the street and train him to be Army Infantry in weeks, not years? I am not saying that it's easy and men and women in the Army are simple but it's hard to believe that after more than three years there's still no Iraqi Army that is effective. The only answer is that they don't want to do it. It's not like they cannot be trained. Besides that, no one seems to mention that Saddam had hundreds of thousands of men trained to fight. Paul Bremer fired them in his "Debaathification" process so he could open Iraq up for business. The excuses of the Bush regime hold no water now. They just don't. The people who defend the president and this war at this point are just pathetic. Could it be that it is next to impossible to train up Shia men to have them potentially defend Sunni from other Shia? That makes some sense to me. The neocons got what they wanted and they let thousands of good Americans bleed out for it.

I read a report several days ago that Senator Kerry went to Iraq and was ignored by the soldiers there. No one spoke to him. He ate alone and worked out alone, but Bill O'Reilly shows up and the line to meet him goes out the door. Whatever. I hate using that word but in this case, it's the only thing I can think of. O'Reilly's your guy? Fine. A non-Vet, bullshit artist is your guy? Perhaps I should reconsider all the time I spend out there with the Military. Perhaps it's just better to leave them to the O'Reilly's of America and call it a day. That thought has been going through my mind a lot over the last few days. If soldiers feel that people at Fox News have the story straight, then perhaps I am just wasting everyone's time with these visits, with this concern and all this sadness that this conflict brings up. Is it better to just leave them to it as they say? This is what has been bugging me for the last several days.

I had a picture on my computer of a female I have kept in touch with sporadically. Occasionally I look at the picture. She has a nice face. I threw it out today. I am trying to kill off everything that makes me want to look at a picture of a female. I would rather kill want than to act on it when it comes to personal relationships. I have it in my head that I cannot experience life the way I want to if I am close to a woman. It's like you can go out as far as you want but it's not really any great distance because you have this tether cord of security that is there for you to pull yourself back to safety with. I don't understand how I can get to the real thing if I know there is a warm embrace waiting for me. Isn't that cheating somehow? I guess I have it in my mind that having a relationship with a woman is a safety net. It's a net that breaks your fall but can also ensnare you. At this point, the bad parts outweigh the good. Fuck it.

01-05-07 Tehran Iran: ?? hrs. The votes are in. The Shadow is a douche bag after all. Hours ago, I was out with Hamid and The Shadow. At one point, I made a call on Hamid's phone to Simin's son to arrange a time to pick up my iPod, as I had lent it to him so he could check out some music. As I was dialing the number, The Shadow kept offering me his phone to use. I didn't get it at first but I figured it out a few seconds later. He wanted to get the number I was calling. The Shadow tried to look at the paper I had the number written on. I know I have to be cool to the guy but I nearly lost it at that moment and as the phone was ringing I started walking toward him asking him what his problem was. He backed off and then the call went through and I walked away to talk without him hearing me. Later, Hamid told me that The Shadow asked for the number that I had dialed and Hamid told him he deleted it, which he did immediately. When Hamid told me that, we were standing in the lobby and The Shadow was standing in the parking lot. I wanted to go out there and shake his ass up but had to restrain myself.

1503 hrs. Waiting for Hamid in the lobby. He had to shake The Shadow and said it might take a while. He told me to meet him here in half an hour. That was about 40+ minutes ago. I hope he's ok. The Shadow's body language was different today. He stood very close to me and conducted himself strangely, like he was following instructions. It could be me being paranoid but I think I'm right about this.

01-06-07 Tehran Iran: 0042 hrs. Hamid has called twice to tell me he is having car trouble and will be here soon. It's a 30+ mile drive to the airport in a car that has chosen this time to have problems. Some might say that this does not bode well but I say this is what travel is all about and you just have to be as cool as you can for as long as you can.

There was a strange incident a little earlier that is at least interesting and adding to the tension of the moment. About an hour ago I was eating dinner with Hamid and his wife. Her brother called to tell her that I was on television in a video or something and he wanted to talk to me. She handed the phone to me and I said hello to the guy and passed the phone back. Hamid was distressed about this. I asked him why. He said that if The Shadow had seen me on screen it would make things complicated. He asked if I would mind getting to the airport early and waiting it out. He thought it would be good to get me checked in and squared away sooner than later. I said sure. He dropped me off awhile ago and was supposed to come back soon but then the car trouble started. I think if The Shadow had seen me on TV we would know by now but it will be good to get wheels up and out of here. It does make these last few hours here a little tense but I reckon I will get out without any problems.

Management just called and filled me in on my hotel information for later today in Jordan as well as my press schedule for Israel and Canada. Both places have me hopping. The Canadians have asked that I do a five days of journal entries about this trip for a Monday through Friday daily story in one of their newspapers. I said yes to that one because it will force me to write. They also asked me, while I was in Toronto, if I would do some man-on-the-street interviews in the same vein as Jay Leno. Well, no. It's amazing to me that I am in Tehran and I am getting a call from Management.

For the next 48 hours I have nothing scheduled so I will spend it in Jordan and see what happens. I don't really know anything about the country. It was either there or a two days in Istanbul, Turkey the land of luggage loss. I have been there a few times already so I figured I would give Jordan a shot instead. I could have gone straight through to Tel Aviv but I will be there for days anyway so I reckoned it would be better to mix it up a little.

0301 hrs. At the airport, waiting for the gate to open. Things at this airport move slowly and you have to be patient. A few minutes ago, a young white male was walking towards me as I walked towards the gate. I saw him look at me. I started walking around him, hopefully to convey that I didn't want to make contact. Didn't work. "Are you Henry Rollins?" I nod. "What are you doing in Iran?" It's a fair question but it kind of ruins the whole adventure and mystery of the trip, doesn't it? It's just another airport now. I asked him, "What are you doing in Iran?" I have had enough of people asking me what and why here. He told me he was an American, apologized for bothering me and moved on. I don't know what he's sorry about but why can't people leave motherfuckers alone? I am sure I am an asshole in his book. I respect him for being all the way out here on his own though, that's really cool.

I am looking forward to getting on the plane and getting an hour of sleep. Iran, for the most part, was worth the trip. The people were great, even The Shadow was pretty cool. He told Hamid that I was crazy. I like that. May The Shadow one day meet the woman of his dreams, master the English language, improve his dental hygiene, and bring spies like me to justice. I think it would be great to come back here some time and see a different part of Iran, to get out of the city and go to Esfahan or Tabriz. I am glad I made this trip.

0819 hrs. On another plane out of Dubai, headed towards Jordan. I don't know what I'll do when I get there. Definitely need some sleep. The plane is sold out, the flight is long, the children are loud, the sun is bright and I don't know how much better things could get.

2117 hrs. Amman Jordan. Bag gone. Hoping it makes an appearance tomorrow. The thing that ticks me off the most is not having a good cup of coffee on the night off. I always bring my own but I won't be having any of it tonight. I had some at the hotel restaurant tonight and it wasn't all that bad but it wasn't nearly as good as what I had in my bag.

I was looking forward to this night off being a little better. I am getting some work done and getting left alone so that's cool. Will see what walking around has for me later. Weather is really bad, cold, raining. In DC it's 69 degrees.

In the hotel restaurant, waiting on the meal. After I eat, I will go back to the room and work on some writing projects and try to get an early night. I am pretty buzzed from lack of sleep. There's a lot I can accomplish this year, another book, I think I can do it. I have a lot of writing stuff to do this year with the radio show and the IFC show and other stuff. I will have to write every day to pull it off.

2233 hrs. In my room. Earlier today, as I was waiting for my no show bag, I took a picture of an advertisement that was on the wall next to the baggage belt. It depicts what looks like a Toyota truck with a crosshair sight laid over the part of the windshield where the driver's head would be. The exact spot where I saw a cluster of bullet holes in the windshield of a Humvee in Iraq once. The ad says, "When going to Iraq, make sure to drive armored." The company was called Asbeck and they are out of Germany. I didn't understand why they would have that on the wall for people to contemplate as they waited for their luggage. This luggage belt, by the way, had a great design feature where it throws suitcases off onto the floor every few minutes in this no man's land area near the mouth of the belt. Also, this comes to mind: as I waited for my bag, there were other people who were waiting and at least three of them, at different times, would go to the place where those strips of heavy rubber hang over the mouth of the belt and pull these great flaps of rubber back to look and see what was coming. I don't understand why they did that. Is it a way to somehow know more than you could by merely waiting it out? Isn't the surprise of your bag coming through those flaps like some kind of birthing something to look forward to post flight?

The outside of this hotel reminds me of the hotels I have stayed at in Nairobi, Kenya. Gates, security and even a metal detector and baggage x-ray in the lobby. I was trying to figure out why and then I remembered the hotel bombings they had here in 2005. I looked it up and sure enough, there were three hotel bombings on 11-09-05 here in Amman. On the internet, a report said that Al Qaeda claimed responsibility for the attacks. After watching the three part series <u>The Power Of Nightmares</u>, it's impossible for me to think about terrorism in the same way.

01-07-07 Amman Jordan: 1010 hrs. They throw in a free breakfast here and seeing how expensive everything is, I'm not going to miss it. Today I will check the news and make notes for the upcoming radio shows. Past that, relative rest and relaxation, show prep, bag watch and other stuff.

One of my resolutions for 2007 is upgrading my level of overall politeness to people. I think I am pretty good at it but I bet I can do better. So far, I have been good. I did slip when I barked at that kid in the airport in Tehran and I am sorry about that.

The coffee in the breakfast room is a crime against humanity. A cup of hot bathwater would be a better option. Perhaps I would be better off hitting the street and seeing if I can find someone from New Guinea to sell me some betel-nut to chew on. That's what I'll do, I'll get hooked up and spit kot juice in an alley all day. Anything would be better than this coffee. 1023 hrs.

2017 hrs. Time is running out. I am out of here tomorrow and my bag is still missing. Worrying about it, dealing with it, or trying to, has pretty much ruined my stay here. I was really looking forward to this 48 hours to catch my breath and not think about stuff so much like I have to on tour. All I did today was call the airport and get pulled around and attempt to get my head around the shows and the work coming up in Israel. I admit I didn't use the time very well. I rarely do. It's hard on morale when stuff like this happens. It's challenging enough out here. The people at the airport don't care, why should they? The same bag was lost in Turkey for a month and amazingly came back to me with all my stuff in it. I wonder if the bag ever got out of Iran.

2243 hrs. My break is done and tomorrow I am out of here bag or no bag. I have spent a good part of the day calling the airport and calling back when they told me to and still there's no news. If I can't get the bag tomorrow then I will have to have it sent to Tel Aviv and I'm sure that will make things all the more complicated. Meanwhile, I have been washing my clothes in the sink and wearing them dry. It was a bad time and it kind of poked some holes in my morale and is a distraction. It's hard to think about the shows I have coming up this week with the hassle of the bag always in the way. I'm going to get to sleep as soon as I can so I can be up early and get back on the phone with the airport.

01-08-07 Amman Jordan: 1353 hrs. At the airport at a Starbucks. A Starbucks in Jordan, no surprise there, they are everywhere. This morning, my nervous sleep was interrupted by the sound of men at work. I looked under my bed as it seemed to be the area where the source of the noise was emanating. There were men underneath my bed building something. I asked one of them what they were building and the man yelled over the noise of his co-workers, "Starbucks coming soon!" This is the third time I have been awoken in a hotel room only to find a Starbucks being built there. The other times the Starbucks were being built in the closet. One time, there was one that was open for business in my room. All that customer traffic in the morning and no one took anything from my bag, I was impressed. In other Starbucks news, another lie was perpetrated on the masses by the conservative media mafia when they reported that Saddam Hussein's last word was "God." It wasn't. It was actually "Espresso." There was a Starbucks next to the gallows and he made his last purchase there. Saddam used to pour espresso into his mustache and let the beverage trickle into his mouth throughout the day. Strange. Anyway, that's what he was saying on the gallows to Paul Bremer, who was casually attired in a polo shirt, slacks and a ski mask. Here is the complete transcript of Saddam's Hussein's last moments, which I cut from a report I found on Teenjihadist.com:

Saddam Hussein is walked up the steps to the gallows platform.
SH: Cold night, eh?
PB: Fuck you.
SH: Fuck you!
PB: You are nothing but an Islamofacist.

SH: You are nothing but a small man who pays women to urinate on him in hotel room bath tubs.

PB: You're going to burn in Hell!

SH: Your testicles will be floating in a jar on Nancy Pelosi's desk by Spring. How do you like them apples?

Onlooker #1: Eat my balls!

SH: No, you eat my balls!

Onlooker #2: Iraq will be freedomized!

SH: Little George, is that you?!

Onlooker #2: I'm the Decider!

SH: It is you! Yellow cake from Niger? Who comes up with this stuff, Karen Hughes?

Onlooker #2: She's a good Christian woman!

SH: And Mary Cheney is a good Christian carpet muncher! How many shots of Stoli did it take you to work up the courage to sow your seed in that beast?!

Onlooker #2: Seven, no, nine, shut up!

SH: Her partner was a first round NFL draft pick!

Onlooker #2: You are part of the terroristizer networkers!

SH: Your wife is clinically depressed and uses a vibrator to pleasure herself!

Onlooker #2: You're about to be justicated!

SH: Zoloft! Zoloft! Your wife is wiped out on Zoloft!

Onlooker #2: Stay the course! I never said that!

SH: Your girlfriend is a negress and your daughters have given their vaginas to many men!

Onlooker #2 is taken by men and put into the back of a limousine that quickly speeds off.

PB: Alright, here we are at the top. Are you ready for your moment of truth?

SH: Do I get a last request? By the way Paul, you look good in the ski mask.

PB: Thanks . . . shut up! No last requests!

SH: How about a hamburger?

PB: No!

SH: A cheeseburger?

PB: You'll get nothing and like it!

SH: I love that film!

PB: Shut up!

SH: You found your wife in a kennel.

The noose is put around Saddam Hussein's neck.

Starbucks Barista: Double espresso is up!

SH: Up here! That is my double espresso!

PB: You can drink your double espresso in Hell!

SH: I paid for that double espresso with money that Donald the butcher gave me! I want my espresso!

Trap door opens and Saddam Hussein hangs.

The Man who drove me to the airport was really cool. He was an older, powerfully built and rugged faced man. His voice boomed when he spoke.

WHERE ARE YOU FROM?!

America.

THANK YOU! I AM FROM PALESTINE!

It was a good time. He pointed out these ridiculous mansions that people are building there one after the other. He said that it's people from Kuwait, Saudi Arabia, Israel, and some Europeans. I asked him why and he said that Jordan is a very safe country for life and money. We parted ways at the airport but right before we pulled up to the curb, he gave me a coin he told me was 2000 years old. He told me he buys them from construction people who are digging up the earth and finding tons of artifacts, mainly coins. He buys them and re-sells them to a coin dealer in Kan Zaman for what amounts to a few American dollars each.

THIS MAN, HE SELLS THEM TO AMERICANS FOR 150 AMERICAN DOLLARS EACH! HE IS A FANTASTIC THIEF!

I went to the baggage claim window and asked about my bag. The man had me get a piece of paper stamped by another man that gave me permission to come into the baggage claim area and look through the piles of stranded luggage. I waded through well over 100 pieces of luggage of all descriptions but couldn't find mine. I had some fun with the man who was dealing with my claim. He knew enough English to see that I was fucking with him a little and I managed to crack him up now and then:

Me: Do you realize all these refugee bags that are strewn like so many carcasses across this filthy floor represent people like myself, unshaven and without clothing? Do you know how many holidays you have ruined with your mishandling of people's luggage?

Baggage Man: Yes

Me: Do you understand that these pieces of luggage are evidence of how you run your airlines?

Baggage Man: It is a busy season, the Hajj.

Me: The Hajj?! Gets really crazy during Hajj season, does it?!

Baggage Man: Yes. (slightly smiling)

Me: Nothing like a Hajj to make the baggage handlers lose the ability to put luggage onto a plane!

Baggage Man: Yes. (now laughing)

Me: Is this (pointing to an open box of vodka bottles by the carousel) compensation you offer to people whose luggage you have lost so they can drink to forget the fact they will probably never see their possessions again?!

Baggage Man: No.

I gave him all my Tel Aviv info and am now at the airport, waiting for the flight.

2320 hrs. Tel Aviv Israel: In the hotel. Interesting thing happened after we landed. The bus pulls up to take us to the airport building. I always get mad when I see that we are not pulling up to a jet way when I see a rows of other planes sitting at them. Anyway, as I am exiting the plane I look through the window, see a van pull up and some men get out. I don't think anything of it and keep moving towards the door. I walk down the stairs towards the bus, anticipating the crush of people inside, the ride, etc. when I see a man holding a sign with my name on it. I walk up to him and tell him that's me. I am whisked into the van and taken to a private check in where I am led to a green room with food and drink as I wait for my passport to get dealt with. This time around, I just got the piece of paper with the stamp on it so I don't have an Israel stamp in the passport which can make getting into some countries difficult and sometimes impossible. Had the Israeli stamp been in my passport at the Tehran airport, there's a good chance I might not have been allowed in. I am going to try to get to Lebanon this year, another place the Israeli stamp isn't doing you any favors. That's pretty fucked up but as they say, that's the way it is. I don't know why I got this special treatment but it was really cool.

When I got to the hotel, I had a little while before the press started. I just finished it all a little while ago. The first thing was an interview with a young female for some kind of TV or online show. It was strange as I didn't understand where she was coming from. I sat next to her on a bench seat and she said, "Don't be afraid of me." I was just sitting there, I still don't know what she was getting at. People are strange, aren't they? I was polite but it was hard to get through the maze of obtuse questions. I have no idea how the thing will come out. After that, I went to a room full of people and took questions from them. Finishing that, I went to the restaurant in the lobby and ate. I liked watching the people at the tables, their conversations were all very animated, old and young people talking to each other, people leaning in, using their hands. I like seeing people intellectually engaged, it makes me think that perhaps good things will happen in the future. It always seems like the wrong people get put in charge of things. Can you imagine if a more positive and switched on group of people had been elected into power in America six years ago?

01-09-07 Tel Aviv Israel: 1950 hrs. In the restaurant, waiting for the same thing I ordered last night. I want to get my meal in early and walk around some before I go back to the room and work on the radio show. I have not done the radio show work yet and don't want to get behind.

I did two interviews today and talked to the Swift River guys who are out here to shoot the Saturday night show. IFC wanted a backdrop. I didn't think we needed one but they asked if they could do one in Hebrew and Arabic that says "freedom of speech" or something. I think it's pretty weak but I'll play ball. I like the IFC people a lot and they have let me do another season of the show, so it's cool. What the audience will think is, well, we'll have to see how it goes. At the end of the day it's always me who has to take the heat on this stuff, I don't know if that ever occurs to them.

I am hoping that management brings me some clothes tomorrow. I wrote the airlines website and asked if there was any information on my missing bag, so far, nothing. It's frustrating. There's nothing I can do about it though. There's nothing happening here, just waiting for the shows to start. Perhaps I'll see something interesting out on the street tonight.

I will start in on the journal entries for the Canadian newspaper tomorrow.

01-12-07 Tel Aviv Israel: 2143 hrs. I did the show at 1415 hrs. Because of the Sabbath, the show had to go on early. I have not had the chance to do any writing here for a couple of days. Last night, I did a show in Jerusalem. It was interesting to be there at night and see people on the street. I was sitting in a restaurant near the venue before soundcheck, watching cars and people go by and heard music blaring from somewhere and then saw a van pass by with two young men on top dancing and waving. I asked someone at the table what that was all about and was told that it was a very serious religious sect. I guess they're all very serious. I forget the name of the sect. Religious matters in and of themselves are of no interest to me. In fact, religion might be the most uninteresting topic for me. I was at the Western Wall the other day and watched these men praying while they rocked their bodies backwards and forwards. I was so glad I had never gone any-where near religion and I felt bad for these people who I think are wasting their lives. I wouldn't try to stop them and as long as they're not trying to take me with them, we're cool.

I met someone interesting today. His name is Ziv Koren and he's very cool and very intense. He's a photojournalist who took photos today and will be out with us on Sunday when we shoot outside shots for the IFC special. He's good friends with James Nachtwey, the pho-

Henry Rollins

tojournalist who was the subject of the documentary <u>War Photographer</u>, which I have seen twice now. It's amazing. Ziv gave me a small booklet of some of his work. The stuff this guy has seen is mind blowing. The booklet contains everything from portraits of Sharon, Barak, and Netanyahu to hectic shots from the heat of battle. He's had shots on the cover of every magazine it seems. Anyway, it was cool to talk to him about Nachtwey, who seems to be one of the most intense people anywhere.

I had some meetings with management and we worked out the basic schedule for 2007. It looks like another uphill stress fest from start to finish. I think it will be a great year of work and challenge. It will be busier than last year. I think if I can maintain the level of activity, I can get a lot done this year. I have to stay with it. Whatever I do or don't do, it makes no difference, it's just what I want to do. Once I get some momentum and get in harness, I am pretty much good to go for the long haul. I don't have anything holding me back so there's no excuse not get it all done. Last year was good but this year has to be better. I want to make the IFC show better than last year and somehow outdo what I did with the radio show last year. I have been working on some future broadcasts that I think will be really good, it's very time consuming but it's worth it to make them as good as they can be. I can get all this stuff done if I just keep to myself and work every day. I can do it if I stay to myself and don't stray from the work.

01-13-07 Tel Aviv Israel: 1913 hrs. Backstage. Just finished soundcheck. They brought in some much needed side fills and it sounds better. There's always a lot of pressure when the show is being shot. A few minutes in I usually forget about the cameras and do the show just fine. I always get too nerved up for shows but this one comes with extra distraction. I finish the show and then get back to the hotel as soon as I can as I have a 0600 hrs. lobby call for a long day of shooting extra footage for this special. We will go all over the place and get as much footage as we can. That will go for about 12 hours at least. My flight for Toronto leaves at 0025 hrs. the next morning so I have enough time to grab a shower and go to the airport. I'll get some good sleep on the flight. So basically, the next 24 hours will be a lot of work with wheels up being the finish line. The press days in Canada will be busy but low impact. Press is easy compared to shows.

Last night post show was good. I stayed in my room and worked on the radio show and other stuff. I tried to get to sleep early but couldn't do it. I started thinking about tonight's show and all the work we have to do tomorrow. It is hard for me to work with other people, they add noise and movement to everything. Everyone who I'm working with is great but it's still difficult having people around the backstage area asking questions and talking when I am trying to get myself together. It's a solid group and everyone's working hard so it's a good thing, just not always easy to handle.

Living this way, in hotel rooms and backstage areas, can make one very lonely. I see it with other people. I can recall echoes of how that felt but would have to read old journals of mine to get a better sense of what it felt like. Loneliness is a natural human tendency and it can be inspiring as much as it can be debilitating. I like to think of lone-liness as something I starved to death by ignoring it until it was too weak to stand up and make its presence known. The way I regard it now, I think it's just something that gets in the way and keeps you normal and moving along with the herd. The world is a lonely place. I live in Los Angeles which is one of the loneliest cities I have ever been to. Just because the world is lonely doesn't mean you have to be. It's not even a matter of not succumbing, for me it was a matter of throwing out a lot of rituals, learned behavior and letting anything else having to do with it just starve out and die off. I think it's a very bad idea to depend on anyone for anything. There are situations where I have to but I don't feel good about it. I sometimes miss peo-ple who have died but that's a different thing altogether. They're not coming back so the entire thought process is different. People are lonely. If you get too close to them, they'll infect you with their lone-liness and that will make it that much harder to get the work done. I kind of remember when I had a girlfriend and would think about her while on tour wondering if we were "cool" and it was distracting most of the time. Better off without. I would rather have a schedule or money or a weapon than a friend.

01-18-07 Toronto Canada: 0502 hrs. At the airport waiting for the 0620 hrs. flight to Dulles. The last three days have been busy and there was not much time to write anything. I basically did a lot of press and slept. The IFC people here are great and we got a lot done. Canadian press is fairly low impact, they are professional and prepared so it's easy to be clear and get a point across.

Last night, there was a reception for me at a bar around the corner from the hotel. I met a lot of people, signed a lot of things and stood for a lot of pictures with people. Afterward, the press gals and I had some dinner at the hotel and went our separate ways. I tried to get some sleep and was largely unsuccessful. I hope to get a couple of hours on this flight.

When I get to DC I have a meeting with someone from National Geographic for what will hopefully lead to some employment up the road and then I am loose for the next couple of days. I am looking forward to seeing Ian and the old neighborhood. It is about as close to the idea of home as I get. I like to walk around the old streets and remember my life before I left town.

The last day in Israel was interesting. I did the 2nd Tel Aviv show, it went well. I got back to the hotel, slept a couple of hours and then started the day at 0600 hrs. We grabbed shots all over the immediate area from the Dead Sea to points in Jerusalem. For the first shot, I floated in the Dead Sea and did some promos for the show, it should look pretty funny. The texture of the water was really something, it was almost like syrup. I tasted it and it was salty beyond salty. People soak in it for the minerals and cover themselves with the mud that sits at the bottom in massive chunks. Luckily, there was a shower there. No matter how hard I tried to get it off me, I could still taste the bitterness of the Dead Sea on my arm later on.

From there, we went to Jerusalem and got shots all over the place. The Western Wall and the Temple Mount, where it's said Jesus Christ was crucified, washed, entombed. Just like the other day when I was there, I saw many people kissing the stone and lining up to enter the grave and again it was depressing to see people acting in this way. It's just pathetic. Ziv, the photojournalist, came with us and for most of the shots, it was the two of us walking and talking. He's a very interesting man. All through the day, when we would be standing somewhere, he would point at the a spot a few feet away and tell of how he had photographed some awful event that happened there months or years before. That seems to be how it is in Israel, the day can go from normal to catastrophic at any time and in any place.

The most interesting parts of the day for me, besides driving around and looking at the rugged landscapes, happened towards the end of the day. We went to a section of the newly built wall, or Separation Barrier as some call it, that separates Israel from the West Bank. In the '80s, I made several visits to the Berlin Wall and I couldn't help but compare the two. I always observed the wall in Berlin from the West German side, where its purpose was to keep people from getting out of the east side. I never understood the idea of walling off a place to keep people from going out into the world, it makes me think of North Korea. The primary purpose of the wall in Israel is to keep people out and cut down on suicide bombings which, apparently, it has helped to do. The section of wall we observed seemed at least twice as tall as the one in Berlin and even more impenetrable. I did some reading up on it and it's over twice as high as the Berlin Wall. We were parked next to a gas station and there were some kids hanging out watching us. They seemed used to people pulling up and looking at the wall. I wondered what the view used to be like when they sat there as the sun set before the wall was built. It was probably great. Now all they have is a tall gray wall to contemplate. The wall has been a great inconvenience to many people who work or have family on the other side. What was a walk or short drive to the destination is now a long drive to a check point and then on from there. I have no idea what that kind of restriction of movement is like. I don't think I would handle it well, or at least it would take a long time to get used to. If I were in opposition to the people who built the wall, it would make me hate them all the more. I don't think there will ever be peace there. If there is, it will have to come from the Israeli side and go from there. They're the ones with all the backing and the advantage it seems to me.

I wonder what Israelis think of all the money that America gives them every year to maintain Israel? I don't think the money and support is a product of America's love for Israel as much as it's indicative of how much the Arab world is fucking hated by the American government, corporate powers and other concerns. Israel is basically an American outpost in the Middle East. They're working to expand that, as any good corporation will do, that's why America invaded Iraq.

The most beautiful part of the day was at sundown. We went to Mount Olive and looked across at Jerusalem. A few moments after the sun had dipped below the horizon the evening prayer started and from a few different mosques the sound of the voices echoing and blending was incredible. We recorded it. I heard Muslim prayers almost every day for about a month on this trip.

From Mount Olive we went to a café for the last shot of the day, the place was called Café Moment. On 03-09-02, 11 people were killed and dozens injured inside the café when a suicide bomber detonated himself. Hamas took responsibility for the attack. I sat with Ziv and we talked about what it's like to live in a place where this kind of thing can happen almost any time anywhere. I truly have no concept of that kind of awareness. The man detonated himself to the left of where I was sitting and as we spoke, I kept looking over there and trying to imagine what it would have been like. I have seen a few photos of the scene, basically a gutted room with the floor almost completely covered in blood. One of the women who was on the crew for the shows and the shoot day told me that whenever she sees a crowd of people anywhere she immediately walks as far away from them as she can. When she sees an unaccompanied bag in a restaurant, she leaves. She said that this is the way a lot of people in Israel are.

I was coming out of the men's room and walking back to the table when Ziv called out to me and pointed out the window. I didn't know what he was on about but I looked out the window and saw a train of black SUVs flying by the café. Ziv said it was Condoleezza Rice and her entourage, who had been in the area earlier that day. I ran out of the café as quickly as I could and yelled "fuck you" at the disappearing taillights as they sped into the darkness. It felt good to let her know where I'm coming from. She's a brilliant woman, too bad she plays for the wrong side, she's a fucking monster like Cheney and the rest of those rotten criminals.

2348 hrs. At the hotel. What a day. I got to DC hours ago. First thing that happened was my bag went missing again. I now wonder if it's because I went to Iran. Perhaps some people want to have a look at it. Hopefully it turns up in the morning. It's almost funny but not that funny. I took a cab down to National Geographic, got there early and walked around the neighborhood for a little while. I love that part of DC. I met up with two of the people who come up with ideas for shows and we kicked ideas around over lunch. I liked them but I don't think we came up with anything that they can use. I am remarkably bad at those kind of meetings, I have not a creative bone in my body. Still, it was really cool to meet them and I hope that something happens. It would be great to have done something with National Geographic before it's all over, that would be so cool. I am not up to their standards but perhaps there's something I can contribute. After the meeting was over and I was heading back to the hotel, passing by so many familiar streets and intersections, I thought that I have come a fair distance from the days I worked at the ice cream store, which isn't a bad place to be. It's been an interesting trip so far. I think of that job all the time. Sometimes I miss it very much. It's when I am here, when I have this incredible reference point to draw from that I see that I have done a lot in the last 25 years since I left here. It fills me with a lot of mixed feelings though. Sometimes I wish I never left because I like being here so much and really like visiting the people I grew up with. They are people I have such admiration for, I am honored that I get to hang out with them now and then. I know that sounds ridiculous but that's how I feel. I think of what I missed by leaving here in 1981. All the bands I never saw, things like that. I miss the simplicity of those times. A lot of that is part of youth, I know. You

Henry Rollins

don't have the world to contend with yet and in the limitations there's a lot of freedom and good times. When you get a little older, there's a lot more happening and you get busier with all of it. I think I did the right thing by leaving when I did. It's been a hell of a time and there's no way I could have done what I have without leaving here and taking several chances. All the same, being here rips me open and makes me feel very vulnerable and sometimes extremely confused and depressed.

After I got back to the hotel I met up with Ian and we went over to his parent's place, as we usually do. We spent some time reading some of his mother's writing. It takes up two full filing cabinets! Many of her journal entries are written in letter form to "Posterity." That's so cool. She willed it all to Ian's niece Ava! How great is that?! Ian pulled out some of the letters, one of which describes the Teen Idles trip to California. I think Ginger wrote all these things to be read now. I think it was long range planning, knowing there was going to be a family there to read it after her passing. Her faith in that was an inspiration to write so much stuff. I think she really liked to write, that's perhaps a good deal of it, but it had to be in her mind to keep the family strong with these stories. Ginger was one of the most extraordinary people I have ever met. I have every letter she ever wrote me. It was amazing to hear Ian read from her letters when she talked about us. It was like someone reading from a legendary time in history. Just that she mentioned me in her writing makes me feel special. I miss her very much. Hearing Ian read her words was incredible. The filing cabinets sit only a few feet from where she passed away.

From there we went to Ian's place and hung out. Ian always plays records when I am there and he always throws on stuff that I have never heard. Tonight he played a band called Third World War who I had never heard of before, no surprise there. One should never think they have heard "a lot of music" because in relation to how much exists in the world, you have not heard but a small fraction even if you are an avid listener. Anyway, an interesting band, sounds like Skrewdriver and Sham 69 heard Third World War. Something that Ian has an almost unnatural ability to do, and he's had this since I can remember, is buy a record that's really cheap and a few years later it's one of the rarest records ever. Stuff he finds for a couple of bucks somewhere, out of the few records he buys a year, are often these astounding finds. I've seen him get a record because he thought it looked interesting or whatever and then you hear it and it blows your mind and then you find out they only pressed a few hundred. In the last few years I have done this game where Ian plays something and then I go online and try to find it and fairly often, I completely strike out.

From Ian's we started walking over to a place called Olson's which is a bookstore. Ivor Hanson of Faith, Embrace, and Manifesto fame was going to read from his new book called <u>Life On The Ledge: Reflections Of A New York City Window Cleaner</u> and we were going to check it out. On the way over, we picked up Guy Picciotto and kept walking. For me, this kind of thing is as good as it gets. As much of a loner as I am, there are some people I brake for and most of them live here. We get to the bookstore and there's some familiar faces there: Ian's sister Katie and Eddie Janney, player on some of some of the greatest records Dischord ever released. Ivor read from the book and it was very cool. I took a lot of photos as I always do when I am here. From there, Ian, Eddie, Guy and I walked over to a restaurant. We walked in and sitting there with his parents was Ian Svenonius of Nation Of Ulysses, The Make Up, and Weird War. How cool is this night turning out to be?! Glad I had my camera with me. From there, we left with Ian S. in tow to our next stop which was Paul Bishow's apartment. We were going to check out some film footage he has that was shot back in the day at Madam's Organ, one of the great early, short-lived DC Punk venues. On the way there, we walked within blocks of Madam's Organ, it was just fantastic. Paul's apartment is located a few doors down from the old Ontario Theater at 1700 Columbia, where we saw The Clash, The Buzzcocks, Gang Of Four, The Cramps, and many others. On our way there we ran into Mick Lowe, one of the guys from the Madam's Organ days. I don't know what decade it was when last I saw him. We get to the apartment and Brendan Canty, of Rites Of Spring, Fugazi, Deadline, shows up. This is one of the great nights of the year so far. The footage was really cool, I saw my 18 year-old self in some of it. There's no audio and I don't know if they have enough for a real documentary but I hope something comes of the footage. I guess it's Super 8 film. What I would have given to have recorded every moment I was in that place somehow, even if it was just journal entries. I saw some shows at Madam's Organ, 2318 18th St. NW, that changed my life. It was one of the places that my life began. It wasn't much, a row house basically, with the stage area in the front window. It's now a hair salon, I think. Underneath it is the very cool Crooked Beat record store. I always try to buy records when I am in there to support the place. It's so cool to walk in there and look up at the ceiling and know that over your head The Bad Brains, The Teen Idles, The Untouchables, Trench Mouth, The Mad and so many other bands rocked that place almost 30 years before. It's where the Bad Brains did their 2nd ever show!

I remember some nights, after the bands had played, people would just stand around and hang out. It was some of the first social interaction I ever experienced. Being a shy person, it was really cool to have people be so friendly, it gave me a lot of confidence and it was one of the places I met people who thought differently. It was like waking up from a very long sleep. The years of private schooling really isolated me from the world and it was in the Punk Rock scene where I began to find my feet on the ground. All these years later, I am still trying to catch up on things.

From Columbia Rd. Guy and Ian S. took off and Ian, Eddie, Brendan and I went back to Ian's and hung out for a little while, then Ian dropped me off here at the hotel.

Earlier tonight Ian gave me a record I had asked for a copy of a while ago. It was the 2nd pressing of the first Minor Threat record. The awful completist in me compelled me to ask him for one even though I hated to do it. Usually if it's something like that, I just find a copy on ebay and don't bother him but for some reason I asked him for a copy. It's the one pressing of that record I didn't have. As he gave me the record, he said that the record was his mother's copy and he thought I should have it. I was really knocked out by that. I tried to thank him and explain what it meant and I am sure the words fell short but that he understood anyway. I guess it's now my most prized record. I sure miss her. What a thing for him to do. Today was so great.

Sometimes when I am here it's difficult for me to contain, control or understand all the things that are in my head. There are places only several yards from this hotel that literally make me stop breathing I am so moved when I walk by. I miss the place even though I am in it at that moment. I think I miss what it was and actually being there only makes that fact more concrete. Sometimes when I am here and I am about to go to sleep, I will bolt from the hotel and walk down the street to look in the window of the place I used to work in when I was a young teenager. I want it to be that place again and I want to go in and work at my old job. It's also the same stretch of sidewalk I walked up in the summer of 1981 to go to the train station to go to New York City and audition for Black Flag. It hits me hard. Sometimes I look out the window of the room down at my old neighborhood and I just want to die. I don't understand these feelings and they are very hard for me to deal with. No place does it to me like this place. The only thing that comes close is the two times I have been back to the South Bay in southern California where Black Flag lived. I went down there one night and drove around after well over 15 years of not seeing the place. I drove by the old practice place, the old SST, the Ginn's house and a few other landmarks. It was intense. A couple of year ago I went down there again with Heidi one night and I showed her the old landmarks. We went to the Ginn's house and looked in the window and there was Mr. Ginn working on something at a table. We watched him for a moment and left. That was the last time I ever saw him. He passed away not long ago. He was an amazing man and without his and Mrs. Ginn's generosity, Black Flag would have had an even rougher ride than we did.

It's great to be here but it comes with a price.

01-19-07 Washington DC: Late. Today was great. Ian suggested that we go out and visit Skip Groff. Skip used to run a record store out in Rockville, MD called Yesterday & Today. I used to go there all the time. A few years ago he closed the store down and now only sells online. If you check out my book <u>Broken Summers</u>, there are photos of Skip and the store. I had not seen Skip since the place closed on 09-30-02. We drove out to Skip's house and he took us to his warehouse where he keeps all his singles. It's insane how many records the man has. I have no idea how many thousand pieces of vinyl were in that place. After we checked that out, we went back to his house and hung out there for awhile and then we came back into town. We went over to Ian's and he played some really good records. This time around, he played some stuff I knew of but not much. Some of the bands he played were: The Hawnay Troof, XBXRX, Jah Scouse, The Bears, and a great single by a band called The Need. They have a really cool song called *Let Them Eat Valium*. Ian also had a download of the acetate alternate version of the first Velvet Underground album that I read about recently. It was online for free and he downloaded it and I copied it. Can't wait to check it out. It's great to get turned onto stuff I have not heard before by Ian because we have been listening to music together since we were young and it's one of the great rituals of my life. We have spent so many hours checking out music together, it never gets boring. From his house we went to the Thai restaurant that we always go to when I am here and it was great as usual. After that, we talked for a long time and he dropped me off here at the hotel.

01-20-07 Washington DC: 0724 hrs. In the coffee place down the street from the hotel at the usual table. After I got back to the room last night I fought back the urge to sleep and went back out again for a short walk in the cold. The air was great and if I hadn't been so tired, I would still be out walking in it. I got back to the room, racked for about 4.5 hours and then wrenched myself from sleep to get up and out. It would be great to still be sleeping but this is better. In 24 hours I won't be here. In less than 24 hours I will take that early morning taxi to Dulles and head west. I hate that ride. It's the beginning of the end of the trip. The hardest part of the DC visit is the night before I leave. I will sit in the hotel room, tired but unable to sleep. I look out the window for minutes on end and then usually throw on my coat and head back out and walk to some point just to be out in it a little while longer. I prolong the inevitable departure for as long as I can by staying awake. I reckon if I stay awake, then somehow it will be easier to deal with leaving. I started thinking this way when my friend Joe Cole was killed. I didn't want to sleep afterwards thinking that if I did, he would really be dead. Ridiculous, of course, but the situation was a first for me. I remember when Ian's mother was dying I didn't want to sleep for fear that sleeping would somehow cause her to depart. I remember trying to sleep after I had arrived here and couldn't get more than an hour. I got back up and went back to the house. I guess I didn't want the story to be over and thought that by sleeping the story would end. I know that's weak. To a lesser degree, that's how I feel on the night before I leave here. The pain of leaving here almost makes it too hard to come here in the first place.

I work at being alone. I am alone when I want to be and alone when I don't want to be in an effort to kill the desire to be around people. The more things I see and learn, the harder it is to be around people on any level beyond work related or casual greeting. Now and then I want to be around people or spend time with a female, but I know that's a weakness I cannot give way to. I will not get anything done if I waste time trying to hold some female's hand. I've never been good at that kind of thing anyway and for me, it's dodging the truth and I can't afford it. The people I put the brakes on for are here and it's always great to see them. Ian is a busy guy with a lot of people leaning on him so it's always amazing to me that he will take some time to hang out with me.

Today has great potential. Susie J. is coming up from Florida to hang photos at the Govinda Gallery for her upcoming show in early February. Susie is the person who took the pictures that are the covers of the first Teen Idles and Minor Threat releases. Her photos are in some of my books. Her photographs are very important to the DC Indie music scene. She has a book coming out next month called Punk Love. I did the foreword and Ian did the author interview. I can't be here for the opening at the gallery but at least I can check in with Susie when she gets here. I saw a copy of the book at Ian's last night, it looks really good. Ivor and Susie both have books out this year, that is so cool.

01-21-07 Dulles Airport: 0705 hrs. Waiting for the flight. Leaving is never easy. The long ride to Dulles is always a drag. Actually, the whole trip starts going south around Saturday afternoon, knowing that it's heading towards a finish. The last few hours with Ian are simultaneously great and sad because I know that I will soon be leaving. It's almost easier when Ian is on tour and I am on my own in DC, it's less of a drag when I am outward bound.

As hard as it is to leave the old neighborhood, it's time well spent with the people I like and hanging out with Ian rather than just walking around on my own. I do like being on my own for part of the time here, just walking, taking things in, thinking. Sometimes when I am here by myself I walk all over, hang out in places until they close and walk by places I used to live in or work at and places of people I know. I figure I should just leave them alone. I usually see these people when Ian sets it up. I figure everyone has their own thing going and I don't want to slow down their lives. I try to be as low impact as possible in situations like these.

LA CA: 1828 hrs. It feels later. I guess it's the time change. I got in around 5 hours ago. I got some sleep on the flight. I have been doing all the things I had on my list to get done today. Basic food and cleaning stuff. Almost done.

This is the finish line for this trip. Honestly, I feel like loading some more songs onto the iPod, re-packing and heading out for something else right now. I wouldn't mind going right back to DC if there was something out there for me to do. That's the problem, I can't handle down time.

Yesterday was great. I walked down to the Govinda Gallery and talked to the owner Chris until Susie J. and Ian showed up. We laid out all the photographs on the floor and checked them out and they looked fantastic in large format. I have not seen Susie J. in many years and it was good to see her again. She looks great and it made me feel good to see her. I hired her at Häagen-Dazs many years ago and we still keep in touch. I am glad I had my camera with me because I got some great pictures of Ian and Susie J. together. The opening is on February 4 and I can't be there because of shoot dates for the TV show. I will check tomorrow with the Swift River people and see what the status is on that but I bet they won't be moving. If there was a way I could get out there for that opening I would do it.

The three of us eventually left Govinda and went to Ian's brother's house to visit the family and see their new baby. She's a beautiful little thing. I played with her older sister Ava for quite awhile. She's 4 and has a very fertile imagination. She told me her name wasn't Ava, that Ava was not around. I asked her who she was and she said her name was Avalina. I asked where Ava was and she pointed to a can of paint and told me she was in there. I called her father over and told him that Ava was in a can of paint. We looked at the can of paint and asked her how Ava could possibly fit in there. She shrugged her shoulders like it was our problem to figure out. I asked her if there were any other sisters around and she said there was another named Angelina but she was asleep. I asked where she was sleeping and she said, "Under the covers, under the bed." I asked, "You have another bed underneath your bed?" and she smiled and nodded like she knew I was buying all this. I asked if there was anyone else around I should know about and she said she had an invisible friend who lived next door but his mother rarely allows visits. I asked if he walks to school with her and she looked at me like I was an idiot who was now boring to her, "Of course!" Then we sat under the kitchen table and used a popsicle stick as a magic wand to make a postcard materialize from thin air. Actually it was her father who dropped it down to us, magic often needs a little help.

Ian, Susie J. and I left to take her to the airport. We dropped her off and then went to Dischord House. I had not been there in awhile. I have been going to that place since 1981. We stayed there for a little while and then went back to the old neighborhood and ate at one of the local restaurants and talked for a long time. We went from there to his car and he dropped me off at the hotel. It's always great to see Ian and be around the old spots but this was one of the best visits I can remember. Seeing all those people was great. It's good to know that I am not so out of it that I can't hang around anyone. I still felt strange around them all, an outsider for the most part, but I could probably get around a lot of that by spending more time being around them. That they are so cool to me means a lot. I have a lot of respect for these people.

At the airport I was waiting for the plane and was listening to a bunch of contractors talk about going to Iraq and Afghanistan for work. One of them came over to me and asked me to sign a page from a newspaper. He showed me an article on the page about DC landmarks and they had the old Häagen-Dazs listed and talked about how Ian and I used to work there. I thought that was pretty cool. I got on the plane and fell out as soon as I could. I didn't get any work done when I woke up because I was too depressed about the trip being over and having to come back to LA. I have been keeping busy all day and am now tired. I am going to fold my laundry and go to sleep. I will be up in a few hours and will go to the office and get back in my LA rut. I feel washed up at this moment.

01-26-07 LA CA: 2230 hrs. I have been back in LA for almost a week now. I have had a hard time getting back into the swing of things here. I was looking forward to the radio show last Tuesday but it didn't go as well as I wanted it to, at least the music was good. I am still thinking about the time I had in DC. It was such a great visit. On Friday nights when I am here, I always think of places in my old neighborhood and wonder what's happening at that moment. I did that tonight, knowing that a week ago, I was there.

One of the things that frustrates me about returning to LA is not the place itself but the act of returning somehow cheapens what I had been doing up until I returned. The only upside about returning is that I live alone and there is no one to deal with or have to explain anything to. I did a full week of "normal" and it's lame how quickly I become absorbed back into this place. The only thing that reminds me that I have been gone is that I am jet lagging somewhat and my sleep is light and filled with bad dreams.

The president's State of the Union Address a few days ago was an insult. What a failure he is. Two days ago, Wolf Blitzer interviewed Dick Cheney and was totally cowed by the guy. No balls. Cheney ate him for lunch.

Blitzer: You know, we're out of time, but a couple of issues I want to raise with you: your daughter, Mary. She's pregnant. All of us are happy she's going to have a baby. You're going to have another grandchild. Some of the ... some critics are suggesting, for example, a statement from someone representing Focus on the Family, "Mary Cheney's pregnancy raises the question of what's best for children. Just because it's possible to conceive a child outside of the relationship of a married mother and father doesn't mean that it's best for the child." Do you want to respond to that?

Cheney: No

Blitzer: She's, obviously, a good daughter...

Cheney: I'm delighted I'm about to have a sixth grandchild, Wolf. And obviously I think the world of both my daughters and all of my grandchildren. And I think, frankly, you're out of line with that question.

Blitzer: I think all of us appreciate...

Cheney: I think you're out of line.

Blitzer: We like your daughters. Believe me, I'm very sympathetic to Liz and to Mary. I like them both. That was a question that's come up, and it's a responsible, fair question.

Cheney: I just fundamentally disagree with you.

Blitzer: I want to congratulate you on having another grandchild. Let's wind up with the soft stuff—Nancy Pelosi. What was it like sitting with her last night as opposed to Dennis Hastert?

Fuck CNN. If I ever go in there again, I will just confront anyone whoever interviews me and force them to deal with me. I have lost all respect for that outlet except for Christiane Amanpour, she's brilliant. Seeing how the media basically let the Bush administration run roughshod all over the truth, they can go fuck themselves. I think yesterday it was announced that four soldiers were kidnapped in Iraq and then handcuffed and executed. Bush and company have to go. They are covered in the blood of thousands. They have to go now. What a mess. What a depressing mess they have sunk this country and so much of the world into. So much waste and destruction. I used to wonder how people could still get behind Bush but now I don't and I don't care what any of them say to me at this point. I get these letters telling me that I am going Hollywood for being against the invasion and occupation of Iraq. That kind of thing used to make me mad but now I just answer the letter politely and tell the guy that I would really appreciate it if he told all his friends to hate me as well. I can only hope he passes that along. Whenever one of these assholes works the Hollywood angle, I know they are fucking weak.

I was thinking of getting out of here again next week when the IFC show shoot dates are done but I have a lot of work to do here and I am pretty worn out. I don't think it was the travel that got me as much as coming back here.

I got a letter from a fellow in Israel the other day telling me that someone working on the shoot in Tel Aviv asked his girlfriend to walk up onstage and give me a bouquet of flowers and that he thought it was pretty lame. I wrote back and told him I agreed. I was wondering how that all came about. I felt so stupid standing there with these two bouquets of flowers in my arms at the start of my show. I found out that it was the producers doing. I wrote them a letter a few days ago telling them to fuck themselves and that it's not their stage to mess with. It really threw me off at the top of the set. It's one of my nightmares, someone getting onstage while I am there. It happens now and then and it's always hard for me to get the set back on track. I managed to save it in Tel Aviv although it threw me off and it will show on the footage. This was the night when the cameras were rolling and it's the one that will be used to make the IFC special to air several weeks from now. The less I need to deal with onstage the better but I guess that's not the same idea the producers have. It's shit like that that makes it hard to deal with them. They are good people but sometimes they are frustrating to work with. We have a long way to go to get through this season.

01-27-07 LA CA: 1904 hrs. I slept as long as I could last night but anxiety and bad dreams got me up fairly early so I have been going for hours. Of all the things I saw and experienced in the time I was out on this trip, a few instances stand out vividly. One is when I was walking down a street in town near the Lemonier Base in Djibouti, a young boy came up to me and pointed at the bottle of water I had in my hand. I just smiled and put it in my pocket, I didn't think to just give him the damn water. As I walked a short distance past him, I looked down and the water was gone. I guess he really needed that water. I can still see his face. Another thing that I remember is how I felt when I was walking with Ian, Eddie, Guy and Ian S. through the Adams Morgan neighborhood. The sound of their voices and their familiarity, the cold air, the streetlights, that we were all together at once and that it meant something. To me, it's more than just some people walking together. I live alone and spend a great deal of time by myself. I work at it. It's not always easy but most of the time I think it's the right thing to do. I don't know a lot of people. It's easier for me that way. A long time ago, when I started traveling all the time, I learned that the less attachments to people I had, the better. I have lived that way for many years now. Many events in my life have turned me further inward so it's often difficult to close the distance I have with people even when I want to. When I visit these people in DC I don't exactly feel like I am with them, it's more like I am next to them but in that instance when we were walking down the street, I felt like I was with them and it was really great. These are some of the best people I have ever met so I am always honored to be around them. When I think of all the great things they have done in their lives I am filled with awe and inspiration. In that moment when we were walking together, I felt like I was from somewhere. I get that feeling now and then when I am in DC.

On a different note, I am listening to Flogging A Dead Horse, the collection of b-sides and miscellaneous tracks by the Sex Pistols. Fuck, what a great band that was. The Never Mind The Bullocks album is as good as it gets I reckon. My favorite tracks of theirs were the b-sides though. *I Wanna Be Me, No Fun,* those are perfect.

I have a lot of work next week so I have to get out of this and get my head in the game. I have to shoot the first four episodes for the

IFC show. I have been writing stuff for it and still have a lot to do but will make deadline. In April I have shows in NYC and LA with Janeane Garofalo and Marc Maron. We were going to call the show Rome but it seemed to cause confusion. Janeane and I were talking about it today and I said that it wasn't a play and there's no music and she said we should use that as the title of the show. So now the title of the show is It's Not A Play And There's No Music: An Evening With Janeane Garofalo, Marc Maron & Henry Rollins. We'll do five shows out there and five out here. I think that's how it's going to go down. It will give me something to prepare for.

This was a depressing week, being back here, the troop casualties. I can't wait to get on the road and go somewhere else.

These are the entries I wrote for the Canadian newspaper:

01-10-07 Tel Aviv Israel: 2351 hrs. I have been in Tel Aviv for a little over two days. The last few weeks have been busy and interesting. The first part of the journey that put me here started on the 19th of last month when I left Los Angeles, California for my 7th USO tour. The USO, otherwise known as the United Services Organization, is an NGO that provides entertainment for American Forces wherever they may be. USO regulars include rocker Joan Jett, comedian and talk show host Al Franken and many others. I do not support president Bush's oil grab in Iraq or his demofacist foreign policy that creates more enemies of America all over the world every day. I do, however, support the troops and their families no matter whether we see eye to eye on any of these issues. USO tours have taken me all over the world to locations such as Iraq, Afghanistan, Kuwait, Egypt, South Korea and Kyrgyzstan.

Anyway, I went from LA to Frankfurt, Germany, switched planes and arrived in Dubai, UAE hours later. For the next few days I spent time with American Forces in Dubai and Abu Dhabi and then went to Djibouti, Africa via Qatar where I spent Christmas and then went to Bahrain, the end of the USO tour. I flew back to Dubai for a speaking date and from there I went to Tehran, Iran for five days. I have wanted to go there for many years. It was an experience to say the least. With the way president Bush is rattling the sabers, it looks like he wants to send other people's sons and daughters to Iran to fight them there before we have to fight them here or take care of the smoking gun that may some day become a mushroom cloud or to stay the course or something. I hope he gets fed well in prison.

From Tehran I went to Amman, Jordan via Dubai where my bag went missing. My two days off in Jordan were spent calling the airport and having strange conversations with the good people at the lost and found department. I am here for three talking shows, Thursday to Saturday.

Today was good for two reasons: I reconnected with one of the more interesting people I have ever met, a man named Michael who drove me around Israel when I was here years ago. I learned a lot from him. He took me to Jerusalem today and we spent the day walking around as he gave me one of his amazing history lessons. Israel is one of the most beautiful countries I have ever seen and Jerusalem is just incredible. I can't wait to come back. The other good thing that happened was my bag turned up and somehow made it all the way to Tel Aviv. Actually, another good thing happened, I was invited to be a guest at a local radio station where I was allowed to play all the music so I brought my iPod and played a lot of music that might be a first for some of the listeners. I was really tired when I got there but woke up as soon as the show started. Radio is a blast. The shows start tomorrow and I can't wait to get it going.

01-11-07 Jerusalem Israel: 1922 hrs. Backstage. The venue is very small and utilitarian. It reminds me of the small art spaces I used to do in Europe back in the '80s. I have no idea what to expect audience-wise tonight. I have only done one show in Israel and it was in Tel Aviv. We got here only a little while ago so there was no time to see anything. I would have been no good for taking in the sights anyway, I get far too wound up about the show to do anything but go to the dressing room and prepare myself. I have been doing shows like this for about 23 years and they have never been easy and I am always nerved up before every single show. I want to be onstage and do the show but before I get out there, I can never figure out how I am going to get through it. I think the constant stress keeps me honest but is probably taking its toll on me in other ways.

My manager is in town as the Saturday show is being filmed for a special on the Independent Film Channel. Hours ago, he and I did our ritual beginning of the year meeting where we figure out the schedule for the too many things I want to do in a 12 month period. Within an hour we were able to figure out that I will have a few days off here and there but for the most part it will be like the previous years: too much, too often—just the way I like it. Actually, it's the only way I have been able to deal with life. I think that work and constant movement is the way I self-medicate. I am an angry man. I have been mad my whole life. I don't kick dogs or punch the walls in a drunken stupor but I do fight against my inherent laziness and my seeming inability to learn. I combat these weaknesses by throwing myself at work and forcing myself to endure as much geographic upheaval as I can stand. Somehow, I think I'm doing the right thing, on the other hand it could be that I can't figure out what to do with my life. Life is a pain in the ass isn't it? All the maintenance, ego, fear, ambition, and utter wretchedness of being human, I guess it's better than being dead.

A talking show in Jerusalem?! Will anyone show up? Will they have a sense of humor? I'm not on until 2115 hrs. So for now, the cold room, the wait.

01-12-07 Tel Aviv Israel: 2039 hrs. Last night's show was good. I had a feeling it was going to be ok when I walked out there and saw so many people smiling. I did the show and after it was over I walked behind the curtain and sat down in a chair and finished my bottle of water. When I looked up I saw there were a bunch of people standing around me, basically a large part of the audience just followed me backstage. I thought it was very funny. They were very friendly and I took photos with them and signed all the things they had and then I packed up and left.

I hit stage here in Tel Aviv today around 1415 hrs. The early stage time was because of the Sabbath. I am not familiar with how it works with things like the Sabbath and some of the rituals of religious rites. While I am not for or against religion of any kind, I must say that it holds no interest to me at all. I was at the Western Wall a couple of days ago and watched the men and women doing their devotions and while I respect the intensity of it all, it's not a thing I want to do with my time. To see people in their outfits walking about, to see how much of their time is spent being religious is, to me, the definition of misery. On the other hand, you can take everything I know about the topic and fit it in a thimble.

The rest of this evening and night I have to myself. I am too tired to walk around and am happy to be alone in my small room with the door closed. I've got some music on and a cup of coffee and it's all I need. I have been out on this trip almost a month now. I will be out again somewhere else in the world next month as I have about two clear weeks in February with no shoot dates for my television show on the Independent Film Channel and nothing I can't work around. I am pretty slammed with work all year and have been working with management looking for spaces in the schedule here and there when I can travel. I think February will be Laos, Vietnam and perhaps Cambodia. I have been eager to go to Vietnam for some time and am very interested in seeing the Plain of Jars in Laos.

01-13-07 Tel Aviv Israel: 1835 hrs. Backstage at the venue. I am not onstage for another three hours. The more nervous I am before shows, the earlier I come to the venue. I am usually nerved up before a show but this one is being filmed so it throws a little more tension into the mix. The talking shows I do are never easy as there's so many ways for it to go bad. I have show amnesia. Even if I am several shows into a tour, hitting stage night after night, I will sit hours out from stage time, wondering how I am going to get through it. When it's time to hit it, there's no place I'd rather be. I feel that way every time I walk out there but sitting here now, I can't remember feeling that way even though I was in this venue yesterday. I have been going onto stages for over 25 years and while I like to be there, it's never

Henry Rollins

been an easy time. On tour, I live inside a held breath of anticipation. It's all about the show and the next one. There is a short time after the show where I feel extreme relief and soon after, I start getting nervous again. I had hoped that it would get easier with age and experience but it has only gotten worse.

The next 24 hours will be very busy and sleep free. I do the show tonight and have to be in the lobby of the hotel at 0600 hrs. We will be out all day, driving all over the place getting exterior shots for this television special. It will be a 12 hour day at the minimum and a few hours later, I am on the aforementioned flight to Toronto for two days of press.

Shouldn't I be writing more about Tel Aviv and Israel? Probably, but it's hard to look around with shows looming. It's one of the downsides of touring for me. If there's a show to do, I stop thinking of where I am and just think about the show. I am happy that I was able to have at least one day off here to drive around with Michael and just see the place. As it is now, all I can think of is that stage. Tomorrow will be better. We will be moving hard but at least we'll be out in it and able to see some things.

Later: Show over. Audience was great and I think the show went ok. Glad to get that one done. I have to be up in a few hours to start shooting.

01-14-07 Tel Aviv Israel: 2204 hrs. Back at the hotel. We were out getting shots for about 14 hours. The idea of the day's work was to film Ziv Koren, the great Israeli photojournalist, and me walking through several locations and talking. We went to many interesting places but what made them all the more interesting was Ziv's experiences in some of them. Ziv has covered many intense and dangerous events that have happened in Israel over the last several years. Many of the religious landmarks we visited were made more interesting when Ziv would recount taking photos in the middle of an intense Israeli-Palestinian clash and point to a spot three feet from where he was standing and explain how he had photographed an injured Israeli soldier being dragged to safety right there. There's a lot of that kind of thing in Israel. Around sundown, we went to a section of the newly built wall to check it out up close. I made many trips to the Berlin Wall in the 1980s and remember it well. This one is taller, stronger and serves a different purpose but the feeling I had when I walked along it was the same as I felt in Berlin. Apparently, this wall has cut down the number of suicide bombings in Israel.

The last shot of the day was in a café where in 2002, a suicide bomber walked in and deployed a device, killing nine patrons and injuring many others. I have seen a photograph of the result and it's about as awful as you can imagine. We sat a few feet away from where that photo was taken. The café was quickly rebuilt to look like it did before and re-opened. Life goes on. This is the spirit of Israel. Our location manager, Sharon, whose office is around the corner and frequents this place, said it took her a year to come back in. There is an intensity and vitality that courses through the many people I've met in Israel that I have not encountered anywhere else. They are people who have been through a lot and will no doubt be going through a lot more. Next stop, Toronto.

03. DC To Superbowl Sunday

02-01-07 LAX: 0512 hrs. Another journey starts. One of the déjà vu moments / rituals of my life. Whenever I sit here waiting to board the flight, I think of flying to DC when Ginger passed away. This trip is a happier one I hope. I have slept about an hour. I feel punchy but alright. This trip was planned only a few hours ago. Susie J.'s opening for her book <u>Punk Love</u> is Friday night at the Govinda Gallery. The plan was that I was going to be working today and tomorrow and unable to make it but the schedule changed around 1830 hrs. last night and all of a sudden I was loose and off I went. Travel plans were quickly drawn up and here I am. Good to go for Dulles. I could have left tomorrow and gotten there in time but I figured I might as well get more time in DC. I can work at the hotel rather than the office and have an extra day in DC, what is the bad part of that? I am doing this for Susie, her book, the scene, the neighborhood, Ian, and the memories the book contains. I know it will make her happy that I am there. This is how I show respect. Having the time available and not to have gone would be unacceptable. 0522 hrs.

1727 hrs. Washington DC. I am at a pizza place that many years ago was an Arthur Treacher's Fish and Chips. I arrived a few hours ago. I spent a little time in my room. I e-mailed Ian then went out. I am tripping on the fact that I am here again after only two weeks. This place does so much to me. When I was at Dulles waiting for my bag, I picked up the airport magazine and noticed my name on the cover. There was a picture of me on the back page along with a short interview. I remember the interview now. The female who interviewed me lives around here and knew all the streets I was referencing and actually walks by the house where I lived in the '70s. It's almost dark outside and very cold.

1814 hrs. Food done. Now in the coffee place, looking across the street at a building I used to work in many years ago. This is another one of my rituals. I have sat in this exact spot many times. I like to look at this section of the avenue and remember all the times I walked on it, skated on it, etc. Before I walked in the door here, I passed a woman and smelled her perfume as she walked by. Perfume smells good in the cold, it's unexpected, like finding an apple in the snow. Talked to Ian. He's glad I'm here. He's jammed up with phone press for an upcoming Evens tour in Australia so I'll see him tomorrow. He suggested I go to his brother's house and check in. I will go to the grocery store and get some food for the house and bring it as a gift. It is now dark outside. What I am looking at through the window right now I have seen in my mind many times as I sit in airplanes with my eyes shut. It's one of the places I go to in my thoughts, it's almost strange to see it for real.

Before I came in here, I stood across the street from the building that used to be the pet shop I worked in decades ago. There was a light on at the top of the stairs on the 2nd floor and I could see the doorway of what used to be the reptile room framed by the light. I looked at it for a few minutes and lost myself in thought. It's best to do this kind of thing alone. It's one of the reasons I try to be alone more often than not. You can't expect anyone to wait around while you stare at a window and go into some Proustian reverie, which I am all about. In a lot of ways I am burned out. I have been all over, heard, seen, done and been through a lot. This place and the people I know here, they make me feel something. I am not burned out on them or this place. Perhaps it's coming here that keeps me from becoming completely burned out on everything else. I have a dedication to this place and these people. It's nothing they would notice or need to make note of, it is for the most part, a code, a sense of duty on my part. I was telling an interviewer earlier today about why I came out here. It's to pay respect to these people, the time back then, the music scene and what was accomplished. The values I learned here are the ones I went into the world with. When I see gangsters with their street tattooed on them, I completely understand. 1839 hrs.

02-02-07 Washington DC: 1236 hrs. Sitting in my room for a

Henry Rollins

moment. I went out for awhile. No way I'm going to sit in this room for very long. I know I should be outside and in the neighborhood but one of the things I like to do sometimes is sit in the hotel room and look out the window and down the Avenue and think about when I used to live here. I basically stew in the juices of the place.

Last night I watched CSPAN for awhile. General Casey was getting grilled by the Senate Armed Services Committee on the troop surge into Baghdad. It was painful to watch the General defend the move. The Military is now just a tool of American corporate interests in the region. It was painful to listen to Gen. Casey have to get hammered by Senator McCain, who is only trying to get votes. I think Gen. Casey knows it's not enough troop strength to do anything more than to catch more bullets and shrapnel but he's got to go out there and take the flak for the Bush camp. When Bush booted Rumsfeld, he bought himself some time. When he said recently that his strategy was "maybe a slow failure" and decided to do something else, he bought himself some more time and didn't have to admit he was wrong but only "adapting to win" or whatever bullshit they trotted out to keep the ball up in the air. No one is talking much about what a 21,500 soldier "augmentation" will mean in practical and financial terms. These men and women will need everything from weapons to protection to vehicles. Is there enough? Or are they going to be given a bag lunch and told to carry on as best they can? The Bush administration will keep this thing going for as long as they have to so they can get that oil. "Daddy, who killed the electric car?" "Well son, that would be Dick Cheney." Exxon had a 39 billion dollar profit in 2006, 6 billion of that was in tax breaks. They will do anything to keep America on petroleum, from paying scientists to discredit climate change studies to starting and prolonging wars. I wonder when the last time America was in a conflict that wasn't about business. If America started using electric cars, companies like Exxon would feel it and that will not do. As long as these companies have so much power, the truth will be mutilated to fit their agenda. That's the thing that trips me out, how they take the facts and treat them like clay and mold them into talking points that bolster their position. It's incredible, actually, deadly.

I think it is a waste of time to worry about what anyone at agencies like Fox or CNN says about anything. At the end of the day, they're nothing more than cowards. Anderson Cooper and people like him know that what they're saying is a softened and nuanced version of what's really happening. When someone brings back the real horror of the invasion and occupation of Iraq and how it's basically nothing more than controlled chaos, they are quickly discredited. Talk about people unable to handle the truth! At this point, I only pay attention to what the Government is doing and form my own opinions. It's the only way I can see things clearly. You can look at what Exxon made last year, what Bush is asking for budget-wise for his invasion and occupation of Iraq and you can formulate thoughts and opinions from the facts. Follow the money and save yourself a lot of time.

The National Intelligence Estimate is in and what little of it American citizens are allowed to read isn't going to put a smile on the face of the Bush administration. The NIE states that security in Iraq will "continue to deteriorate" which says to me that there will be increased amounts of casualties compared to last year. I wonder if there will be any questions asked of the president. I wonder if press secretary Tony Snow will find some way to smile and patronize the press corps as he waves away their inquiries as to why Bush never listens to the experts, like the dozen plus intelligence agencies that put the NIE together. This current administration, they sure are experts in every possible field. They know more about the environment than all the leading scientists concerned with the topic. They are the masters of war and finance. It's amazing how well they are handling everything. The Bush Administration does not listen to anyone but themselves. This is the way of empire. 1311 hrs.

Late. What a night. Ian, Amy and I got to the Govinda a little before 1800 hrs. We walked in and Susie J. saw us and freaked out when she saw me. She was very happy that I managed to make it. Just the look on her face was worth the trip. At that moment it hit me how badly I would have felt if I were unable to make the event. Soon after we got there the place started filling up and I started to see some familiar faces. I saw John Stabb of GI and talked to him for awhile. I was signing books and talking to people there. The next time I looked up the place was wall to wall people and I saw many I recognized. I saw that Nathan, Ian, Geordie and Jeff of The Teen Idles were all in the same room. I don't remember the last time I saw them all in one place. I don't think they were all at Ian's brother's wedding and that would be the only time I can think they would be in the same place at anything I was at. Susie J gathered them all for some photos and I stood next to her and took as many photos as I could. I got in a few pictures with them too. The four of them standing there, I was looking at my youth. I was at almost every one of their shows. I looked around and saw Guy Picciotto, Eddie Janney, Danny Ingram, Alec MacKaye, Amanda MacKaye and a few others I recognized from back in the day. I felt in the right place at the right time. I talked to all of them and little by little the place emptied out and around 2100 hrs. it was down to just a few of us. All the books had sold and the attendance was way more than they than expected. Those of us who were left went around the corner and ate at a restaurant. I had a chance to talk to Susie J.'s husband who is a really great guy. After we finished there, Ian and I walked back to the old neighborhood, which was one of the highpoints of the night. Ian and I go on some pretty epic walks, it's one of my favorite things to do with him. Most of the time I walk alone but it's cool to spend time with Ian on foot. When we got near my hotel we parted ways, I came back to my room and here I am. I am tired but still tripping on the evening. There were a few people who didn't show up who I thought I was going to see there. I am sure all this stuff holds a lot less meaning for some of the people from back in the day. I can understand that.

I am tired but I don't want to sleep. In 24 hours I will be back here knowing that I have to get up in a few hours to take a taxi back to the airport. These visits are hard on me. There's a short amount of time I enjoy being here and then an almost equal amount of time I spend saying goodbye to the place while I am still here. The best part of trips here is usually the first night and then I get to feeling empty. It got worse after Ginger passed away. Now, every time I come here I think of her and it makes me sad.

02-03-07 Washington DC: 1248 hrs. Last night was so great. I am still tripping on seeing all of the Teen Idles in one room. I know this sounds really bad but it's true: of all the history I have ever studied, the one I find most interesting is my own. I am not saying that I am more interesting than anyone else out there but it's amazing to see these people years later and catch up and get their take on what the past meant to them. I am part of their past and they are part of mine, that's the part that I find so interesting. We're all out there in different parts of the world, doing different things but we have a shared past that feels somehow larger than all of us. It's something I trip on when I am around these people. It makes me remember that I was at the first Minor Threat show and I was at the shows in a lot of the photos that Susie took. I watched her take the famous photo of Alec MacKaye that is on the front cover of the first Minor Threat EP. It's things like that and seeing all those people last night that makes me feel lucky I was born where and when I was. I wouldn't trade any of those memories for anything. We were all quite lucky, I think.

The two year period of summer 1979 to summer of 1981 is a time of my life I have returned to many times. I have written about it, tried to retrace steps, pick up clues and document as much of that time as I possibly could. This two year period is post-high school and pre-Black Flag. After I joined the band in the summer of 1981, everything changed. I started missing DC the day I left for my life out in the world. I knew I was doing the right thing, I had to leave, but all the same I knew I was going to miss my hometown. I have been back many times for many reasons, shows, birthdays, weddings and some occasions not so festive. Summer of 1980 to summer 1981 was a great time for DC music. It was the time to go to as many shows as possible. It was great to live the music.

Whenever I am here, I am filled with mixed emotions. I am happy to be walking on the old streets that hold some kind of familiarity, perhaps more self created than real but real enough for me. Behind that joy of the familiar are feelings of sadness and loss of passing time. 1351 hrs.

02-04-07 Washington Dulles Airport: 0659 hrs. Much better now that I'm at Dulles. DC is miles behind me which makes it easier to deal with in a way, knowing that I am not leaving, but have left.

I tried to sleep but only dozed off for short periods. Before I leave the hotel I am always filled with dread. I always think of the apartment building I lived in while I was in high school. It's only a few blocks away. I feel like I have come full circle and really haven't gone anywhere in my life. Also, I think about Ginger and how bad it felt to leave DC while she was so sick. Staying would have made no difference but still, I felt bad leaving that morning and I always think about it when I am about to leave the hotel for the airport. Being here at the gate is allowing me to think more clearly and disengage from the DC experience somewhat.

I don't think it's a good idea to be close to people. I do not hate them but I think I am better off keeping my distance and staying to myself. I think the best thing for me to do is be as much help as I can when and if I am needed and leave it at that. That's what I do for the most part but I am honestly so glad to see these people from DC that I break code. They are great, their kids are great and I would give them anything I have. I know that's a heavy thing to say but it's the truth. That's why I went to DC on a moment's notice this time, it was a chance to show respect and show that I don't take anything from there for granted. I have no feelings like that for LA. If I never saw the place again it wouldn't matter to me at all. It truly is nobody's city. Not mine at least. I am always happy to leave. One thing I like about the place is that it alienates me and that keeps me sharp. I feel like a mercenary when I go after that Hollywood work. It's the money I make from those jobs that I like the most.

02-05-07 LA CA: 2145 hrs. I am back in the grind of things and everything is back to LA normal.

The big news today, besides more American KIA and many more Iraqis dead, is Bush's 2.9 trillion budget proposal. It tells me that he has no plans of getting out of Iraq. He doesn't care about the middle class, the poor, the sick, the elderly. Fuck it. Don't get sick. Don't fall down. Get the fuck out of the flood plains and whatever you do, don't be African American. The Democrats will get run over again. Bush and his murderous fuckers will get what they want, they always do. I think we deserve it. If those who don't like what's happening can't overthrow the regime then they deserve the regime: Iraq under Saddam, Russia under Stalin, North Korea under Kim Jong-il and I feel the same way about America. If the Dems can't control that budget and what it's being spent on, if they can't change the situation in Iraq and Afghanistan, I won't be surprised. There's so much money at stake. The Bush administration will take all the money away from America and re-distribute it to themselves and the ones they favor. They are changing the way the world works, they have changed everything in only a few short years. If it wasn't so true and if so much of the damage done wasn't so irreversible, then it would be interesting to marvel at the coup they managed to pull off but it's all death and loss and sadness and pain and darkness so it's no good to think about how well they brutally manipulated, lied, and stole. All the people who are broke now, that's that. Nothing will change for them unless you consider things getting worse a change. There are some people who actually think the war on terror is being fought in Iraq. I wish they weren't so naïve and thick.

I got up early and went to the doctor to get my left foot looked at. I can't get much movement out of it and it often makes me trip and fall. Basically, I can't tap my foot. I noticed it a couple of years ago but I didn't think much about it. These days I come down hard on my left foot. I can't balance on it either. I notice that when I am trying to put my shoes on after I get through security at the airport. Ian noticed it two weeks ago and asked me about it. He said I should get it checked out. He said, "You still have a lot of walking to do." I reckoned he was right so I found a doctor who looks at these things.

I went to see the guy today. He looked me over and said that my sciatic nerve is palsied. He explained that the nerve starts in the back and goes down the leg. Makes sense because there's a chunk of my back that's numb and a part that hurts all the time. I looked it up and sure enough those are symptoms of sciatic nerve damage. I asked him what I did to damage my sciatic nerve. He asked me if I had been in any accidents or anything. I have not. He said it can happen in all kinds of ways. He said basically that the nerve isn't talking to the muscles and that's why the foot won't move. It's a strange thing, trying to move my foot and being unable to. I asked the doctor what can be done and he said that sometimes they can operate and clear scar tissue off the nerve and if they can't do that, they can give me a brace. A brace means there's no healing, just maintenance. He said I have "drop foot."

I think it's great. My body is falling apart on me. I did some reading up on all this and it's all bad news. Now I understand where all that pain was coming from. I don't know what will happen to me next. I go back next week to have someone else look at me. I'll know more then.

Sitting here at my desk, I am still thinking about DC. I had such a good time there. I don't know when I will get a chance to go there again. I have been thinking about the two visits there in two weeks and it's a lot to deal with. It is a great place but being there confuses me. When I walk on the same sidewalks that I walked on 30+ years ago, it just trips me out and I feel like I am dying right at that moment. Sometimes when I am walking by myself there, I can feel my heart pounding in my chest really hard. I am not a very emotional person at this point, I am fairly deadened, like that sciatic nerve that's quitting on me but walking around with Ian in the old neighborhood or down by 18th and Columbia Road, everything was vivid and poignant. There were moments where I felt myself becoming somewhat overwhelmed.

When I was at the Govinda Gallery surrounded by all those pictures of myself and others taken over 25 years ago and also amongst many of the people in the pictures, I felt like I was in the past and the present at once. At moments I felt like I was amongst people I had known at a certain time and we were all back in one place but not together. At one point, I wondered if we had all converged on this spot to find something or to seek out some kind of answer. Perhaps

A Preferred Blur

that's what those class reunions are like. I watched people's faces as they looked at pictures of themselves and tried to listen to what they were saying to the people they were with. I wanted to know what those times meant to them. I don't know how much it's supposed to mean to me or exactly what it's supposed to mean at all. It was intense to see Nathan's mother after at least 25 years. These were the people I was around before I left DC. Summer 1981 was the time that my life changed. I left town. My life is divided into two parts, before and after I left DC. I have spent many hours of my life sitting on airplanes and in hotel rooms wondering if I should not have left DC. I think of all the shows I could have seen and everything else and I always come to the conclusion that I did what I did and here I am and that's it.

Those last few hours in the hotel room the other night, I was very depressed. I didn't want to go but of course, I had to go. I have to stay tight and keep driving forward. It's great to see all those people and hear their voices. I like them all very much. But I have to go. Other currents push me and other voices speak more clearly and I have to go. 2237 hrs.

Henry Rollins

04. Getting Evens

02-21-07 LA CA: 0017 hrs. Been back from the radio show for some time now. Trying to get to sleep but not tired. I came up with an idea several days ago and am now acting on it. I will detail the idea here in a minute. Nothing earth shattering, just trying to keep things interesting.

In the last several days there has been a lot of things happening in the world, a lot of things happening in America. I have been listening to the president ramp up the pre-invasion of Iran rhetoric and it's making me sick. The other day he said that there was no doubt that Iranians were supplying Iraqi insurgents with bombs to attack American Forces.

This is Bush at a recent press conference: "I can say with certainty that the Quds Force, a part of the Iranian government, has provided these sophisticated I.E.D.'s that have harmed our troops. And I'd like to repeat, I do not know whether or not the Quds Force was ordered from the top echelons of the government. But my point is, what's worse, them ordering it and it happening, or them not ordering it and its happening?"

This quote from General Peter Pace is very intense: "We know that the explosively formed projectiles are manufactured in Iran. What I would not say is that the Iranian government per se knows about this. It is clear that Iranians are involved and it is clear that materials from Iran are involved. But I would not say based on what I know that the Iranian government clearly knows or is complicit." I wonder if this their next bullshit "slam dunk."

From the way I was hearing it on the news, and from the way these guys are positioning this information, it's as if Iran is the only place that manufactures explosively formed projectiles, otherwise known as EFPs. I did some internet research and learned what an explosively formed projectile is, it's not all that hard to understand. I also found a site that had a soldier talking about how American Forces have been discovering EFPs in Iraq for years. I did not hear that on the news at all, although I did hear Randi Rhodes mention it a couple of days after I read about it online. I imagine a lot of people have done the same exact sequence of sleuthing and now know a bit more than they knew before. I think these motherfuckers are full of it.

I was listening to ex-Marine Scott Ritter on the radio the other day, he was saying some really intense shit about the consequences of invading Iran. Ritter is one heavy mofo, Fuckin' Marine, UNSCOM weapons inspector in Iraq charged with finding WMDs, a Republican who is a very outspoken critic of the Bush administration. He said that he has little doubt that Bush wants to invade Iran. He also said that going into Iran will be nothing like going into Iraq. He said their military is strong and well equipped. Then he said, and I am paraphrasing here, "If you think Iran is going to passively allow a Christian country to bomb them, you're wrong."

What the fuck do I know? I know what I read and what I come up with sitting here thinking. I wonder how the hell American forces could possibly go into Iran when there are men and women who are going into their 4th rotation in Iraq. Does America have the troop strength? Are the Bush people just barking mad? There's an interview Amy Goodman did with Ritter that I found online at Democracy Now! that blew my mind.

I don't know if I can explain this idea clearly to you but I will try. Sometimes America makes me feel like I am suffocating. I try to think of somewhere I can be in America where I won't have to be in America. I don't hate the place but when I see the news about how many troops died that day and what the White House is saying about the invasion and occupation of Iraq and the bullshit they're starting about Iran, when I think about the Katrina disaster, and all the rest, I know I need to consider the world my home and not America. I need to see the entire planet as the place to be. I feel that I am not an American but a transient. That's what I now consider myself. I am passing through. As often as I can, for as long as I can, I want to keep moving. I want to fly on planes, live in hotel rooms, walk streets in cities at night all over the world. America is being destroyed from the inside. It's a great place that's being ruined. If I attach to it too much, it will ruin me too. So now, more than ever, I want to go far and wide. In the years I have left, this is it for me. I will walk the streets of this world as it is destroyed. I am nearly fifty now. I don't know how much longer I will be able to keep moving but I am going to give it all I have. There is nothing else for me to do. I have no one in my life. I am not attached to anyone and no one is attached to me. No one is under the slightest impression that I am all that much a part of their lives. This is something I have worked at and maintain. I don't hate people and the few that I know, I care about a great deal but I gotta keep moving and not suffocate. When I am somewhere for too long, I feel like I have surrendered, that's as best as I can put it. I feel like I am going along with someone else's plan. When I come up with an idea, like going to Iran, then I feel alive again and it makes me want to keep coming up with things like that to do until I am dead. It's a way to distract myself from myself, which is always a good thing.

The power is in the idea. There is nothing I like better than thinking something up, going out and executing the idea. To live life on your own terms you don't have to be all that intelligent, you just have to think differently than they do. If that means being a bit crazy now and then, so be it. Looking back at that pass through Tehran, that was the right thing to do. It's the only way I learn anything. I have to go into it. I read books but can't retain much, I try to enjoy life living in one place and it just depresses me and makes me feel like I am dying. There is only one way for me to understand anything and that is to go into the territory. If you're not going to be smart, you will have to be tough.

1039 hrs. I woke up this morning coming out of a dream where I was staring at a painting of a boy sitting on a highway guard rail with a plane in the air behind him. I have no idea what that's about. Then I thought of the articles I read about the soldiers at Walter Reed and started getting angry and disgusted and I got up and got going.

Back to what I was saying last night. I am still struggling with the idea I am trying to express. I try to pay attention to what's happening in the news, Iraq, Iran, etc. If I didn't, I would feel as if I was endorsing the criminal activity of this administration and being complicit with the slaughter and mutilation of all these people. By absorbing all the awful information that comes through, the thought of these kids coming back dead, amputated, guts ripped from their bodies, the smell of it, the horror these young people go through, what it does to them and that they will deal with it for the rest of their lives, it makes me sick. The only way for me to decrease the amount of toxicity all this truth fills me with is to keep moving and to get out of America when I can. When I leave America for another country these days, I feel as if I am leaving the earth itself. I feel alive again. I can't get that feeling here anymore, at least not at this time. Leaving America feels like being pulled out of the water and discovering that there is life after drowning. When I am here, I find myself spending a lot of time just reacting to all the bad things happening these days. I don't feel "home" anywhere, I never have and I don't want to but I do feel less like a target when I am out in the world. If I spend too much time in America, I sometimes forget that there are other places to go.

This begs the question, "If you don't like the place so much, then why don't you just leave for good?" I can't do that. America is the best idea on the planet and by just leaving altogether, the wrong people get what they want and the wrong people get destroyed. It's nonstop conflict and genocide here, I understand that. The good is being killed off by the bad, I know and I'm up for fighting the good fight but being an American all the time will break you. I know that to be human is to be broken over and over, I just want to be broken by something more noble and honorable than cowardly men and their actions so I have to travel the world as much as I can until I die. I have to constantly combat my mediocrity, my apathy and slothful tendencies. I am quick to get angry at anything that distracts me from this struggle. I also struggle with that anger and I'm angry at that struggle.

02-22-07 LA CA: 1320 hrs. Yesterday afternoon Heidi and I went over to Linda Ramone's house to pick up tapes of Johnny Ramone being interviewed for a potential autobiography.

Soon after Johnny passed away in September of 2004, Linda told me that Johnny had been working on an autobiography with a writer. She asked if I would look it over. I read it and for the most part, I thought it was good. It needed some work, the writer had written himself into the book quite a bit and I thought it was distracting but the Johnny parts were great, pure Johnny Ramone. Johnny was a straight talker, very blunt, always to the point and didn't care what anyone thought of that. I got back to Linda and told her the book was good but needed some work done on it. She asked if I would work on it. I said I would even though I was already very busy. It would have been impossible for me to have said no. It's a good way to say thanks to The Ramones for all that good music and it would be an interesting bit of work. The literary agent and her management looked it over and showed it to some publishers, they all passed and cited the writer's additions as what they didn't like. I was instructed to basically cleanse the manuscript of his input and make the book more Johnny.

I got a file of the manuscript and started reading and re-reading it, making notes, and getting an understanding of what the book was and what it could be. I went through the book chapter by chapter in February of 2005, when I was on the Trans Siberian Express. When I got back to America, I gave my version to Linda, she read it and liked it. I think the writer read it and didn't like it so much. Linda said that the writer and Johnny had done a lot of interview stuff on tape and she was having trouble trying to get the tapes back from him. She asked me to call him and so I did and had a not-so-great, tension-filled and very long conversation with the man but didn't manage to get the tapes from him. Linda's agent tried and failed too. Linda wanted to get the tapes back so I could listen to them to see if there was anything else on the tapes that could be used.

Over the next few months, tension built as the writer wouldn't release the tapes, nor was he ok with the changes I made to the manuscript. Johnny had done some kind of 50-50 deal with the guy. Linda was now taking Johnny's place as half owner of the book. She told the guy that unless I was involved with the book, there would be no book at all. He didn't like that. I was hoping we could just get to work on the thing and finish it. It turned into a stalemate and I went back to other things and stopped thinking about it, figuring if something changed or if Linda needed me, she would call me. Around that time, I got a call from the owner of an independent publishing house who puts out some really interesting titles, several of which I have. He told me that he had been in contact with the writer and wanted to publish the book in its original form, he thought it was great. I told him that Linda had the ultimate say on what, when, and where. The publisher said I shouldn't be too sure of that. I like the guy and in the friendliest possible way, I tried to explain to him that he was wrong and he really didn't want to mess with Linda Ramone and her management and lawyers. He would indeed be in breach and Linda would have to unleash lawyer hell on him. She would, too. I don't know whether he took me seriously or not. I called Linda and told her about it and she got pretty mad.

Anyway, fast forward several months to a few weeks ago. Linda calls and says she got the tapes back from the writer, he's cooled off, and would I come get the tapes and check them out and finish the book. This is what lead Heidi and I to go over to her place and pick them up. There were about 9 micro cassettes. Also in the package the writer sent was another Johnny Ramone manuscript he wrote which I had not seen previously. It's kind of a dramatized "fact-based" type of thing. I started reading it out loud to Linda and Heidi. It's, well, it's not for me to judge but I think it's a good thing that it never came out. To paraphrase, "Johnny's restless gaze searched the room, his hard eyes glinted in the dim light of the backstage..."

I had not been to the house in awhile. This is the house that Johnny passed away in. One of the times I was there, we were going through boxes of stuff and came across a spiral notebook. I started turning the pages and saw that it contained Ramones lyrics and other writing. I asked Linda about it and she said that it was Joey's. I turned to a page that had two different sets of writing and asked her about it. She pointed to one set of writing and said that was Joey's and that the other set of writing was Lester Bangs', who sometimes wrote songs with Joey. I have been thinking about that notebook ever since. I borrowed it and Carol scanned it into the computer today so now it's backed up.

I put a couple of hours of audio from the tapes onto CD last night and came in early today and went back to it. It's all in real time so it takes awhile.

1710 hrs. About to head out of here. I spent the day working on radio, upcoming schedule stuff and the Johnny tapes. I am 8 hours into it, about half way done. My mood has changed from having listened to quite a bit of the tapes. The writer is now pissing me off. On the tapes, it's easy to tell when Johnny is medicated, tired or in pain. This fuckin' guy goes barreling right along and from the questions he's asking, it sounds like he's very unprepared, he switches topics, asks really stupid questions, chimes in, etc. It's frustrating to listen to. I am not looking forward to plowing through all this stuff but I have to. I hope Linda doesn't listen to the CDRs I am going to give her. There are moments when I can tell Johnny's in pain. When he was hurting, his voice would raise in pitch. He gets along with the guy and I think this writer is doing the best he can but fuck that, he's not a pro and it shows. We're just lucky that Johnny was such a brick motherfucker and could be so lucid and direct under such conditions. I was being cool to this writer fuck but as you can tell, that's over with. He's getting his proper credit in the book as he obviously worked his ass off on the project but listening to the method he used, if there was one, it's easy to see that the interviews could have been so much more or at least not so hard on Johnny.

02-23-07 LA CA: 2337 hrs. I didn't get all the work done at the office I wanted to but I got enough done. I did an interview with a nice female from the New Republic. I went to the radio station and pre-taped the show for next Tuesday with Engineer X and then came back to the office. Heidi told me to call Janeane, who wrapped out of her show yesterday, to ask if she would to come over to the office to say hello. She came by awhile later and met Carol and Heidi and then she and I hung out for awhile and then she went back to her hotel and

A Preferred Blur   **117**

then off to the airport. It was great to have her in town. I don't hang out with people all that much but I liked hanging out with her. She's very funny and easy to be around.

I am packed and ready to go for the most part. I will go over it one more time on Sunday morning. Looking forward to getting out of here. What else? I got another hour of Johnny tape banged onto CDR today. I have about 7 more hours to go. I'll get it done when I get back. I can't think of anything else I want to write about at the moment. I didn't get a chance to hear much news today. I know that we lost another soldier at least. It was hilarious to hear Cheney say that the fact that Blair pulled some of his soldiers out of Iraq is a sign of success in the region. If America does it, it's cutting and running. I got it.

02-24-07 LA CA: 2236 hrs. I went to the Spirit Awards today. I did the press line and the photo line as well. The press line was interesting. I told a nice man from the BBC that I thought Tony Blair was a douche bag and asked him if he would please put that on the radio when he got back. I stood in the general hang out area for a little while and talked to the IFC people and some others I ran into. I met Sarah Silverman and told her I thought she was great and that I had seen her the other night at Largo. I spoke briefly with John Waters and then went into the theater space. I was at the same table as last year. Sarah was funny again like she was last year. Dennis Hopper came out and reprised the role of Frank Booth for a moment, "Don't you fuckin' look at me!" which warmed my heart. He was then joined by Laura Dern and they did a tribute to David Lynch. Loretta Switt and Robert Downey Jr. did a tribute to Robert Altman. At one point, Sharon Stone was up there for way too long. Minnie Driver sang very well as did Rosario Dawson. The whole thing lasted about two hours. After it was over, I was taken to the after party. There were a lot of people waiting outside wanting autographs and pictures. Many people had pictures of me on hand, they must have found out I was going to be there. I signed them, I know they are going on ebay. What these guys don't know is that no one will buy them for more than a couple of bucks. I went inside the after party area for about ten minutes and then left and came back here. I was out the door at 1130 hrs. and back at 1700 hrs. It was all pretty painless, I guess. If the IFC people didn't ask me to I would never go to something like that. I really like the IFC people and they ask very little of me so I don't mind. I think those kind of things water you down. I don't want to get used to things like that, I think if I go to too many events like that, hang around with people too much, it will soften me.

When I was young, I didn't need to think that way but now I do. It's like caloric intake. When you're young and hungry you don't have to count the calories because you're not going to get enough to satisfy your hunger anyway but when you have resources, you have to watch your diet. It's easy to become tamed and normalized. Where there is light and laughter there is danger for me. I don't trust it and don't want it. I don't want it because I know anything I want can't be all that good for me. I don't mind seeing the few people I have known for many years, like in DC, but even that is difficult for me because I feel so bad when I have to leave, it's almost easier not to see them and not feel so torn up later. I guess one could say that's real life and you have to dive in and take all those emotional vicissitudes as part of the package. The party-event environment is like junk food to me, upon leaving, I feel like I have wasted time and overindulged. Do you remember that scene in <u>Das Boot</u> when the captain of the submarine has to leave vessel and go to that party with all the over-fed high ranking officers? Do you remember how feral he looks in comparison to all the soft men? When I first saw that film, that was the scene that stuck out. I never want to be one of those soft men at the party, that's the bottom line.

I have been reading up on coalition troop levels in Iraq. I wanted to know the numbers because British Prime Minister Tony Blair pulled some of his soldiers out of Iraq and John Howard, Prime Minister of Australia, said mean and nasty things about Barack Obama and I wanted to see how many of his brave Australian forces he had in the region. Perhaps John Howard should add the same percentage of soldiers to his troop force in Iraq that Bush will add to American troop forces with the surge. That is, unless he doesn't have the stomach for war that Bush and Cheney have. Anyway, I found the numbers of troops that other countries have in Iraq, they should put that shit on the news. There's hardly anyone there but American forces. America is fighting this thing on their own. Cheney and Bush are not vice president and president of the United States. They don't represent America. They represent a few corporations, not even all that many, either. They should take those American flag pins off their jackets, they're not in any way patriots nor do they love America or care about the American people. They just treat Americans like suckers. I wish some people weren't so naïve.

02-25-07 LAX: 2045 hrs. I am out of here for a little under a week. Next stop, Sydney Australia. Last year when I was in Cannes, France at MIPCOM, the Australian company who is carrying the IFC show there asked if I would ever go to Australia for press. I said sure. Several weeks ago, when I found out that The Evens were going to play in Australia, I called management and asked if the Australians might be interested in me doing the press around The Evens shows in Sydney and they said yes. So, I am going to Australia to do press by day and hopefully see The Evens play two shows in Sydney. I didn't tell Ian, I thought it might be more interesting if I just showed up. I wrote my agent down there and asked him to get me a ticket to each show to make sure I could still get in if the shows sold out.

I will get there Tuesday morning and start press a few hours later. The Evens are playing Wednesday and Thursday nights. I will do press by day and see the shows at night. Friday, I fly to Melbourne for press and then back to Sydney for more on Saturday and then I fly back here on Sunday. I wish I could stay longer but I have chores in LA all week. I am glad this worked out so I can get the work done and see the shows. Perhaps there's a show to see in Melbourne on Saturday, I am looking forward to finding out if anyone's playing.

As always, it's great to be leaving town and it's always great to be going to Australia. It's a long flight but I don't mind. I like the chance to think and write. Whenever I fly to Australia now, I always think of the great Mick Geyer, my old pal from Melbourne. He died a couple of years ago. I miss that guy. He was an extraordinary person.

I am hoping that a geographical change will help me knock myself out of the depression that has been chewing on me for the last few days. Today I could barely move. It woke me up early. Last night and this morning, I just wanted to be dead. I know it's wrong to think that way but I feel like that a lot. I have figured out ways to get myself out of it. One of them is to plan to kill myself but only after I have properly taken care of all my affairs. I make lists of who I would give what to and what I would do to make things easy on anyone who would have to deal with anything I leave behind. It would take awhile. I would have to fulfill obligations, meet some deadlines, etc. Then I would have to figure out a way to dispose of myself without traumatizing anyone. By the time I have worked though that a few times, I am onto other thoughts and I find something to do with myself. It's awful to think these things seeing what other people have to go through every day and I feel ashamed of myself when I am this way. I need to stay busy to keep depression at bay. It's one of the reasons I go all the time, it's the best way I have found to deal with it. In a way, it's dodging the issue, dealing with it by not dealing with it. I know that's no good but when I am still for too long, if there's nothing challenging me or making me have to prove myself, I don't know what to do with my life. Time to get on the plane. 2128 hrs.

2157 hrs. I like that. The flight attendant remarked that he sees me on this flight pretty often. That's pretty cool, I'm a local in the air. One of the best parts about travel is the points in between. On long flights like this one, I feel weightless and alive. I am on the way to somewhere. I am sitting still but in motion, I am going. It's a relief. It allows me to sit next to my mind. You do what you want, think what you want, it's all choices, I get that. I miss processing information without filtering it through current events. With things the way they are, it's difficult for me to read fiction. It makes me think I am slacking off somehow. I purposely brought two works of fiction with me: Proust and a book by Dawn Powell that Janeane Garofalo gave me called <u>Turn, Magic Wheel</u>. I also have some magazines and articles I dragged off the internet about Iran, Iraq, and all the other usual, awful stuff. Since 9-11, it has been difficult for me to write much besides journal entries and travel writing. I feel the need to mark time, events and motion in writing. Never in my life have I wanted to stay on the move more often than in the last few years. I am trying to be a fugitive from the confines of my inherent mediocrity and amazing ability to stay in a state of comfortable torpidity for appalling amounts of time.

What occurs to me to do is to be a crazy man who doesn't stop moving, doesn't stop working. I want to wear myself out as often as possible in as many places as possible. Travel keeps me off balance and always reaching for it. I am trying to learn something here. Slamming myself into everything I can is the only way I can do it. I am not naturally curious, I work at it. I have to struggle to keep myself learning new things. Much of the time, everything in me tells me to sit in a small room and not move, to listen to a handful of records and not to read anything that is hard to understand or to just shoot myself in the head. I also know that most of my instincts are wrong. I am bad with names, directions, maps, or anything that requires common sense. In a way, this makes things easy. All I have to do is think about what I want to do and then do the opposite. Sometimes I get letters from people asking my advice. I do the best I can but always warn them that I am the last person they should be asking as I am as messed up as anyone.

12:04 hours into the flight. I guess I needed the sleep. In a dream, Raymond Pettibon gives me a magazine and excitedly points out an article about me. It's a one page profile. I remember it being a well written series of put downs. The one that I remember is "Achievements: Smashed roadblocks on the road to progress and replaced them with bigger roadblocks." The magazine was called Dropout. I went back to the magazine in another dream and found that the article had been written by me.

When I woke up a few minutes ago and looked at my stopwatch, I realized that there's only a little while before the plane lands and I felt the need to do something. I don't know why but I started wondering if it ever occurs to an elderly person to get out of bed and get going that day because there may not be many days left. I wondered if being old gives a whole new meaning to the idea of sleeping your life away. Now and then, I get a letter from my mother and she tells me what she's up to. She tells me about the last couple of books she has read. She reads voraciously and writes very well. She is a very intelligent person. I don't know her very well so reading the letters are like getting book tips from an enthusiastic professor or something. Much of my early youth I have walled off so effectively I would probably need surgery to access it so I can't remember if she and I ever discussed any topic to any great length or depth or much of anything she ever told me. She is the only living relative of mine I keep in contact with. I have not seen my father in about 20 years. I met his mother a couple of times, I met my mother's mother a couple of times, I also spent a couple of Christmases with my mother's sister and her kids. That was in the late '60s, early '70s. It doesn't matter to me, there's nothing I want to know about those times or those people. Anyway, my mother is in her seventies and seems to kick much ass but I always remember her as being that way. I wonder if she gets up early and gets it going knowing there's not decades to go.

On my better days, I try to disappear into life. Not by spending time with people but by traveling great distances and experiencing the destinations on my own. I don't mind spending time with people now and then but I really like to watch people walk by and live their lives. That's what I tried to do as much as possible when I was in Tehran and it was great. Some places I have been are harder to blend in than others.

I'm feeling better now that I am somewhere and have a full day ahead. I have press starting a few hours after we land, not as much as tomorrow but enough to keep me busy.

There's always a lot to think about when I am in Australia. I first went there in early 1989 when the band was just starting. We had just finished recording the Hard Volume album. Since then, I have toured there many times, recorded live albums with the band and on my own and produced an album for The Mark Of Cain, which is still one of my favorite records. I have been lucky to see some really great shows there, Beasts Of Bourbon, The Mark Of Cain, Kim Salmon And The Surrealists, Nick Cave And The Bad Seeds, Mass Appeal, and even acts from outside of Australia like Nirvana and The Stooges. One of the only friendships I ever had was in Australia with Mick Geyer. I can't even begin to say how much he taught me and how generous he was with his time. I learned so much about music, literature, film and history from him, he's one of the bright lights in my life. He's dead now and whenever I am in Melbourne, it hits me hard. When I am there on Saturday, I hope I don't stay in St. Kilda, that's where he and I used to hang out at the cafes on Fitzroy street. It's hard to walk around there at night and think about him being gone. He died of cancer in his early '50s. I kept all his letters, he was a great letter writer. When I read them, I felt that I was the only thing on his mind at the time, that's what a great letter is all about to me. You can take any one of those letters to a book or record store, get the titles he recommends and that's your weekend, week, month, what have you. I have tried to list all the books, records and artists that he turned me onto and at this point it's impossible. From 1989 to 2003, he recommended things for me to check out.

There is also a sense of finality I get when I am in Australia. I bet I will never do band shows in Australia again. I remember last year, when it looked like the band was going pretty good, I asked management to see if there was any interest in any other countries as I wanted to tour the world with the band. If it had worked out, I would like nothing more than to be training for a tour this coming summer. Anyway, management asked our Australian agent if there might be any interest and he said he doubted it and added that ticket sales for the talking shows go down every year, so I don't know how many times I will be coming back. At least one more round of talking shows and then that will probably be it. One of the hardest parts of touring is the numbers. Always the numbers. I know what they mean when they say numbers don't lie. In this business, you live and die by them. I have to work hard to deal with the numbers but at the same time not let them affect what I do. It's one of the reasons I throw myself into whatever work is at hand with all I've got, you never know if it's the last time around the track. Nothing that I do is a sure thing for longer than it takes to do it. I'm shooting the IFC show now, that's work until summer, then it's over. Will there be another season? Who knows? I'll tour this fall, will anyone show up? I can't spend too much time thinking in that way but it's bad battle strategy not to think that way part of the time. I wish things were different. When I see bands go out every year and do great, a comedian type pack it out year after year, do I want a piece that? It's probably a great thing but it also seems like a perfect way to take things for granted and get soft. Success isn't what makes you successful. Instability, discomfort, dissatisfaction and uncertainty are the ingredients. Success is a tricky quantity. If you're only working for it, that's pretty boring in my opinion, like a band who only makes a record in order to sell a million copies, if that's the motivation, how good will it really be? If you achieve success, it can potentially ruin everything you do even more than failure can. The bottom line is I would rather do what I think is right and be considered a failure than do what I think is wrong and be considered a success. From reading the short history of the writer Dawn Powell located on the inside of the book of hers I am reading, it says that even though she had fans like Hemingway, she never achieved much success with her writing. I am about 50 pages into Turn, Magic Wheel and already know I will be reading more of her work, she is a fantastic writer. We will be landing soon.

02-27-07 Sydney Australia: 2011 hrs. I landed in the morning and met up with Fiona, who will be taking me through all the press chores here in Sydney. She dropped me off here at the hotel. I had about an hour off and then had to meet up with some of the people who run Movie Extra, who will be airing the IFC show here. I met with them for awhile, they're good folks, they like the show and seem to be behind it. After that, Fiona and I went to shoot some interview stuff for Optus Austar Magazine and Movie Network. We shot the interviews at the Summit Restaurant 1 Orbit Lounge, it's like the restaurant at LAX, it rotates slowly. I didn't really notice it turning, I was jet lagging so everything was spinning a little anyway. After that, Fiona and I got back together with the Movie Extra people and we ate dinner. I just got back.

The hotel I usually stay at is sold out so I am down the road from there which is a drag, I really like that neighborhood. The one I am in now is busier and noisier. I don't mind, I am just glad to be here.

One of the major upsides of this trip is that tomorrow night and the night after The Evens are playing here at the Glebe Town Hall. Ian doesn't know I am in town. I am hoping to get to the venue tomorrow and surprise him and Amy. I think this will be the first time I have ever seen Ian perform outside of America. That should be interesting.

I want to go out and walk around but I am fried and have a long day of press that starts early in the morning and when finished I will go right to the venue with Tim Pittman. Somehow, I have to get all the stuff written for next week's IFC shoots. I have to do four Teeing Offs and two letters. I have the radio broadcast notes done for the upcoming show but am not ready for the next one that I have to do a couple of days after I get back from here. I'll just have to hope jet lag gets me up before the press starts so I can get a lot of it done.

Jet lag always depresses me. I have strange dreams and sometimes I feel in two places at once. Being in Australia usually fills me with relief and lowers my overall stress because it feels so far away from everything, which doesn't make any sense at all but that is how it feels. It's warm and moist outside and it makes me want to stay up late but I have to get my head down. The schedule is very ambitious. I am very excited to be seeing The Evens tomorrow night. The other day when I was in DC, I knew I was going to be making this trip and it was funny to ask Ian if he was looking forward to coming here, knowing the whole time I was going to see him. I hope it all works out tomorrow so I get the drop on him!

02-28-07 Sydney Australia: 2348 hrs. Today was long but ended well. All the press people I spoke to actually seemed to like the IFC show so the interviews went smoothly. I was hoping for some static, I always do, and I was sure to call John Howard a douche bag at every opportunity. It needs to be done. At the end of the press day, I was at Drum Media Magazine which put me close to Tim Pittman's office. I walked over there and he and I set off for The Evens show.

We went to the Glebe Town Hall and waited for Ian and Amy to show up. Tim had been in touch with the woman who was putting on the show and she had been keeping Tim up to date on where Ian was. A few minutes after we got there, Tim called her and found out they were only a couple of minutes away. We went around the back where they would be pulling in and when I heard a car pull in and heard Ian's voice, I walked out there and yelled, "Are you guys going to play *Waiting Room* or what?!" I will never forget the looks on Ian's and Amy's faces when they saw me. They were both completely blank for a second and then they looked surprised and then happy. It was very funny.

We ran all the gear up the two flights of stairs to the top floor of the building where there was a stage and a good sized floor. The Evens bring the entire show with them. They have a small PA which also serves as the monitors. They used the overhead lights in the venue for the lights which I thought was going to look strange but actually turned out to be ok. We set up quickly and they soundchecked. The room was quite boomy but we hoped all the people in attendance that night would dampen that somewhat.

After soundcheck was over, we went down the street to get some food. Glebe seems like a cool part of Sydney. I am not familiar with it but I liked it. We secured some food and then came back to the venue which had started to fill up with people. We kicked it backstage for awhile and then soon enough, it was time for the band to play.

The place was pretty full when they went on and the audience was very happy to see the band. One of the things I like about The Evens is that the low volume of the music and the low key nature of their set up makes for a casual mood and gives Ian a chance to talk between songs without a lot of volume and drama like a Fugazi show used to have. The stuff he says is almost, if not as cool as the songs themselves. He has a great way with an audience because he isn't there to bullshit them and they can tell. Also, he's a very funny man and that's not always the conclusion someone would come away with at a Fugazi or Minor Threat show. His sense of humor is one of the things that I have always liked about Ian and something that people find surprising when I describe him. There are some great sing-along moments in their music and tonight, the whole place was into it. This was the first time I had heard a lot of the new songs done live and they were great. I have listened to the first album so many times. I kinda burned out on it but it was great to hear some of those songs tonight. I can't wait to see them play again tomorrow night.

I have another long day of press tomorrow. I am doing pretty well on not a great deal of sleep. I can do this for about three days and then something gives. I usually do this kind of thing in NYC. I just go and go and not seem to need sleep and then it hits me.

03-01-07 Sydney Australia: Late. I am up in a few hours to fly to Melbourne. I did press and photos all the way to the end of the day. The last stop was a radio station and Ian was there doing an interview in the studio next to the one I was in! He was pre-taping and I was live. The walls between us were glass so we were fucking with each other as we were doing the work. It was so great to see him there. It's such a trip seeing Ian in Australia. I went right from the interview to load in at the Glebe Town Hall. The Evens were great again tonight. Only a couple of songs from the night before. It's so great that they have so many songs and can do two nights in a place and make it worth going to both. Tonight's crowd seemed to be a little more just checking it out where last night's show was full of people who were perhaps more ready for what they were going to get. There were a few of those cheerful Australian drunks at the show. They are fairly unique to Australia I have found. Not belligerent really, just annoying, responding to everything said from the stage like they're having a direct conversation. With The Evens show being on the quiet side, this can become wearing quickly. There was one guy who was non-stop, so after several times of him talking to Ian and Ian being very gracious but getting slightly frustrated at this guy disturbing the evening, I told myself that if he yelled out three more times, I was going to have a quiet word with the guy. He did his three times and that was it. I slipped into the crowd and went looking for him. I found him quickly as he yelled out again. I kind of stood on him so my body was leaning against his. He didn't understand at first but he got it soon enough. I just told him to be quiet and he said ok. He then went and told his friend and his friend came over and looked at me. I just looked back, he said something, I told him to be quiet and stared at him. They were quiet after that and I stayed with them for the rest of the show. I fuckin' hate lightweights. The show was really good and I met a lot of people afterwards who were the typical cool Australian. I loaded out with Ian and Amy, said goodbye to them and came back here. I have been operating on a very low level of sleep for a few days now and it's getting to me but it was worth it to see the band play these last two nights.

There was a moment earlier in the evening that took me quite by surprise. We had just finished loading in. I was standing in the back of the hall, Ian was onstage. The sun was almost gone and the air was very warm and moist. All of a sudden it felt like we were in DC and there was a show that night and there was Ian and there I was and it was like being at a Teen Idles show or something. Here we were, all these years later in a venue with a show happening that night. I can't count how many times I have been in a venue with Ian in a situation just like this, in weather just like this, over so many years. For a moment, I was standing in the past and the present at the same time. It made me think that I was very happy to be born when I was, where I was, and that everything worked out the way it has for the most part. I live for moments like those because no one else can have them exactly that same way, there's no way those things can occur to any-one the same way and it's one of the few things in life that are truly yours and they can never be taken away. That moment may be one of the best times I have ever had in Australia. I have to get some sleep. Tomorrow starts soon and it will be a long one.

03-02-07 Melbourne Australia: 2032 hrs. I was tired enough to get lost walking out of the restaurant to the hotel even though the hotel is directly above it. My alarm clock is set for 0500 hrs. and I have to be up and out of here at 0615 hrs. This is the hotel I was staying at the last time I saw Mick Geyer. Mick was one of the few people I would go out of my way to see. I had many great nights of conversation with Mick from 1989 until 2003. It's been so long now, there's no way I can even start to list all the musicians, artists, directors, writers and other things he turned me onto. There are so many things I learned from him that I probably think I found them myself. I really want to walk down Fitzroy past some of the place we used to hang out in and think about him but I have to get some sleep. I only slept a few hours last night and today was flat out all day until quitting time. I have a lot of memories tied to St. Kilda, where I am now. I guess it's a suburb of Melbourne. I can walk to the first place I ever played here and past venues where I have done so many shows. I don't think I will be coming back here again for music and I don't know how many more times for talking shows. It's always with a bit of sadness I walk around here. I have been to this neighborhood frequently for 18 years, it's a part of me. Being familiar with a place like this is a very big part of what I am all about and why I travel. It's the idea I was trying to explain before, about needing a place the size of the world to breathe in. I like it that I can walk the streets of countries all over the world and know where I am. It's something you have to earn by putting the time and the miles in. That's what it's all about for me, the time, the miles. Over time, I am field stripping myself into the world. America is great but it's full of sadness and pain and death and liars and weaklings. I am a stranger wherever I go so the world is my home. Walking on streets in cities at night and returning alone to small rented rooms is one of the best things I have ever done. I feel more at home in a hotel room than in my own. I believe more in the temporary part of a hotel room. It's great to get your bag and walk out of the thing and leave it behind you and get onto the next one.

Today, when I got into the car to head into town, I found out that a truck had overturned on a main highway and all traffic heading back into the city center was at a standstill. The gal who was in charge of press, Erin, started re-arranging things on the fly as we were going

Henry Rollins

to be late to everything. She managed to do it and even though it was a busy day, we got it all done.

0930: MMM FM

1015: RRR FM

1100: 3LO FM

1200: Herald Sun

1225: MX

1300: Sunday Herald Sun

1400: The Age

1425: Beat

1440: Sunday Age

1445: InPress / Geelong Advertiser

1545: Fox FM

1615: 3PBS

1630: Billboard

1730: RRR FM (again)

It was good work. I am tired and somewhat depleted but really wanting to walk around. I have to be up in a few hours and back to Sydney so I better try and shut off my mind and sleep.

03-03-07 Sydney Australia: 2131 hrs. Today was long but it went surprisingly quickly. It started off with a photo shoot with my old pal Tony Mott, the first photographer to take my picture when I came here in 1989. After the photo shoot, I did a bunch of on camera promos for the show. They were well written but I did some changes here and there and some of them I just re-wrote.

Below me, the streets are full people, it's the start of Mardi Gras, which here is a gay oriented thing I have been lead to believe. I think there was a parade earlier today, I didn't see any of it. This is a good room, I am listening to a mix of tunes on my small stereo system I brought along. I don't have to get up so early tomorrow so I will hang out with my mind for a little while longer before I try and fall out. This trip was a blur punctuated by the two Evens shows. That's how I live my life. I prefer the blur and running semi-wrecked from one thing to the next, it's easier for me to deal with life this way. I would rather serve or protect than befriend. Now and then I go to DC and spend a couple of days there just walking around. I walk by houses where I know the people inside but I don't bother to visit. I just like to see that the lights are on. I look at the house for a minute and walk on. It makes more sense to conduct myself in this manner because a lot of the time, I feel like I'm dead anyway.

03-04-07 Sydney Australia: 1550 hrs. Sitting on the plane, waiting to take off. About 15 hours from now I will be back at my office getting ready for the next thing. This was a good trip that allowed me to get away from myself for awhile. I have a very busy week coming up and now my sights are set on quitting time this coming Friday. Heidi says that all I do is try to get through things and never stop to enjoy them. I guess that's true. As soon as I get somewhere and do what there is to be done I want to get onto the next thing and then get that thing done, aways trying to lose myself in the moment of it and then at the end, find myself in a small room, alone with some time to mend and prepare for whatever comes next.

2130 hrs. LA CA: Flight was uneventful and I got nothing done. It hit me how exhausted I was. After I got home, I wrote up all the rest of the stuff I had to for the IFC show, did my laundry and outlined all the things I have to get done this week. I am feeling pretty bad but I have to stow it for now and get some sleep as soon as I can and try to be sharp for tomorrow. It's depressing to be back here, hopefully there will be enough things happening to stay away from myself for the next few days.

I got a phone call from Inger, the gal from The Nymphs, I have known her about 20 years. She told me that Rodney Bingenheimer is getting a star on Hollywood Blvd. on Friday and Rodney wanted to know if I was going to go. I told her I would be there. I have never been to one of those things but I definitely want to be there to cheer on Rodney, he has done so much for music in Los Angeles and everywhere else. I remember when I first came out here in 1981 and went to KROQ with the other guys in Black Flag to be on his show. I was really happy to meet him. I see him now and then, usually at a

Ramones function and I always make sure to say hello to him. He's been on the air for so many years, it has to be at least 30 or close to it. There is a lot of sadness and death and pain in this town.

05. New York New York

04-04-07 LAX: 0601 hrs. And so it starts again. I don't know why I am so awake but I am. Last night, after the radio show was over, I got back to the house and worked on the show notes and finished packing and tried to sleep but was largely unsuccessful. I was up before the alarm at 0400 hrs. and getting ready to hit to road. The driver was a Vietnam vet from Washington DC. At check in I ran into Stewart Ross, who was the tour accountant for Jane's Addiction back in the day. He's a good guy. He was on his way to Buenos Aires to meet up with Tom Waits who is taking part in a film festival down there. He has been working with Waits for over two decades. As we walked to our respective gates we talked about Gerry Georgettis, a Jane's crew guy. Gerry is remembered by many as the man who had a disagreement at a car dealership, ran his truck into the showroom, literally, and did a lot of damage. Amazingly, he made bail and then hopped a flight and killed himself in the airplane's toilet, you can look him up on the internet. Anyway, Stewart took off to his gate and here I am.

I am happy to be on the move. My bag is very light and it makes me think I have forgotten something very important. I went through everything over and over and I don't think I have left anything out. I am going to New York so I will be able to find whatever I need. I have been off the road for a few weeks and have been grinding it out at the office and the house. I take the work home with me and then take it back to the office. I am not doing much else. I have been working on the IFC show, the radio show, editing a book, and trying to get some reading done. Days go by and I don't really notice. My spells of depression now last longer and hit harder than they used to and I have been spending a good amount of time dealing with that. I don't know if it's depression or just seeing things very clearly and not blinking. Perhaps that's just me trying to tell myself that I am ok.

04-07-07 NYC NY: 0241 hrs. In the hotel room. This is the first opportunity I have had to write since I got here. I have been getting up between 0500 and 0600 hrs. for press both days I have been here. Usually that's not hard to do but it is hard to do it when you only got a few hours of sleep total over both nights. I tried but couldn't get myself to sleep for longer than a few hours. Depression and nightmares were factors.

The interviews were good, I think. Rarely have journalists expressed much enthusiasm for what I do. It's not important, you get on with whatever it is you're doing no matter what and I am used to their apathy and/or dislike of me and what I do. That being said, the ones I talked to over the last couple of days really seem to like the IFC show. That's pretty cool and it made the interviews go smoothly. I don't mind when they are combative but none of them were this time around. There's still more to do next week so there's always time.

I have been out of the news loop for a couple of days. Last night I came back here and literally dropped my bag, brushed my teeth, got right into bed and headed back out the door a few hours later. I did see that the British sailors, newly freed from Iran, are being knocked about by people on the internet. Some people are calling them cowards, for what I can't really understand, and others are calling England, Europe and America weak for not declaring war on Iran right then and there. These people are pathetic. The Fox News bitches dare to make comment, these soft men who have never seen anything more intense than a boxing match. White House spokesman Gordon Johndroe said that it was "unfortunate and extremely disappointing they were treated inappropriately in any way." The White House has a lot of balls to make any fucking comment. Inappropriate treatment of prisoners?! British sailors are cowards? For what, not trying to take out the guards and break out of Iran? People live in a dream world. Some people are criticizing the sailors because they made televised confessions and didn't try to attack their captors. It's always people who have never been in any shit that say things like that. I remember once when Steven Segal asked me if I had tried to take the gun off the guy who was on me the night Joe Cole was killed. I told him no and he asked me why not. There's a guy who lives in a movie. What a douche bag. Since Bush has been in office, he's given all these sissies like O'Reilly and Hannity so much false bravery. It would make you mad if you took them seriously but you know what they're made of so you can't. They lie and people die, it's that simple. They will do and say anything to keep the conflict going. It's just business.

04-08-07 NYC NY: 1123 hrs. I forced myself out of sleep, I didn't want to sleep late as I did yesterday. I was out for a good ten hours yesterday and didn't get out of bed until late afternoon. It was great to sleep but I felt bad getting out of bed so late in the day.

I could tell I wasn't going to get much done last night and needed to get out so I went down to my old neighborhood in the village and checked that out for awhile. I visited with Janeane Garofalo for a couple of hours and then hiked back up here. I am seeing promotional posters for the IFC show all over the place and noticed on one I walked by last night that someone had put a swastika on my forehead like Charles Manson. This is an amazing city. I have been pretty far and wide but have never seen a city like New York. It's one of the greatest inventions ever.

For the last couple of days, I have been busy with press and trying to get enough sleep so I make sense during the interviews. Chris Haskett, the guitar player I was in a band with for many years, was in town and wanted to meet up. I couldn't see him due to scheduling and sheer exhaustion and now he's gone back to Australia. Thinking about it now, I am glad I didn't have the chance to see him. I don't dislike him, quite the opposite, but at this point I don't know what there is to say. We did that tour last year and I think it was, at the end of the day, a waste of my time. I played hard and gave it all I had for sure and the shows were good but I don't think everyone's heart was in it all the way. For some, it was a way to get a paycheck and for others, it was a way to evade reality for awhile. The more the weeks went on, the madder I was getting at most of them and at the whole thing in general. All in all, it was pathetic. So, it's probably a good thing I didn't see Chris as I am sure this would have come out.

The band being done with is one of the things that makes walking around this part of New York intense for me. There's a lot of memories, feelings of failure and finality that hit me hard when I am here. Last night I walked by places I used to live, get my groceries, what have you, and it only then occurred to me that it has been a decade or more since I had an apartment here. It feels more like three or four years. Some of the best and worst times of my life happened here and it's sometimes difficult to walk by all these landmarks of elation and misery. Last night I walked by the apartment I was living in when we wrote the <u>Weight</u> album. I remember how motivated the band was, how much everyone pulled together and were putting all they had into each day of songwriting. I remember how we all were working hard to make something really great happen and knew we had the stuff to do it. It was a great time of inspired effort. I also walked by the apartment I lived in when we were working on the <u>Come In And Burn</u> album, which was quite a different experience. We had great difficulty writing songs and some people in the band started to lose motivation and focus. It turned into a very long and painful process that should have been an indication that the unit should no longer work together. I think we all knew it but didn't want to face it. I remember walking around for hours on end on the weekends just trying to lose myself in the city and somehow distance myself from my pain. There is a Starbucks on Lafayette, near that large metal cube statue, that stays open late. I would go in there and write until they closed at two in the morning. I got a lot work done in that place. After that album was done, I moved out of the city and have never been back except to do shows and press. I still like it here very much but sometimes the memories are hard to deal with.

Living alone in this hotel room makes me thankful I am single and not attached to anyone. One of the best things I know is to be alone in a city that I don't live in full time. I am a transient and hope to be that way for as long as I have left. I don't want to feel any more or any less "at home" anywhere.

04-11-07 NYC NY: 1746 hrs. In the basement of the Vogue Theater.

I can write here. I am finding I can't do much in the hotel room now that the shows have started. All I can think of is the show, the huge wave coming my way and I have to get down here early. This is good. I think the performer should fear the stage, the night—all of it, lest one takes it too easy and betray the work and the audience.

Last night was the first show and I think it went well overall. I liked my set ok and will be better tonight. Janeane had the idea of going into the audience with a hat that had the performer's names on pieces of paper in it and let an audience member decide the running order. That's what we did. It was Janeane, then me, then Marc. I think it was fine. Janeane was good, I held my own and Marc just slayed. He's a very funny man. It was a great audience, the kind a performer respects and wants to give everything to. For me, there's little better in life than an audience who wants you to go flat out and give them everything. There are crowds you can be in front of who don't have any expectations, they just sit and take it. That happens on college campuses a lot and it's like punching your way out of a paper bag. A week's worth of shows in NYC is great.

I am having difficulty getting to sleep before some ridiculous hour. Even if I work out like a bastard like I will tonight, it doesn't seem to help. This causes me to get up late and messes me up. I will get up early tomorrow morning because I want to go to Air America with Janeane for one of Sam Sedar's last weekday broadcasts on the station. I think his last show is Friday before he's rotated to the weekend. I want to witness a little radio history. I slept too late today but while I was lying there, I came up with some good ideas for the shows.

An interesting thing happened after the show last night. I was on my way out, talking to people who were hanging around afterwards, and met a young woman who told me she was from Iran and thanked me for saying nice things about my visit to Tehran and the people I met there. While she thanked me, tears were streaming down her face. We talked briefly about how the Iran that I encountered was nothing like the one I see on the news. After I met her, I walked outside and met a few other people. Then Janeane and I got some food and I went back to my room. I tried to write but could not.

A Preferred Blur

04-12-07 NYC NY: 1738 hrs. In the venue again. Last night's show was good but there was something about the audience that was a little slow. They were not in any way abusive or bored but I think there were a lot of guest list people there for the IFC thing they had post-show and that might have been part of it. I thought Janeane and Marc were great. Marc really hits it hard and gets the audience with him almost immediately. I brought out a new idea last night about the relationship between Paris Hilton and her father Rick and that seemed to work as something I can build into.

After the show and after party thing, I walked with Janeane for a few blocks and then headed uptown to the hotel. I got up early and met her in front of Air America this morning and we went in for the last hour of Sam's show. Janeane did her Katherine Harris impersonation and was very funny. We did the last hour with Sam, hung out with him in his office for awhile and then split. I went back to the room and did an interview and then packed up and came down to the venue. Not much done today, it's all about the show. The news items seem to be Don Imus being fired from both his television and radio shows and all the missing e-mails that pertain to the Gonzales case. How convenient that, whoops, all those e-mails that are so important seem to have gone missing. I hope that with a good forensic agent they can be recovered. The interesting thing about Imus is that he got fired for his racial slur against the Rutgers women's basketball team, fair enough, but Rush Limbaugh says all kinds of horrible things as do talk show hosts Michael Savage and Neal Boortz but no one goes after them. I bet some of the advertisers went to the people who put Imus on the air and said they would put their advertising dollars elsewhere and that was the end of Mr. Imus. It is about that fast in that business. If anyone understands, it's Imus. He makes millions a year, I think he'll have a few meals before he exits. The missing e-mail thing is just another Bush administration move. At this point it's not surprising, just sad, that it's what all the people in his administration will be remembered for. I think history will be pretty hard on Bush. He might not get it right now but his father does and that's why he lost it on television months ago. He knows. He knows that the history books will list the Bush family as lying imposters who got soldiers killed and bled America of its resources. There will be the defenders of the Bush Crime Family but no one will take them seriously. Not many people take them seriously now, the fan base is continually shrinking as oceans no longer protect us...

It rained like a bastard here today. NYC in the rain is an amazing thing to behold. Umbrellas self-destruct in the wind and are utilized in the downside-up bowl shape until they collapse and are then slammed into trashcans. People wear bags, newspapers against heads, suits are soaked as cars toss gallons of water at people waiting for the light to turn green. No one stops though, everyone charges on to their destination undeterred. I saw something great today. A newspaper vendor had stacks of the New York Post, they were soaked and he was giving them away for free for people to cover themselves with. He was yelling, "New York Post free! Stay dry!" Finally, a good use for that paper.

04-13-07 NYC NY: 1733 hrs. Sitting in the same spot here in the venue as I was yesterday about this time. I am listening to the new Dinosaur Jr. album Beyond. It's a great one!

Last night's show was good and I am really liking the new material. It's great to have new ideas to jam on up there. I can't wait to get out there tonight. I went on 3rd last night. I think that's the way Marc wants to do it. He and Janeane really ripped it last night and the audience was into it. Every night this week, I have pulled out new ideas and I have a couple of new ones for tonight as well.

Last night after the show I walked around with Janeane and we met people on the street and talked to them as we walked, they must have thought we were nuts. One guy said he wanted to see the show but he was a starving student, so Jeanane gave him a 20 dollar bill so he could get a ticket. We met another student who was in film school and I asked him who some of his favorite directors were and he mentioned Werner Herzog, so I guest listed him for one of the shows. After that we ate at the Lyric Diner. I have not been in that place for at least ten years. From there I went back to the room.

I had to get up early for press and, as usual, it was hard to sleep. I slept pretty well for a couple of hours and then it was off and on until 0700 hrs. when the alarm got me up. I started the day at 0750 hrs. with an interview with Whoopi Goldberg for her radio show. She was very cool and I hope I was making sense while talking with her. I did three hours straight of press and then thought I would grab a little sleep but it was not to be. The phone started ringing, deliveries to the hotel, press woman, etc. Then there was the afternoon press stuff and so sleep was off the table. I managed to get about 40 minutes on the couch and then I had to get up and get down to the venue. Between the press and the shows I am not getting much else done. It's hard to think straight past a certain hour with a show at night. I have a lot of work to do in the coming weeks, a whole lot. I fly back to LA on Monday and have press as soon as I get back to the office. I will have to finish radio stuff for next week on the plane or tomorrow if I can pull myself out of bed early enough. I have to perform the wedding ceremony for Joe Lynch and his fiancé next weekend, have to get ready for that. I think there are IFC shoots next week as well. I know that Gene Simmons just confirmed but I forget what day we are shooting. I should try and do a little radio work now.

04-14-07 NYC NY: 1747 hrs. You know where I am. Listening to The Fall doing Surmount All Obstacles. I am really looking forward to the show tonight. On the way back to the room last night, I stopped in a deli to get a sandwich, one of my favorite NY rituals. To be walking down the street late at night and know that within a block or two, you will come upon a open store with every possible sandwich option available is an amazing thing to me.

04-16-07 JFK Airport: 0534 hrs. And like that, it's all over. The press, the shows, all of it is done and I am now on my way back to LA. What was it, like 12 or 13 days? I am not aware of the time at all. I spent damn near two weeks in that room and I can't remember any of it. The shows went by in a blur and I think they were good but as soon as they started, they were over and I can't remember much of any of it. I don't understand why. I kept a daily record of things but sitting here now, I can't remember much of anything I saw or did.

We wrapped the last show several hours ago. It was a good night and again, the audience was great. It's an honor to be in front of them every night. That people would come to see you every night is as good as it gets and doing shows in one place night after night is a great experience. The older I get the more I want to give onstage and the more important it all is to me. I think the new material I was hammering away at is solid and I know I can make it better. I always worry if I was good enough and if I wasted anyone's time.

I had a good time with Janeane. Tonight I went over to her place and then we ate at a restaurant in her neighborhood, same place as we were a few hours before the show.

04-18-07 LA CA: 2217 hrs. I have decided to keep writing here as the last several days have been very strange and I want to see where it's all going. I got back here Monday morning and went to the office. Carol and Heidi were very busy packaging up the new DVDs of the IFC show first season and the live special from NYC for mail order. I packed them all in my car and took them to the post office. I really don't remember much of what I did that day, I painted some shelves, did an interview with the <u>LA Times</u> on the phone with Janeane conferenced in and the rest I can't remember. Yesterday I took the car in to get checked and got a rental car and came back to the office and worked on swatting down e-mail and answered questions sent in by Onion AV Club readers, after that I did photos with the <u>LA Times</u>. I went from there to dump the mail and got into some trouble.

I was turning right from Hollywood Blvd. onto Wilcox. I was in the far right lane, turn indicator on. The light turned green and as the street was clear, I started to go. At that time, an SUV in the left lane made a right turn and basically drove over me. I guess he didn't see me. I heard my car crunch like a tin can. We pulled over and looked at the damage. All he had was a scratch on the side of his truck and I had some of his plastic siding marks on my car. He kept saying that my car looked fine that we should leave it at that. I told him it was a rental car and I had to check it out. I looked all over the place where we made contact. I rubbed the plastic streak marks and they came off and the car looked fine. I knew I had to get all his stats but as I was telling him that, he was saying that it was alright and was moving to his truck and before I knew it, he was inside and down the road. I was so mad that I didn't get his plate number or anything, I totally let him get away from me and there's no one to blame but myself. From there I went to the radio station to pre-tape next week's show and then go live. I did all that and came back here and worked on the radio show notes and sent them in to Carol for her to post.

I got up this morning early to return the rental car and pick up mine. I showed the rental car guy where the damage had been done and in the light, I could see there was a small dent on the front edge of the door, it was very small but it was a dent all the same and it happened on my watch. I told the guy everything that happened and then filled out a report and walked back to the leasing place and picked up my car and went to the box to work on the IFC show. I have been feeling very bad about the whole car thing. I was fucking lame to not get the man's information. I didn't do the right thing and will have to pay for the damage he did to the car and I deserve to. I learned a lesson from that. I have to do the right thing as much as I possibly can. It will be expensive even though the dent is tiny, I am sure they will find a way to make it expensive.

Today I interviewed Gene Simmons. It was interesting to say the least. I have met Gene a couple of times over the years and he's always been cool to me. He's a very smart and funny man and he was in top form today. He speaks at least four different languages, which is really cool. He has found the two things he loves in life: money and Gene Simmons. He goes on and on. I just let him do his thing, there's no use in stopping him. He's something else. I am sure we will get a lot of response from this one.

After he left, I did some interviews with Gene's producer for his show. Some of the stuff we shot will be used on his show at the end of this season. I finished the day by doing intros and outros and then left the box and waded into traffic. I got back here and got in a good work out which made me feel a little better. I am stressed and depressed but have to get a lot done so I have to keep slamming myself into it even though I don't feel like doing anything. I know that is my weakness trying to hold me back so I have to fight it. I have a lot of work to do for quite some time. It is all work I signed up for. I want to do it, I will do it. I don't have anything else to do so I make more work for myself so I don't have to think about myself and can only think about the work. As it is right now, I don't know what else to do with myself. I will keep this file open and account honestly as often as I can until there is some down time. It's late and I have to be up early.

04-20-07 Santa Cruz CA: 2123 hrs. In a hotel room. I got up early this morning and drove to the airport in Burbank and flew up to San Jose. I picked up a rental car and drove here. I went to the courthouse and met up with the bride and groom to be and got deputized so I can marry them tomorrow. I wrote up a thing that I will read to them before they exchange vows and put rings on each other's fingers. After they are married I'll hang out for awhile and then drive back to San Jose and fly back to Burbank and go back to the house.

It was interesting to walk around on Front Street hours ago, it's very much like how I remember it when I sat out on the street here 21 years ago waiting to play a Black Flag show. Adult hippies and students walking slowly, everyone very relaxed, almost under a spell. It's very "California" here. I have had some intense times in this place, like the time many years ago when the police tried to work me over, I barely got out of that one. Then there was a time I was here in 1992 with Tool. The man who ran the venue and some of the staff were coked out and as the night wore on, it got more and more edgy. Santa Cruz is a perfect example of the California that appears beautiful on the outside but conceals a dangerous darkness. It's a beautiful piece of real estate, one of the most beautiful parts of California but a lot of drugs move through here and there are some very heavy people who live and do business in these parts. That's always the California I register when I am here.

I have a lot on my mind and have been working since I got back from the courthouse and lunch with the wedding party. Monday, I have an interview with Don Cheadle and then I am interviewing Iraq vets First Lieutenant Paul Rieckhoff and Sergeant Jason Lemieux. Paul sent me his book, Chasing Ghosts when I was in NYC last week and we have been exchanging letters for a few days. I want to have his book read as well as Cheadle's book Not On Our Watch by Monday. I am a good way into Watch, I will have to get that one finished by tomorrow afternoon and then when I get back to LA, I will lay into Ghosts and get to the end of it by Sunday night. I know I don't need to have Rieckhoff's book read by Monday but I want to anyway. I also have to write up two letters for the show on Sunday. On Monday I will do all that and then go see The Stooges at the Wiltern. Tuesday I am doing something for the IFC show and then that night we start the run of shows at the Silent Movie Theater. All week there are shows at night and IFC stuff during the day. It's going to be a long week. I can pull it all off if I just make a list of all the things I need to do and then do them. This is a good way to work. I like to get a schedule that fills me with dread. I work away at it all day, go to sleep thinking about it, get bad sleep and wake up nervous. It keeps me from myself and that's what I want right now. There are many bad sides to working this way but it keeps me honest and pushing ahead but mainly it keeps me distracted from myself. It's becoming harder and harder for me to live with my thoughts, what I've seen, what I know. It's not anger, it's something else. I am trying to figure it out.

I want to write more here but I should go over my notes for tomorrow and get more of Not On Our Watch read. Perhaps tomorrow night I will get a chance to write more here.

06. LA LA

04-25-07 LA CA: 1846 hrs. At the venue getting ready for night #2. I thought last night went well. It's a small place but it was sold out and the audience was fantastic to all three of us. I will have to take a little off my set time as it's a late night if I don't. I am dealing with a good deal of stress and depression at the moment. It's hard to battle both at once and I am having a rough time of it. I am losing track of days. I am forgetting what happened two days ago if I don't take notes. I think I am trying to forget things as soon as they happen. I have a lot going on and the IFC show requires several tasks to be done. I have to be at all of the music tapings this week which has me going downtown and then back here for the show. It will be a lot of running around which makes none of it enjoyable.

I like Marc and Janeane but I don't want to do any more of these shows with multiple people. I don't like all the people backstage and dealing with everyone's thing, whatever it is. It's not like anyone is hard to get along with but it's all I can do to have it together and it is all the harder with people around. I have been working one way for so long, it's hard to change. I don't want to change. I will do these shows and that will be the end of it. I have enjoyed seeing the two of them do their thing, they are really great.

I got a lot done at the office today. Tomorrow will be fucked because I have to be downtown at the set at 1400 hrs. which is the perfect time of the day to get nothing done on either side of it. I got up today at 0618 hrs. and felt pretty good. I should have stayed up and got to work but I dozed off for a little while because my body was telling me to stay down. I got up a little while later and felt doped. I went to the office and got some stuff done. Janeane came over and helped me and saved me a bunch of time. Soon enough, it was time to come here and get ready for the thing again. My thoughts are scattered and I am tired from being stressed. I put it on myself, my fault, my problem.

04-26-07 LA: 1850 hrs. Back at the venue. Last night's show was really good and the audience was great. I am hoping for another good night in this place. Today was a fucking waste of time that has left me frustrated and more tired than anything else. I had to go downtown to check out Rufus Wainright who was taping for the IFC show. I don't mind and I am a fan of Rufus but it's hard for me to go down there and then come back into LA and get anything done. I was told that Rufus had requested I be down there and I was happy to do it. His flight was late getting in and I ended up hanging around there uselessly for some time and then when I had to go, he turned up and I said hello basically in passing. So, I got fucked out of my day and have gotten nothing done and that has me all fucked up. One cool thing was that one of the Rufus crew is Ali McMordie, the bass player from Stiff Little Fingers. I had not seen him in a long time so it was cool to say hello to him. I saw them do some good shows many years ago. I have heard their recent shows have been really good. I got back into traffic, went to the house for a minute and then to the office. I notice I forgot to shave. It's par for the course. I am blowing it left and right at the moment. I am booking over other things and then it all has to be re-done and untangled. I say yes to having lunch with someone to do some business and then a few days later something comes up that makes me have to cancel it and be a jerk. From now on, I won't say yes to anything that's not a show or press. 1907 hrs.

04-27-07 LA CA: 1842 hrs. At the venue. It was a pretty good day and I got some work done on both sides of the music shoot I checked out at the studio downtown. Heidi, Janeane and I went to the Bombshelter to check out The Good The Bad & The Queen. Paul Simenon of The Clash on bass, Damon Albarn from Blur on piano and vocals, Simon Tong from The Verve on guitar, and Tony Allen on drums. Tony Allen, what a history. He was with Fela Kuti from the start. He is easily one of the world's greatest drummers. It's a very interesting line-up to say the least. I think this all came together at the behest of Albarn but I'm not sure. I went into the room where the band were set up and the first person I saw was Paul Simenon. I introduced myself and we talked for awhile. He was really cool. It meant a lot to me to meet him. I should have told him about the first time I saw The Clash play 02-15-79 at the Ontario Theater in DC. I met the others in the band and they were great as well. I talked for awhile with Damon and Paul and told them about the TV show. One of their crew was out on the 1992 tour where we opened for the Red Hot Chili Peppers in Europe. The Good, The Bad & The Queen were so great. The way Simenon and Allen were locking up was amazing. Simon was playing some really great stuff and Damon is completely impressive. It's interesting to see that much talent in one spot. I made sure I introduced Heidi to Paul so she wouldn't kill me. He was very cool to her. I am listening to the first Clash album at the moment. It's sometimes hard for me to listen to The Clash because hearing them makes me sad that Joe Strummer is gone and that music like this isn't coming back ever again. There's a few bands that get me like that, The Clash are definitely one of them. I have been listening to this album for over half my life. But anyway, The Good, The Bad & The Queen were fantastic and I am lucky to have seen them.

I went back to the office and worked on next week's radio show and then talked to management about things happening later in the year. I am doing a few nights at the Edinburgh Festival in Scotland. That works for me. I will work hard as I can all year and hopefully get some things done. I have to stay focused in order to keep it all together. I can do it if I keep to myself and get it done. I need to close my eyes for awhile.

04-28-07 LA CA: 1927 hrs. Backstage. Last show tonight. I am glad this run is over. I don't like being part of a multi-person bill. It's not a matter of the people I am working with but I don't like waiting to go on, sharing a dressing room, etc. I won't be doing this again unless it's a festival setting and there's no choice.

The blur continues. I have to get out of these shows and get on with the next thing. I have to re-immerse myself in all things Maxed Out. I am presenting that documentary at the Maryland Film Festival this coming Saturday. I will be flying to DC on Friday, cabbing it into

DC and checking out the old neighborhood. I will meet up with Ian and on Saturday we will go to Baltimore for the film thing. I was tempted to fly out on Thursday so I could have a day to walk around in the old neighborhood but I have too much to do and wouldn't have a good time so I am just going to go out there on Friday.

I will have to take it one day at a time for awhile. I am feeling more stressed than usual and the depression has been worse than usual. I don't know why. It's been hard to get out of bed every day and get out there but I have done it. My depression has gotten worse over the last few years but in the last several months it's been damn near crippling. It gives me a lot of strange courage in that I just don't give a fuck about things that might hold me back. I am not saying I don't care about doing good shows and hard work, I mean that when I am usually shy or self-conscious, I no longer care and walk right in. I know I can do all the stuff I have lined up to do, so I don't know why I am so fucked up all the time. I need to get ready to go on soon. 1951 hrs.

07. Maxed Out

05-02-07 LA CA: 1951 hrs. At the house. I did all I could at the office and after I work out, I will get some more done here and then I have to get to sleep as early as I can.

The shows seem like a long time ago. I put a lot of distance between myself and them as fast as possible. I had to so I could get all the work in front of me started. My sleep is bad. It's hard to get to sleep and hard to get up. I am more depressed and stressed than usual. There are a lot of things happening, nothing I can't handle I don't think but it all seems to be burdensome. Basically, I don't want to do anything and I don't want to do nothing. When in doubt, go.

Some things that have happened: I got a letter from a woman who is distressed because her son wants to join the Army and she doesn't want him to. She wants me to write him, I told her I would. I have to get on that. I know what I want to say so I have to find some time, perhaps later tonight, and get it done. I don't think he should join at the moment. I think the Military is being used like cheap labor by this administration. I like the Military, but under this regime their talents, bravery and very lives are being squandered by cowards and it's not a good time to be part of it. You're going to go to Iraq and you're going to be a standing target and get paid a fraction of what private security personnel will for doing the same thing. There was another letter I got that I should mention, a drunken, idiotic ramble. I don't remember if I answered or not. A couple of days later I got another letter from the same man telling me that he was sorry. He had been drinking and was feeling distracted, disconnected and anticipating what he was up against. From what he said he was going through, I took a guess and wrote him back a single word, "Iraq?" Here's the letter I got in reply:

Leaving in August for 18 months. No interest in women or other people any more. Too much of a taste for violence and I just can't make the ethics of it work. We need to defend ourselves against assholes but most Iraqis just want us to leave them the hell alone. That region will never be stable until one group establishes itself as the power in the area; we're not going to make that happen with an Army. Reading "Solipsist" and "Get In The Van" right now. Keeps me company when I can't sleep.

This is my history. This is the screaming bloody story. This is the result of lies piled on top of each other and left for others to make truth of. It all ends in death and darkness, rehabilitation, skin grafts, suicide and attempts at normalcy. George W. Bush will be seen as the worst president in the history of my United States. He is seen that way by the world at the moment but it will take Bush's decreasing support base to finally admit what millions have known for years. The Bush Library will try to wash the blood and miserable failure from his record but try as they might, they will be unable to.

The Bush administration has no intention of leaving Iraq. Many Iraqis have no intention of staying and are fleeing the country every day. That's great for the Bush administration. If they hold out long enough, there will be no more Iraqis in Iraq and they can do what they want. The Bush administration are criminals and they are breaking America into pieces according to plan. I don't think we have seen nearly the worst of it yet. All the troops are in Iraq, someday, they will come back and there will be hundreds of thousands of men and women suffering from injury, mutilation and PTSD. It will be a part of American life. There will be suicides, increased incidents of domestic abuse and who knows what else. The cost of this? Besides the money it will take to care for these men and women—funds that many of these people will struggle to get their hands on, if they still have the hands to struggle with?—we'll just have to wait and see what that will be. Every day that passes, the angrier and more fucked up about it I get. It's not the weakness of this administration that gets to me as much as the cowardice and dirty dealing. Bush vetoed the war spending bill as everyone knew he would. It's incredible that such a cowardly idiot has so much power. Harry Reid, the Senate majority leader, said about the veto: "If the president thinks by vetoing this bill he will stop us from working to change the direction of the war in Iraq, he is mistaken." That means not a fucking thing to me. I have no confidence in the Dems to stand up, no confidence in the media to tell the truth and very little confidence in the American people to see this thing for the nightmare that it really is. It's not a matter of pulling out of Iraq and getting onto the next thing. This is our "thing" for years to come. We have fucked Iraq up. It was in better shape before we went in. The rebuilding of the infrastructure has failed, as planned, and buildings are caving in, which is perfect for more tax dollars to be spent building it again. The administration no longer counts car bomb casualties in its death tolls of Iraqis. Here's what Bush told Charlie Rose about that: "If the standard of success is no car bombings or suicide bombings, we have just handed those who commit suicide bombings a huge victory." That is one of the most incredible leaps in logic I have ever heard. The way Bush's mind works fascinates me.

So, what else happened today? I talked to Gore Vidal. I want to interview him on the show so I asked Janeane if she knew anyone who might have a number for his management or publicist. Janeane made some calls. A woman who works with Rachel Maddow at Air America called me and said she had just called him and he said it was ok for me to call him and gave me his home number. I called him, introduced myself and asked if he wanted to be on the show and he said, "Sure, why not?" He handed me over to his assistant and we worked on some potential shoot dates and hopefully it will work out. That was pretty cool. I wrote Ian about it. His mother and Gore used to exchange letters. The next few days will be somewhat blurred.

05-04-07 Washington DC: 1546 hrs. Sitting at the usual table at the coffee place down the street from the hotel. The weather is top shelf, sunny, not too hot, dry, perfect. I arrived a little less than two hours ago. Ian will meet me here fairly soon. I don't know if it's paralysis or being content but when I am here, I feel like I could come here every day and that would not be so bad. I could sit here and not think about all the other places I would go, should or could go. I could just be here instead. That's something. Sitting here, I am thinking of all the streets that I'm going to walk on tonight, the music I listened to in the apartment I lived in a few blocks from here and my life before I left here.

I am staying at the Holiday Inn, instead of my usual spot up the street from here, the Savoy is sold out tonight. I like to walk around this neighborhood when I can. I don't know if I learn anything from it but it's good to see some evidence of myself. That's probably this place's biggest appeal for me. I am always trying to deal with life as an adult. I am trying to deal with this place as an adult and also in the present and not exclusively as a place in which to trap or recapture what is gone because it is gone. I know that I always say the same things about this place in this journal, over the years, these thoughts have become a mantra or something. It's also a howl of sadness and looking back. I don't like to be that way but when I am here, that's a part of it. My life changed very radically after I left here. I am sure I lost a lot along the way. Whenever I am here, I am always reminded of passages of Thomas Wolfe from his book Of Time And The River. "Returning, always returning…" 1608 hrs.

05-05-07 Washington DC: 1226 hrs. In a different coffee place. I have been in here many times. I have to go to Baltimore soon but I wanted to hang out in the old neighborhood for just a little while longer before leaving. I hope to be back here in July for The Evens show at Fort Reno.

Yesterday was great. I met up with Ian and we visited his brother and family. I had a great time playing with their daughter, she's a crack up. We went from there over to Ian's and as always, he pulled out some music I had never heard before. He played Karp, some live Pink Fairies, some Groundhogs and some George Brigman stuff I had never heard before. From there, Ian, myself and Amy Evens went out to dinner. It was a great night to be out walking around. There is no city I have ever been to that lights up like DC at night. I think it's the way the street lamps illuminate the trees that are all over the city. Sometimes, for blocks at a time, you will walk through what looks like a tunnel lined with green leaves that are all lit up. It looks like it was designed to look exactly this way. For me, it's the most beautiful city I have ever been to. On the way to the restaurant, we ran into Justin

Moyer from Antelope and Supersystem, again, just another typically great DC moment. After we ate, we walked back to Ian's place through the Adams Morgan District. The place has really changed since the days we were down there checking out the Punk Rock almost 30 years ago. It was a pretty dodgy part of town then and I am sure you can still find some trouble there pretty easily but now it seems to be over-run by college aged youths like it's an extension of Georgetown University or something. It's still great to walk through it at night though. I have a lot of memories tied up in that neighborhood. All the shows I saw in there: Bad Brains, Teen Idles, Clash, Buzzcocks, Cramps, Minor Threat, Untouchables, Gang Of Four, The Mad. I wish no matter where I was at any given time, I could walk out of the room I was in and be in DC. 1312 hrs.

1448 hrs. Sitting in the lobby of the Holiday Inn, waiting on a cab to Baltimore. It's cool and overcast outside, another kind of weather I love in DC. I wish there was nowhere I needed to go today so I could just walk around and smell the air. Joe Fugazi is doing a show here tonight, it would be great to see him play. After Ian dropped me off here last night, I went to my room, dropped my bag and went out for a walk. I went up to the hotel I usually stay at and then back down the avenue again. The air was so great, I wanted to breathe it more because of how good it smelled and how good it made me feel than for the fact that it keeps me alive. As I walked, I thought of songs that I used to listen to when I lived here. It's a lot of the same music I listen to now but it takes on an increased poignancy when I am here. The same thing happened to me that has happened many times in the past, I get to a certain point on Wisconsin Avenue and I have to stop because I am nearly in tears from all the things I am feeling at once. It happened again last night. I just stood there for a minute and then kept walking. It is at those moments when I feel very alive. It's very painful and I feel as though I am drowning. There are many ways to regard and deal with time. I have noticed that for some, time is an elastic, fluid thing where past and present are all happening at once. For me, it is quite different, it's an inflexible and cruel thing, the past being that which mocks from the ether. I know that's bad but that's how it is for me.

2342 hrs. Baltimore MD: I am back from the Maryland Film Festival. It was a good time. Jed, the guy who runs it, is a great guy. I spoke for a little while before and after the film and hung out with people in the lobby until they all left. I am back in the room, listening to a Japanese compilation CD of The Damned called The Damned Super Best Of. I have to be up in a few hours to go Baltimore Washington Airport and back out to LA. I am sitting here in Baltimore but I am thinking of the walk I took last night up Wisconsin Avenue and I wish I was back there right now. I wish I could get in a car right now and jam back to the old neighborhood and walk around. Last night, I almost went into the old neighborhood to take my normal walk but I couldn't do it. I was too depressed to go there. I didn't want to see all those trees and the streetlights and the streets, all the while knowing that I was going to be leaving in the morning. Sometimes I can do it and sometimes I can't. That I can have that kind of feeling for the place makes me see that I am not burned out all the way, good to know because I feel dead a lot of the time these days. It sure was great seeing Ian and everyone else. It was a strange little trip, in and out so quickly. It was a treat to see the place even if it was only briefly. As much as I would like to be back there all the time, I don't know what I would be able to get done there. It's probably better just to visit now and then and leave it at that. I like it when I am there and miss it when I am not there. On the weekends in LA I am alone at the house and I listen to a lot of old music and think of DC and when I am out here on a weekend, it's especially heavy for me. I am now listening to Perfect Teeth by Unrest, that's a great record. Being out here on a weekend always makes me think of my old job at the ice cream store and how much I miss those times. Walking past some of those old landmarks last night was really heavy for me. Last night I walked by an apartment building I lived in with my mother when I was about 5 years old and that tripped me out. I let all this stuff get to me too much but I can't help it sometimes. A few hours from now, I will be back on a plane and headed to LA. I will get in a car and go back to my house and prepare for the upcoming week but my thoughts will be back here. There's nothing in LA that affects me emotionally. I have memories of places and things but there's no place there that I ever miss. It's just a place to exist and work. The memories I have of LA are usually connected with death, failure and regret. I should get some sleep.

05-08-07 LA CA: 0014 hrs. Today was fairly productive even though it was hard to get out of bed and I am fairly exhausted. My body wants to be still for a lot longer than I am allowing it to be so there's going to be some resistance there. I got a letter from the press lady that said the People Issue of the LA Weekly will be out this week. I was selected to be one of the "people" for this year's issue. Apparently, they pick five people and each one gets a cover and I am one of the covers. I saw a jpeg of it. I look old.

I am still thinking about DC. I wish I had one more day there to walk around but I have a busy week here. I get operated on Thursday morning. A doctor is going to open up my leg and free a nerve that apparently is restricted and not allowing me to move my foot. I hope it works. He says it might help but added there's a good chance it might not. He said that I won't be able to drive so I need to get management to get me a car to take me there and back. I don't want to ask anyone I work with. In situations like this, it's better to just pay someone to do the job and not ask anyone to help. It's really the last thing I would think of doing.

I have been reading a lot of Gore Vidal lately as I want to be sharp when I interview him on the 20th. His interview confirmed the other day, I am very happy about that. I think he will be great and people should hear what he has to say. I don't know how much longer he'll be around. For the last two days I have been re-reading Perpetual War For Perpetual Peace. That's a good read. I want to get his new autobiography read before I meet him. Ian read it and liked it. I will get it today if I get a chance between all the stuff I have to do. I have a feeling Thursday will be spent on my back. The doctor offered me a prescription for pain medication but I told him I didn't want it. I will get by with Tylenol or something. I don't know how much pain I'm in for but I am not concerned about it.

I have been slightly less depressed for the last two days. I don't know what brings it on as heavily as it comes and I don't know why some days are better than others but I know it has never been as bad as it has been for the last few months. Fuck it.

08. The War On Everything

05-13-07 LA CA: 0047 hrs. I have seen Dinosaur Jr. two nights in a row. They were great the first night but much better tonight. People are very friendly to me, the last two nights they have been coming up to me and telling me how much they like the IFC show or the radio show and things like that. It's very cool. I forget that people in LA can be good to me. When I go to the venue again tonight, I will have my defenses up as always. I don't understand any other way to be in this city.

As I watched the band play earlier, I saw people moving about all through the concert, they went upstairs and downstairs, they talked all through it. Made me wonder what they went to the show for. I figured they would want to get more out of the event than to just push through the crowd back and forth. It's not any business of mine but still I wonder. On the first night, I was trapped behind four people who just talked and carried on through the whole show like it was an inconvenience to them. They were distracting but I still had a good time.

As soon as the show was over, I hit the street and went to my car. I walked by Dan Tana's, the restaurant that Phil Spector took that woman out of before she got a bullet through the head. It's funny, every time I walk past that place there's always these men in front that look like they only eat at Dan Tana's, they look beef fed and like they're about to explode. They stand in the middle of the sidewalk like there's no one else even thinking of using the sidewalk. I go right through them, fuck it. It was a Saturday night so all the bars were packed. I drove by clubs that had people in lines down the street. It was almost midnight and these people are spending their night standing in line to get into a place to drink. They should just have a bar where the line is and stalls for people to go fuck in so they don't have to waste so much time standing around. On the other hand, I don't give a fuck what these people do with themselves.

I got my left leg operated on two days ago. I am noticing a little bit more movement in the foot than I had before but for the most part, I still limp around.

I have been pushing hard against depression and the last couple of days have been pretty good but I feel myself slipping. I stayed busy today by working on the radio show and reading, trying to keep myself from myself. I have been thinking a lot about the president and his pack of cowards that are helping him kill American soldiers and keeping his fake war on terror going. More and more I see that America, for all of its good points, is just a sad, hateful, very racist racket. It's that "war on" whatever you can't really fight a war against that has been at the center of my thinking lately. The war on drugs, there's no war on drugs. Drugs are around just to keep minorities killing each other and filling prisons. It's just slavery. The war on terror is just a cash in for the pigs and they know that people are onto them but they don't care. America is at war with its denial and hypocrisy and it's losing. America is conducting genocide on its poor, non-whites and now, its returning veterans. You might say that is a bit extreme but I'm right. Every day I am becoming more and more disgusted at the cowardice of those in power.

05-18-07 LA CA: 2345 hrs. At the house. I didn't sleep much last night but just kind of dozed off now and then. Soon enough I had to get up and go to whatever station it is that Adam Carrolla's show is on. I got there at 0645 hrs. for an 0715 hrs. interview. Danny Bonaduce, the Partridge Family guy, is also on the show. I guess at this point, he's better known for that show <u>Breaking Bonaduce</u> that chronicled him melting down or something. I watched a few minutes of a couple of episodes but couldn't stay with it. It's not my kind of show. It's like watching an animal get tortured. Anyway, he's a nice enough guy but he's incredibly intense and loud and takes up a lot of space. I was looking at his body and he looks like he's on a steroids cycle or something. Apparently that's a well known fact I found out later today. The show's topics are things like Rosie O'Donnell, Tyra Banks, and other popular culture bullshit. There were ads on the show for Danny's bachelor party now that he's getting divorced, got divorced, or whatever the status of it is. It was really great to leave the building and I will never go back on there again. It was very depressing. I hope Danny takes care of himself. I have met him a couple of times over the years and he's always really cool to me but it's hard to be around that kind of thing. I like Adam a lot and have known him quite a long time but it's not my kind of radio show.

I went to the office and worked on radio stuff and looked over information so I can be sharp for the interviews I have to do on Sunday and Monday. I'm interviewing Serge Tankian and Tom Morello on Sunday afternoon about their site Axis of Justice. I really like those two. They are good guys, smart and fighting the good fight. That will be a great interview, it can't fail. After that, I interview Gore Vidal. I am looking forward to it but I just hope he's in a good mood and that I don't make him mad or something. I don't know what he's like but I have learned a lot from him, that's for sure. Reading his books Perpetual War For Perpetual Peace and Imperial America really helped me understand why we're in Iraq and what Bush's foreign policy is all about. Thinking about it, of all the stuff I have read and tried to learn about all these ruinous cowards, it's Gore Vidal's writing that has been the clearest voice for me. His article, The Enemy Within is amazing. I downloaded it and read it very carefully. I hope that interview goes well. Monday I interview Russell Simmons. I met him once and he was an asshole to me but I don't care, he's an interesting person and he has had a huge impact on American culture and that's what I want to talk to him about. I have been trying to read his book Do You! all about personal power and the keys to success or whatever. It was hard to get through because it's so corny, so I gave up. I read his autobiography years ago and thought that was very interesting. Basically, the next few days will be very busy.

I have been battling with depression. It's now a constant in my life like a metal pole stuck in the front of my skull. That's what it feels like, it's always there now. Being alone helps though. The more I am on my own, the better. I am looking forward to getting this Fangoria thing done with tomorrow so I can be back here and be on my own. All the things I do now are things I have to do and the reward is getting back here and being by myself. It's my incentive for getting things done. I have been busy and doing good work but it's been very difficult because of the depression but as long as I have time to myself, I can do it. I don't want to go to this event tomorrow, not in the least but I am going to because I like the director of the film and he asked me and that's good enough for me. The thing I am looking forward to is walking out of there and getting back here and not having to be around anyone for a few hours. Sunday will be full-on all day. It will be good work and I want to do it but I am not looking forward to it, I wish it was all happening tomorrow so I could get it over with. I don't know why I am this way with everything. I don't dread the radio show. I like doing that. Just two people in a room talking and playing records, that I can handle. Everything else, I dread. Even going to something like this Fangoria thing, which will be fine, but for some reason, I just want to get it done immediately and not have to think about it. I know that working is the best thing to do. I know that doing things like the IFC show and helping Joe, the WT2 director, are good things to do so I just have to keep hitting it. I can do it but I have to admit, depression has become a considerable obstacle. I am fighting back by working in spite of it. The best anti-depressant I have is that I don't give a fuck when I die and knowing that makes me feel better. I'm feeling better already.

09. One Way Ticket To Paradise

05-23-07 LA CA: 1606 hrs. At LAX, watching Glen Beck on CNN Headline News. What a psycho. I said I would never watch CNN again but it's on and I am in front of the screen. Beck is incredible. He's flexing poll results: Of Muslims under 30 years of age living in America, 26% polled said suicide bombings against civilians were sometimes justified. He works the numbers to show how many potential terrorists live in America right now and comes up with 280,000. Then he includes the people who answered "I don't know" and inflates the number to "about half a million." It's only a matter of time, according to Mr. Beck, before we're all killed! Other Beck stats included that 47% of Muslims consider themselves Muslims first and Americans second while 47% of Christians polled think of themselves as Americans first. This is important to keep the hate and fear going. He then interviews Nonie Darwish, author of <u>Now They Call Me Infidel: Why I Renounced Jihad for America, Israel and the War on Terror</u> and Zuhdi Jasser, president of the American Islamic Forum For Democracy, about all things fear related while the screen shows images of Osama Bin Laden and bombed wreckage. He gets some brief bits of useless information from the two of them and then thanks them very much and almost immediately front sells an interview with Jerry Bruckheimer he has coming up after the break as "PATH TO WAR?" burns across the bottom of the screen. Is there a planet these people can go colonize so I can have Earth back? Luckily for me, it's only a television show. Glen Beck is, thankfully, a minor annoyance. It's interesting to watch corporate news after not having watched it for awhile. It's one long advertisement. There's no real difference between the commercials and the actual news content. One can get by in America with very little smarts, Glen Beck proves that. It's too bad this crap passes for information.

The last few days have been busy and eventful. I have not had the time to write anything because of the schedule but over the next few days, I will try and catch things up a bit.

I am on my way to London, England and from there onto Wales and then onto Scandinavia. I get in Thursday afternoon and have the night off in London and then I have a show on Friday. I am looking forward to having a few hours to walk around in London and getting a meal in my favorite UK restaurant, Wagamama.

Last Saturday, I set the finish line at walking out of the radio station after completing my broadcast. I did it. The next stretch starts Friday when I am game-on for the show in Wales and on from there. Compartmentalizing workload is something I have started doing to minimize stress. I try and deal with it 3-4 days at a time so I don't get too distracted by the overall. I am nervous most of the time anyway but this helps somewhat.

1714 hrs. Now sitting in my seat on the plane. I ran into Ross Halfin, the photographer, on the way into the cabin. He was out here photographing ZZ Top. I remember seeing a photograph he took while on ZZ's Eliminator tour of the bass player and guitarist Dusty Hill and Billy Gibbons with Phil Lynott of Thin Lizzy in the middle of them. Phil looks pretty wasted, Hill and Gibbons look uncomfortable with having Phil's arms around them. I can't remember the last time I saw Ross. He's an amazing photographer. He used to take pictures of my band when we were doing well. Once you drop below a certain budget you can't afford Ross. He did the photos on the inside of the Rollins Band album <u>Weight</u> back when we were fab.

So, the last few days. I went to the Fangoria convention. I have heard it referred to as "Fango" as well. It's all about horror films, comic books and the like. I went because Joe Lynch, the director of <u>Wrong Turn 2</u>, that film I did last summer, asked me to be on a panel with an actress in the film, Erica Leerhsen. I think she's a great actress and she really kicked ass in the film. I didn't want to go and didn't want to be on a panel but Joe asked me to and I like Joe a lot so I said I would. On Saturday afternoon a car came to take me to the event which I think was at the Burbank Airport Hilton. I walked around the area for awhile before the panel started and checked out the scene. A lot of people were decked out, metal fans, goths, etc. I really like all that stuff. I like seeing the metal guy and his metal girlfriend walking hand in hand. How cool would it be to be all into Black Sabbath and meet a cool girl who was into Black Sabbath? You would be set. I always like seeing large groups of people who might be considered "strange" or otherwise alternative. It's great to see that there are still people who are going about things in a different way. When I was younger looking Punk Rock could get you into a fight, then it became "normal" or at least common enough to where people wouldn't mess with you as much. Now I think it's winging back to where looking different can get you very noticed. I appreciate those who dare to stand out be it with an opinion or their look. A lot of people recognized me and asked for photographs and shook my hand, they were all very friendly. I did the panel thing with Joe and Erica and then we sat at a table and signed autographs for over two hours. That got to me. It's not the people, they were all great but there's a limit on that stuff before I just want to bolt. It's a long time to sit still and meet people. I got through it and eventually got back to my place and prepared as best as I could for Sunday's work.

On Sunday I did an interview with Serge Tankian and Tom Morrello about their website Axis Of Justice. I really like those guys and admire both of them very much. They are both very intelligent and putting their money where their mouths are. The interview was great, both of them are very inspiring people. The interview that came next was the one that I was nervous about. Gore Vidal. Mr. Vidal is a writer and intellect of great power and I have read a lot of his work and gotten a lot from it. Several months ago, I started hearing Mr. Vidal interviewed on Air America and gathered that he was back in America after having lived in Europe a great deal of his life. I wanted to get him on the IFC show so I asked the producers to see if they could locate him. They tried and could not. I called Janeane Garofalo and asked if she could help. She passed word to the folks at Air America and they had his number and actually called him on my behalf. I got a call from Logan at Air America and she gave me Mr.

Vidal's number and said it was ok to call. I was nervous but I called him. I introduced myself and asked if he would like to be on the show and he said, "Why not?" I asked if he had an assistant and he said he did and told Mr. Vidal I would handle all the details with him. He passed the phone to his assistant and I passed him onto the producers. A couple of weeks later, Gore Vidal was in our studio.

Gore came in by wheelchair with an assistant. He was friendly enough but seemed to be in a certain amount of discomfort. I imagine getting around for him at this point is not all that easy.

I had no idea how he was going to be in the interview environment. Janeane had interviewed him before and said he was very friendly. He was great with us. I did a lot of preparation for the interview, more prep that I have done for any other guest. Knowing the man doesn't have years and years to live, that every hour counts, I sought not to waste his time, but also I didn't want to get caught out there by Gore Vidal, you wouldn't be able to walk that one off.

He was a great interview. I told him I was from DC, knowing he was also from there and we started talking about landmarks. He told me about the grave plot he has reserved and I told him I knew that having read about it in his book Palimpsest. He told me which grave-yard it was and it happened to be the one I lived across the street from for a few years and used to walk around in when I was very young. I would like to get a transcript of that interview. At the end he again mentioned that we were both from DC and I added that so were Ian MacKaye and Duke Ellington. I am a fan of the man so it was great to meet him. It's times like that where I feel very lucky to be doing what I am doing. At one point, I asked him if he recalled getting letters from a woman in Washington DC, last name MacKaye and he did. Ian's mother used to write him now and then. She once showed me one of his letters back to her. It was great to tell Gore a little about her and what she means to me and that she recently passed away. The part of the interview I knew was going to cause a stir with the viewers was when we were talking about John McCain and he mentioned that it was obvious that he was not presidential material. I mentioned that he was a prisoner of war and he shot back that he was caught, what good was he? I laughed in disbelief that he would say such a thing. I thought of all the mail I was going to have to answer. All in all, it was a good interview and I don't think I wasted his time, which was my main goal. It would be great to meet him again some time but I bet that won't happen.

5 hrs. 42 min. into the flight. The best I ever feel is when I am moving. It's the time when I don't want to be dead. No matter where I lived with my mother it never felt like home. Never felt like home when I visited my father either. I always liked being outside better, that's why I always had jobs, it kept me out of my mother's place. So, the streets and the places I worked were home to me. It's not like I was looking for some place to call home but I always felt better out in the world than when I was with my parents. I grew up, left where I was born and moved thousands of miles away. The years went by and now the world is my home. I am going to London and that makes me feel pretty good. I have had a lot of bad times there but still I am glad to be going. Since 1981, I have been on the move and it's what passes for normal for me. It's hard to be in LA day after day. Some days I want to do all my work and some days I don't want to do anything but sit alone and try not to think of anything. The best possible thing for me is to be on my own and on the move. I have some shows and some press days coming up in Wales, Denmark, Sweden and Finland. Hopefully I will be busy enough to stay distracted from myself. I guess all the movement and work is the way I self medicate. I figured that out a few years ago. When in doubt, just go. Fuck it.

05-24-07 London UK: 2354 hrs. I got in about 12 hours ago. I went to some record stores and found some of the CDs I was looking for. I got The Fall re-issues of <u>Code: Selfish</u>, <u>Shift-Work</u> and <u>Extricate</u>. The track listings don't seem all that interesting as far as unreleased stuff but there might be something on them that I have not heard so I have to check it out. CDs are very expensive here.

I went to Wagamama and ate and it was great as always. I have eaten in that place so many times now over the past decade. I came back here to the room and passed out for a few hours. After I shook myself out of that jet lag coma sleep that I love but have to avoid, I sat here for awhile listening to music and then I got lonely for the outside so I went out walking.

It's always the same around here in the summer. It's packed with people, tourists and youth out for a night of clubs and alcohol and general hanging out. I like seeing all those people. A great people watching location is outside the Gap clothing store at Piccadilly. There's always hundreds of people walking around and you can lean on the railing and see them all at once, it's pretty cool. As I was walking up one street, I saw a young woman walking with an older man in a suit. He looked drunk. She had her right arm around him and her left hand was holding his tie and it looked like she was steering him to the place where the business would transact. In this neighborhood, you never know what you're in for. I wondered if she was going to take him to get robbed in Soho. I wonder where he is at this very moment.

After walking around for awhile, I came back here. There's no place to get a cup of coffee and hang out around here after a certain hour so I reckoned I would come back to the room. I am listening the first Generation X album on my i-Pod stereo thing. It's a thing of beauty for a small room. I will probably be up for awhile, perhaps I will check out Eno's Here Come The Warm Jets after Generation X is done. I always like to check out Punk Rock records when I am in England and try to imagine what it must have been like to see all that go down.

I have spent a lot of time in London and have a lot of memories from here. The good ones make me miss those times and the bad ones make me mad that I can't forget them. Most of my memories are band related. Sitting here thinking about it makes me miss the times we had the band really happening and no one in the band had turned into a useless piece of shit yet. London was a place we did really well in and I think some of our best shows ever were here. There was a feeling of feral invincibility in those times that I really miss. It's hard to get a group of people together to make a band that really wants to go out and kill it every night. I have had bands that did it but they couldn't stay with it and I have always had to endure their weakness and it's not worth it to me now. I learned my lesson with that bullshit last summer. The first time the Rollins Band played London was a couple of months shy of 20 years ago so I guess it's all in the past now. Many years ago, I had relationships with some women here and those didn't go well. It was all my fault but walking by some places around here brings back some feelings. For the most part, those memories are very faded, I have not maintained them very well and they have atrophied.

I am glad that it is night and that I am alone and that I am in England. Walking alone and unknown on streets at night in cities all over the world is a way to live without being alive. Coming in off the street alone to a rented room is perfection.

05-25-07 London UK: 0134 hrs. I fall in love with an idea of myself and stick with it. The self-created story becomes the story. My self-perpetuated reality is the one I live in, no matter what's coming at me. London is hard. Hotel memories. I sure regret the times of feeling so fragile and open. Dead is better. Tired. 0137 hrs.

05-28-07 Helsinki Finland: 1000 hrs. At the airport. Flight to Stockholm, Sweden boards in about 70 min. By the time I have been done with work I have been too wiped out to write anything. I did the show in Wales on Friday night, that went well. It was part of the Pontypridd Festival. Small theater, great audience. I hope I get to go back there some time. I spent the night at an airport hotel and flew here on Saturday. I got in around 1800 hrs. I went out to eat with the press lady and some others and when I got back to the hotel, I was jet lagging hard and couldn't stay up any longer. It was too bad because right before I fell out, I looked out the window and saw that a very thick fog had come in and I wanted to stay up and look at it. A Friday night in Finland, complete with fog. It would have been great to stay up for awhile and listen to music and look out the window but I was too tired.

Yesterday was a very long day of press. I got to the end of it all, went back to the hotel, ate and then I went back to the room and immediately fell out and slept through a rainstorm. I got up this morning and finished up proof reading another section of the Fanatic! book and sent that in to Carol. I want to get that one off to the printer so I can concentrate on other stuff.

I can never help but notice the difference in the way things are built in Europe. From the sinks to the windows. So many things are new, ergonomic, efficient and made to last. I may be naïve but one might conclude that people here think that progress and stability is a good thing. In a lot of parts in America, progress of this kind is considered "gay" and not to be taken seriously. It makes me see how completely resistant America can be to change and innovation. It's frustrating to know that things could work so much better. This occurred to me every single time I came out of the elevator on my floor at the hotel into darkness only to have the lights all turn on because of the motion detector I had tripped. When no one is in the hallway, the lights are off, that's pretty smart. I wonder what that would do to the electric bill of a large hotel over a decade? It would probably only serve to make the electric companies angry. If America took some of these tips, the place would be a lot cleaner and energy efficient but there are a lot of people who don't want that because they make their money from the problem.

05-30-07 Copenhagen Denmark: 0857 hrs. At breakfast. No internet in room. Restless. Shows have been good. Sweden, good, last night, almost as. Tonight will be better. Over jet lag pretty fast. Yesterday pretty normal day of travel hassle: SAS on strike, waited 2 hours for flight change. Thankfully, I was able to be slightly proactive and get on a plane. Contacted the promoter via internet and we worked it out. Change of airport, 2 flights. Promoter somehow didn't see me at airport. Had to cab it to venue with less than 2 hours before stage and no chance to check out record stores. I did the show and it was a good time anyway. I remember my first talking show here in the late '80s. I was surprised how well it went. Actually, talking shows have always gone well, I don't know why but it's a good thing.

05-31-07 Aarhus Denmark: 1117 hrs. I am out of the hotel and in the back of a cab on the way to the airport. I don't have a show tonight. It's a travel day back to Helsinki, Finland. I don't think I have any press to do today so it's basically a day off with two plane flights that will hopefully go without a hassle.

The show last night was a good time. I have never done a talking show here so it was good to get one done. I have done a lot of band shows in Aarhus though. Perhaps I will be able to come back here again some time. Arhus is an interesting place, it's very quiet and wide open. The drive from the city to the airport is almost an hour and the views are great on the way. I am looking out the window as I write this and there are trees everywhere, it reminds me a bit of Washington DC with all the green. What I have seen in Scandinavia in all the years I have visited is very beautiful but it's also very placid and I can see that one might get a little stir crazy. Yesterday on the way into town, I was thinking of what it would be like to leave America and live some-where like this. I get so bummed out about things there that some-times I think about leaving. It would be a heartbreaking thing to do but on the other hand, it sometimes feels that way to live there. When I am outside of America, I think about it differently than when I am there. I think one of the best ways to really see America for what it is, is to get out of it and consider it from a great distance.

I have been out on this trip for about a week. I don't remember much of it. Between jet lag, the daily airport hustle and the work, it's been all I can do to try and keep up. I have not had any time outside of the tasks at hand. I worked on Johnny Ramone's book yesterday and I will proof another chapter when I get to Finland later in the day. I don't know how many times I have been through this book now but I think it's almost done. The original manuscript was very fleshed out by interview segments from a lot of people. The writer on the project did a lot of work to make the thing as well-rounded as he could. However, Linda Ramone's agent took it around to all the publishing houses and they all had the same complaint, they all said there were too many people talking in the book and they all wanted to just hear what Johnny had to say for himself. Fair enough. So, I have been going through the book and cleansing it of all the interview bits and trying to make it make more sense by doing some re-arranging of things here and there. The original writer made some very strange choices in what he put where and I am really noticing it on this draft. I have worked on this thing on and off for over two years now. I want to get it done so I can clear my mind and get onto some other things.

Wow. Vast, rolling fields to my right. So wide open and so completely green. It looks like the entire surface of the earth has been painted bright green. A few houses and barns here and there but for the most part, just space and green with blue sky. I have a house in the country. I never have time to go to it. I don't know if I spent more time there if I would be any the better for it. Spending time there might make me crazier than I am now. I keep it in my thoughts though and look at pictures of it now and then. Now there's dense forest on my right. Thousands of trees. If you had this many trees in America, you would have to guard them with your life. 1150 hrs.

1212 hrs. When I walked into the airport, there were two people behind the counter and one man walking towards it. After I checked my bag and got my ticket, that took about 70 seconds, I took some pictures of the scene so I could remember it later. I am now in the waiting area. It is practically silent. I guess there are not all that many flights in and out of here. Interesting thing happened at check in. I was asked to put my index finger on a touch pad to record my print. I asked the man what was going to be done with it and he said that when I get to Helsinki, the print is thrown out. I don't know if I believe that. I told him that if they did that in America, the print would go onto at least a few data banks and straight to Dick Cheney's laptop. The man said nothing.

06-01-07 Helsinki Finland: 1657 hrs. In the venue. Soundcheck and lights are done. So, yesterday, things went south pretty quickly at the airport. The flight to Copenhagen canceled. I had to get rechecked on another flight route that added hours to the trip. By the 3rd flight, from Gothenburg to here which I barely made, I knew my bag did not make the flight and I was right. I filed the form and left the airport for the hotel, some food and some sleep. I did something interesting this morning before the next salvo of press started, I brushed my teeth with shampoo. I had no toothpaste. I can't recommend doing this.

1821 hrs. My bag came back to the hotel and I went and got it. I am in a better mood now that I know where it is. I am out of here at 0515 hrs. tomorrow and would have hated to leave it behind me. I am looking forward to the show tonight. I am glad it's sooner than later. For some reason, I am bottoming out on a wave of jet lag. I thought I had it beat. I'll be ok by show time. I have to go from here to Heathrow tomorrow, that's the worst airport in the world if you have to transfer and go to another terminal. The airport was built only to torture travelers. Dead, moist air, small busses, all the idiotic hoops you have to jump through to get out of there. I don't look forward it.

After the show tonight I have to meet some people from the company that is putting on the IFC show here and then I will have a little time to myself before I try to get some sleep. I am already thinking ahead to what I need to get done if I get back to LA in one piece.

06-02-07 Helsinki Finland: 0709 hrs. We are supposed to be boarding soon but I can't see any signs of life at the gate. Last night was a good show and the audience was fantastic. There was a small reception thing for me afterwards that the people who are carrying the IFC show put on. It was mainly their staff and some press people. Everyone was friendly. From there I went back to the hotel, packed and got a few hours of sleep. I didn't sleep much between work dreams and anticipating the flights. I am glad to be on the way to the next thing.

Last night, I was very tired which was too bad, I really wanted to stay awake and enjoy the night. It's so strange to see the sun still up past 1100 hrs. I wanted to walk around a little but I was just too wiped out. I haven't had very much sleep on this last run and it all kind of caught up with me yesterday. On the way back to the hotel last night we passed by what looked like a restaurant or a coffee place that was so cool looking, I stared at it until it was out of sight. It was mostly glass with an amazing stone skeleton. Inside where hundreds of small lights. It looked like a small universe. I really wanted to go in there. It looked like something out of a dream the way it glowed in the low light of the evening. There is something strange and secret about this part of the world. I don't know how to describe it but I always feel it when I am here. Perhaps it's reading all those Knut Hamsun books and listening to The Sods and Sort Sol albums so much that I have attached a certain idea to Scandinavia. I have been coming to this part of the world since 1983 and have been fascinated by it ever since.

1202 hrs. London Heathrow Airport: Finally on the plane. It's an amazing airport. Genius in the way it reduces the flow of human traffic to an almost standstill! Incredible how it inconveniences the harried traveler to the point of despair beyond frustration! You emerge from the plane and walk endlessly and then you are greeted by a mass of unmoving humans, it's a line you must wait in to make sure you only have one bag so you can continue onto the next... line. This next line is the security check and it's an insidious, winding, treacherous piece of work that is a doped river of loud student travelers, would be rappers and all the rest of us, the huddled, the brutalized and damned. You go ten steps forward and then turn left, ten more steps and then turn right, repeat until it's finally over, days later. This line is like the entertainment industry. You see the same people again and again, so a mere glance can turn into quite something else by the time you get to the metal detector. Finally, you are past the security check and just when you think you are free to overpay for something at the duty-free sprawl, you must again face another line to get your next boarding pass. On this day, all the screens were dead blank forcing the traveler, now a trembling and submissive heap, to walk down the line of attendants and ask if they can direct you to the airline you seek. Disinterested fingers point this way and that and finally, you have a boarding pass in your hand. The clamminess of the air almost overtakes you as you hear the woman detail your next assignment. You must now go down the escalator to catch a bus to another terminal. And so, down you go into the steamy bowels of the very poorly considered Heathrow Airport. The bus arrives and the humans dive into the bus like sardines volunteering for can duty. The bus lurches on, a brake-punching stop-start journey to the interminable Terminal 3, a moist tomb, its air fragrant with the odor of ancient carpet and all things stale. (On today's ride, a Hell Ride, to borrow from the late Wesley Willis, I stared down at a woman whose botoxed forehead, nipped, tucked and peeled face and button nose sat like a fright mask in juxtaposition to the rest of her exposed skin, which was the texture of battered leather.) The bus comes to a halt, the travelers fall out of the doors, collect themselves and lurch towards the escalator to ascend and prepare for another multi-kilometer walk to their respective gate. I was awarded the random search for the second time today. If uniformed men didn't touch me, I would have barely any contact with humans past shaking their hands. I am so grateful. And now, I am on the plane. Nearby is a body builder I have seen in magazines. He's talking to the female pilot. It is at these times when I need the strength that Allah gives to his chosen.

5 hrs. 30 min. into the flight. I have been working on radio stuff. It occurred to me yesterday that I have to put together damn near one dozen radio shows for all the weeks I will be on the road this summer. I will have to get up earlier and get to my desk earlier. I will try and keep the jet lag hours that this trip will hopefully have afforded me. I will get some more radio stuff done when I get back to the house and hopefully I can start in on the writing for the next IFC episodes. If IFC doesn't ask for any extra episodes, which I don't think they will, I am done with the show in a couple of weeks. That went pretty fast. I don't know if IFC wants to do it again next year and I don't know when I will find out. Fuck it, if there's work there, I'll take it, if not, I'll do something else. I like working because I think it's the right thing to do and it keeps me away from myself but I don't get much enjoyment out of it. I never have. Doing music was never enjoyable, it was a release. It would have been far more dangerous to have kept it inside. I don't enjoy doing the IFC show. Interviewing people makes me nervous. I think we are doing a good thing with the show and I don't think the guests are getting their time wasted. I think I am doing a good job but I don't look forward to going in there and doing it. It's work and I'll take it. I'll always take the work.

I have no feelings about this trip that is now coming to an end. It was good work, good shows and the audiences and all the people I worked with were great. Past that, it was ten days of how I am getting through life.

Henry Rollins

10. Incoming

06-16-07 LA CA: 2121 hrs. I have been at the desk on and off for the last 12 hours or so, working on upcoming radio broadcasts and travel plans for July. A lot has been going on as of late. I have been deep in the work and little else.

The shooting for the season of the IFC show is almost done. There are two interviews to do next week and a couple of bands to tape and that's pretty much it. So far it's looking like Arianna Huffington and someone else will be the guests and the bands will be Sinead O'Connor and someone else. The someone else thing happens a lot with this show. Somehow, we always find a willing band.

We had some very interesting guests on the show over the last few weeks. I interviewed Christopher Walken a couple of days ago. It was hard to concentrate on the next question because I was so captivated just watching him speak and listening to the way he phrases words. He was very cool and straight forward but I was nervous interviewing him because he is just so different than anyone I have ever spoken to. Samuel L. Jackson was very interesting to talk to for a lot of reasons. Besides his acting skill, he was in the middle of the Civil Rights movement in the '60s. He knew H. Rap Brown and Stokely Carmichael a.k.a. Kwuame Ture. I don't think I have ever met anyone who knew Ture. Jackson was an usher at Martin Luther King's funeral. It's so great to get this stuff on tape and on the air. I don't know if anyone asks him about that part of his life. It was interesting to talk to Larry Flynt, who had only a couple of days before written a nice piece on the passing of Jerry Falwell, who he had an interesting relationship with, to say the least. Gene Simmons was hilarious and brilliant, that interview should come out very well. I have met Simmons a couple of times before and he's very smart and very funny, sure to make some people angry though.

In the mean time, things grind a long here. I am working hard to get the next volume of <u>Fanatic!</u> out the door and to the printer. I am trying to get it out of here by July 1. I don't know if we'll make that but I should be able to give it a lot of time next week.

Another episode of the IFC show aired last night and it featured the interview with Iraq Vets Paul Reickhoff, author of <u>Chasing Ghosts</u> and the Executive Director and founder of the IAVA (Iraq and Afghanistan Veterans of America) and a Marine named Jason Limieux. The two of them were perhaps the most potent interview we have ever done on the show. We talked about Iraq, the sustainability of our troop forces, equipment, etc. It was mind-blowing what they were saying. So glad we got it all on tape. Anyway, it aired last night and I got some interesting letters today. All of them were very into the interview except for a couple of citizens who said it's a volunteer Army and that America is safer, I am unpatriotic, I'll never get another season, etc. Please. You all have to get some better shit. I told Reickhoff about it and he just said, "Fuck 'em." That's good enough for me. It's good to be having some impact, I hope it does some good although I don't know if it really makes a difference. All I can do is try.

I got a letter from Jim Wilson of Mother Superior the other day. I did a lot of records with him and his bandmates, they are the band who played on the <u>Rise Above</u> WM3 benefit album. Great band, great guys. Jim is one of better people I have ever met, the boy can play some guitar. He told me that they were in Germany and that the opening band at one of their shows had Greg Ginn playing bass. I asked him to send me the full report when he had a chance. He got back to me today. Ginn is such a trip. They were loading in and Ginn walks up to them and asks, "Are you guys Black Flag?" acting like a fan and the MS guys all laughed thinking it was friendly. Then he said, "I've always wanted to open for Black Flag, this is awesome." Then the conversation switched to load in and other stuff and Ginn lightened up. Then Ginn asks very seriously, "You guys didn't answer my question—are you Black Flag?" Jim said no and then Ginn said, "Ok then." Then Ginn got all friendly again and then turns around and asks Jim, "Hey where's the cowboy hat? We need the cowboy hat

Henry Rollins

for the complete Black Flag experience!!" I think Ginn saw us once and Jim was wearing a cowboy hat. What a swell guy that Greg Ginn. He's 52 now, you would think he... hell, who cares? When he was good, he was really good though.

I have been working on plans for a bit of travel in July. Parts of it could be a little tricky but whatever. I want to do it and I don't care about what happens to me. I am usually nervous about something most of the time but when it comes to anything that is potentially threatening to my life, I don't give it a lot of thought. I keep the schedule packed so I can get through time. I don't know if I really enjoy anything I do. Most of the time I am just a combination of nerves, depression and anger. I have not spoken to anyone in about a day and a half. That's pretty good. Fuck it.

The "war" is going great. I think we're winning! They're partying in Baghdad! I just dragged this off the internets: "Never in my life have I heard such a sound," said Ali Jawad, a 48-year-old who was selling phone cards nearby. "A big fireball followed. I saw blood and a decapitated man thrown out of the bus." Sounds like freedom to me, fuckface!

People In Front Of Mosque: *I had been wandering around in the Al Hamidiyeh souk and came out the other end to see a group of people gathered in front of a large mosque. The man on the far right holding the microphone whipped the crowd into a weeping mass. I took photos and recorded the audio.*

A Preferred Blur

Theater in Virginia.

Henry & Steve Eller: *That's Steve, he was my boss at Häagen-Daz, the last straight job I ever had before I left DC to join Black Flag. He helped me get my first apartment. I learned a lot from Steve and he was a great man to work for. He gave me a lot of trust and respect and that helped me incredibly. When I told him I was leaving for California to be in a band he told me if it didn't work out, I could have my job back. That was very cool of him because I figured there was a good chance I might have to take him up on that. He means a lot to me and I am glad that we still keep in touch. This shot was taken backstage at The Birchmere Theater in Virginia.*

11. Three Years Gone

06-27-07 LA CA: 2253 hrs. Sitting on the floor in a room in my house. I am listening to The Damned. I only come into this room at night, it's a great room late at night. It's Wednesday night. Very early Saturday morning I will be flying to Washington DC for a few days. For the last three years, June 30 has been a hard day to get through. It's the day Ian's mother, Ginger, passed away. I will hopefully get out there in time for whatever function the family will be having this year. I think Ian said they will be having a picnic or something. I miss her all the time but on 06-30, it's especially hard.

I am looking forward to walking around the streets of my old neighborhood and seeing all those beautiful trees in full bloom. The air will be hot and moist. In the summer, DC hits that almost unendurable threshold of heat and moisture and you just have to deal with it. I really like it.

Carol and I have been working as hard as we can getting the next volume of <u>Fanatic!</u> finished. We still have another couple of drafts to go but I think we're making progress. That and working on future radio broadcasts for when I am not in town has kept me very busy and distracted from myself.

The last several days have been busy and eventful beyond the work. A few days ago, I went to the premier of <u>Ratatouille</u> with Janeane Garofalo. She provides the voice for one of the main characters, Collette. Patton Oswalt is the lead, a rat named Remy. The premier was at the Kodak Theater. I have never been in there before. The red carpet thing was the biggest one I have ever seen, I guess Disney was pulling out all the stops. I watched Janeane walk out onto it and the cameras started flashing away. I heard people calling my name from the roped off area where the fan types were so I went over there. I am not going to pretend that I don't hear them. One guy pulls out a stack of pictures of me to sign and I asked him how the hell he had them on hand. He told me that he saw the guest list and knew I was showing up. I didn't know it worked that way. I signed a couple of them, he had a lot of them, it's a racket and I don't mind doing some but after a few it's just a drag. I am sorry that's the way the guy makes money. I don't get mad at that kind of thing, the guy's just getting by as best he can. I signed a bunch of stuff for people and then walked back to the red carpet area to watch people do their thing. I was spotted by some of the photographers and they started yelling my name so I went out there for a minute and goofed around with Janeane and then stood around for some photos and snuck away when their attention was diverted by someone else. After that, I stayed out of the area and used other people's bodies as cover as I watched famous people get their pictures taken. It's crazy how many of the women I saw had some kind of plastic surgery done to their faces. They all look insane because of it. None of them look good, they just look nuts. Some of the older women were rail thin with breast augmentation, the implants look like they want to tear themselves away from the body. Combine that with the creaseless forehead and tight skin around the eyes, they all look like they just woke up from a nightmare where they saw themselves naked.

Ratatouille was really great. I have never seen one of those Pixar cartoons. Janeane was fantastic and so was Patton, hell, everyone in it was great. Five years in the making, that thing. It was completely impressive and I was happy for both Janeane and Patton for getting that work and doing such a great job.

I saw them both onstage at the Troubadour last Sunday night and they were both really good. Patton is one of the funniest people I have ever seen. I was sitting on the stairs on the side of the stage when he was on and I am glad I didn't have to stand, it would have been hard for all the laughing I did.

I want to write more but I am tired and need to get up as early as I can so this is it for now.

06-30-07 LAX: 0502 hrs. So, again, at an airport. Three years ago today I flew from Dulles to LAX and went right to a film set. Three years ago today Ginger MacKaye passed away while I was in the air. My depression is very heavy at the moment. I almost didn't make this trip. Last night I didn't want to move I felt so bad. It's not good feeling this way, but it's what I've got at the moment.

Last night was the Ramones get together at Hollywood Forever. Joe Sib and I handled the proceedings. I told the audience what they were going to be seeing, when it was shot, etc. I knew that Marky Ramone was going to go up and speak before the 2nd feature but I figured he wouldn't be all that informative and I was right.

Last night's presentation consisted of a documentary called <u>Too Tough To Die</u>, directed and shot by Mandy Stein. Mandy's father, Seymour, signed The Ramones to Sire. The documentary covers the 30th anniversary Ramones benefit show done at the Avalon in Los Angeles on 09-12-04 and also shows scenes of Johnny Ramone's memorial service at Hollywood Forever Cemetery. It's an interesting scene at Hollywood Forever, people bring blankets and hang out on the lawn in front of the screen. Punk rockers and their families, it's really cool. I have been there for a few Ramones functions and it's always a good time.

1537 hrs. Washington DC: Just spoke to Ian, will see him soon. Will space out here at the coffee place for awhile. It's Saturday. Mood is pretty good. Last night was really bad. I could barely move. I wanted to stay in LA I was so depressed. It's a hard day thinking of Ginger but I am getting a little better with it as the years pass. When I am here, I always try to imagine living here again and try as I might, I just can't do it. The world calls out to me too much and I don't know how I would pass the time here.

07-01-07 Washington DC: 2311 hrs. Back in the room. This is the same room I was staying in when Ginger was dying. Today was really great. I went to Mt. Pleasant where The Evens were playing a free outdoor show. They are trying to ban music and live performances in bars and venues in the area and some of the local artists got together to push back. Bands and rappers performed in a small park all afternoon. The Evens were the last ones on and they were great as always. I saw a lot of DC people I knew at the thing and met a lot of cool people as well. It's a great neighborhood, all kinds of people live there, it's a great DC melting pot. The local stores are diverse, it's like real life. 2323 hrs.

07-02-07 Washington DC: 2321 hrs. Back in the hotel room. The end of a great day. I went over to Ian's around 1300 hrs. We went out and walked for quite awhile. We walked through Malcom X Park, also known as Meridian Hill Park, and Ian pointed out where Fugazi had played years ago. We walked from there to Red Onion, a record store, but it was closed. We went to Crooked Beat, another record store and checked it out. It's a great store. One of the things that makes it interesting to me is that it is below the sidewalk and the floor above it is where Madam's Organ, the old punk hangout, used to be. I had some of the best times of my life in that place. From there, we walked over to where the Rumba Club used to be and picked up Eddie Janney (Rites Of Spring, One Last Wish, Happy Go Licky) who works in the building and we went down the street to get some food. We hung out there for awhile and then walked back towards Eddie's workplace. On the way, Ian called Ian Svenonius (Make-Up, Nation Of Ulysses) and he came out of his building and we went forth. I live for these moments. These are some of my favorite people in the world. It is hard for me to be around people. I have always been self-conscious around them and I don't know how to be myself in people's company but I do enjoy being around these people very much. They are all so brilliant and talented. I have known them for many years and I always feel so lucky to be around them. They see each other all the time but for me it's a rare occasion, so I try to take in as much as I can. We dropped Eddie off and the three of us proceeded back to Ian M's place. I always like getting suggestions for films and books from Ian Svenonius because he has checked out a lot of stuff. He recommended The Great Silence with Klaus Kinski as well as two Luis Bunuel films, The Discreet Charm Of The Bourgeoisie and Phantom Of Liberty. I have never seen any of them. I have a lot to learn. I always listen carefully to the things that Ian S. says, he has a very interesting way of thinking.

Eventually he left and Ian, Amy and I went to Fort Reno to get the gear onstage for the show that night. We loaded onto the stage and started setting up as the sun was setting. The weather has been incredible the last two days. I took a lot of pictures of Ian, Amy and John Hanson setting up the gear. They seemed meaningless at the time but I always enjoy looking at them on the laptop when I am far away. It was cool to have loaded The Evens gear twice this year in two different countries. Soon after we had set up, Joe Lally came with his gear and we got his stuff onstage too.

People started showing up very soon after and it looked like it was going to be a very big audience. By the time Joe was onstage, the field was filling up with people. I recognized a lot of people there. I saw Alison Wolfe of Party Line, Guy Picciotto, Brendan Canty of Fugazi, Eddie and Ian S., Mark Sullivan of Kingface, Jessica, a woman I used to work at Häagen-Dazs with, Justin Moyer of Antelope and all the MacKaye's. It's such a great scene. It's a free show, the parking is easy and it's a no hassle way to experience live music. Before The Evens played, a lot of people came up to talk to me. The people at these shows are always so friendly to me, I really like to meet them, even though I am fairly shy, it's easy to be friendly to friendly people, they make it easy I guess. When the youngsters call me "Mr. Rollins" it makes me feel old but it's also very funny and fuck it, I am old. They see that gray hair and it's always "Mr."

The Evens were great again. By the time they were onstage, the place was so full of people it looked like a festival. I asked some people around me if it was this crowded for the band last summer and they said no, that this was the biggest crowd they had seen there since the last time Fugazi had played there. The word is out that The Evens are great. Also, besides the band and the music being so great, Ian is a man of his time. He really is one of those people they will be talking about long after he is gone, that's why I always listen carefully to what he says and don't take time spent with him for granted. He means a lot to a lot of people. It's great to see it on the faces of the audience. I have seen it so many times in my life, the effect he has on people. It's nothing he tries for, it's just the way it is. It's an amazing thing to see.

He has made a real impression on more people for all right reasons than we'll ever be able to measure. At the end of the day, Ian will have inspired and reached more people than a lot of politicians and leaders, fuck it, he IS one of those leaders. Everyone had a great time at the show. All too soon it was over and I was back onstage, breaking down the gear with John. We packed up, left Fort Reno and after storing the gear Ian and John dropped me off at the hotel and here I am.

I was on ebay the other day and saw that a member of a band I was in many years ago, called SOA, was selling his test pressing of our EP as well as an original copy of the record. It's his to do whatever he wants with but it's too bad that it doesn't mean anything to him more than a way to make some money. I kept my eye on the auction and he got over 1100.00 bucks for the test pressing. I hope he's happy about it. I talked to his sister who was at the show tonight and she said he was in town but didn't come to the show because there would be a lot of kids and people he knows there.

Got this letter today:

A sniper killed my friend yesterday. That's three that I've lost now, its straight up insane and I honestly can't understand it. Today, my squad and I were clearing a rooftop for a building we were going to use when the damn building exploded. Wounded two and rattled the hell out of the rest of us. When we finally got back, they half-assed screened us for concussions. The medic didn't give a shit about the bullshit test he was giving us, my ears are still ringing and everyone's talking, so its impossible to focus on the questions, so I pretty much botched mine, made me feel like a freaking moron. We're all fine though. I'll be sure to write about it more in depth in a bit, but I did remember you saying to fill you in if anything interesting happened, so there's a quick heads up I guess.

We really lucked out, so I'm feeling pretty grateful about that one. Gotta talk to the family real quick. Wish me luck.

I got this e-mail from the man in Iran who got me my visa, pretty interesting:

Hi Henry,

I hope all is well with you. Today I heard about you in the most important news section of the Iranian state radio! They were talking about the good things you have narrated about Iran and your trip! Well, there you go. I am sure that this goodwill message is sitting on some screen of an American Intelligence agency computer as a steely eyed hawk figures out ways to have me rubbed out.

07-03-07 Dulles: 0512 hrs. Have not slept much but feel pretty good. Still have a long day ahead of me. All in all, it was an amazing trip and not full of the sadness of the other visits at this time of the year. 0514 hrs.

07-04-07 LA CA: 2242 hrs. I got back yesterday but had a lot to do and couldn't get it together to write. I don't remember any of the flight back here or much of the details of the hours before the flight from DC. I had a 0415 hrs. pick up. I didn't sleep much before I left. I got on the plane and slept on and off for the 4 hrs. and however many minutes it took to get back to LA, it didn't seem real how quickly it went by. I have not been on a plane that empty for a long time.

I got to baggage claim and there was a man with my name on a card there. He and I walked to the car and headed into Hollywood. We got to talking about things and he tells me he was in Special Forces for a number of years and got out about a decade ago. I noticed when he started talking about it, he became hesitant and his voice raised in pitch and he seemed nervous. I remarked that there will be a lot of men and women coming back from Iraq who will have problems readjusting and will have to deal with PTSD. He said that some people suffer from that and some don't, it was all down to how ok you were with killing people. Ok. He told me he has an older brother who was in the Military and came back with a lot of problems. His brother is homeless and lives in the Hollywood Hills. I asked him if he ever tries to make contact and he said he has tried but his brother just wants to be left alone. He dropped me off here and I thought about all the things he said for quite awhile before I could get anything done. I understand about wanting to be left alone even when good people want to reach out to you. A lot of the time, it's a hard to balance the feelings and thoughts I have. 2256 hrs.

12. A Night In The Ruts

07-06-07 LA CA: 2120 hrs. I have been wanting to get this story going for a few weeks now. It involves a band called The Ruts. Heard of them? They were one of the great UK Punk Rock bands and easily one of the best bands I have ever heard. I have played them on my radio show many times, written a lot about them, tried to track down every possible pressing of their records and get every live tape and demo of theirs I could. The band's first release, a two song single with *In A Rut* and *H Eyes*, is one of the best debut singles I have ever heard. I can't remember when I first heard The Ruts or what particular record it was. Back in the early '80s, I had all their records and then as now, played them all the time. There are no bad Ruts songs in my opinion. Some of the early songs that can be found on the demos are not as great as what was to come but even those are pretty great. The band's one real album, <u>The Crack</u>, released on Virgin in 1979, is one of my favorite albums of all time.

The Ruts career came to an end when the vocalist, Malcolm Owen, overdosed on heroin and died on 07-14-80. He was 26. The rest of the band, guitarist Paul Fox, bassist Segs Jennings, and drummer Dave Ruffy, carried on for a couple of albums under the name Ruts DC, the DC standing for Da Capo, or new beginning. The songs were good but without Malcolm, it wasn't the same and the band called it a day. Over the years, the band's music keeps getting added to all those retrospective box sets and people keep discovering the band's amazing songs.

I was young when I first heard The Ruts and at this point, I have heard a lot of music and made a lot of music and all this has only made me appreciate them more. I guess you could call me a Ruts Fanatic.

Recently, I got an e-mail from a man named Mark Wyeth, who knows the three remaining Ruts, and we went back and forth about how great the band was and all. I asked him to please pass on my regards to the members, none of them have I ever met before. I thought it was great to have been able to get word to them and thank them for all that great music, short as the band's time was.

A few weeks ago, Mark wrote me and told me that Paul Fox's health wasn't very good, in fact, it was very bad. Paul has untreatable lung cancer. He said the other Ruts were thinking of doing a benefit of some kind and would I like to be a part of it. We went back and forth as to what it was going to be and it boiled down to a benefit show with bands playing and hopefully the three Ruts with guest singers. He offered me a chance to do a song or two with the band. I wrote him and asked how well the band could play, were they serious about really having the material together, etc. He assured me that they would indeed have it together. I thought about it for a few days, looking at schedules and all the things I have coming up but I was still on the fence about it. A venue is found and a night is confirmed, the Carling Academy in Islington for the night of 07-16-07. They want to do a press release and they need my yes or no. I give it one last think and say yes, deciding that I wanted to be part of it to help out Paul and to be part of this event that is most likely a one time only situation.

Mark tells me I will probably be singing up to three songs. I tell him that's fine and request that I get to sing <u>In A Rut</u>. So far, I had not heard from any of the band. On the morning of 06-21-07, I get an e-mail from Dave Ruffy and Segs telling me that they are happy that I am part of the event, that they are getting things together for rehearsal and looking for another guitar player to sit in if Paul isn't feeling good enough to play.

Days go by and Segs, Dave and I exchange several e-mails a day, going over lyrics, etc. One thing leads to another and it looks like I will be singing most of the set. So far we are going to try for: *In A Rut, Staring At The Rude Boys, S.U.S., You're Just A..., West One, Society, Dope For Guns, Babylon's Burning* and *Jah Wars*, which will be sung by someone else. I must say, getting a letter from Segs asking if I want to sing *Staring* rates high on the list of moments I'll never forget.

Sarah Pink, who is putting the show together, writes to tell me that The UK Subs are confirmed and the show is sold out.

So now it's late on Friday night and I am getting ready to head out of here. I have been practicing as best I can on my own, singing along to the records every day. I have been going back and forth with Segs and Dave getting lyrics together, and I think I have my head around it all enough to get me to band practice. I leave Monday and I think we will practice for almost all the days leading up to the show the following Monday. I don't know how well oiled those guys will be and what Dave's abilities are so we'll have to see what shall be when we all fall in at band practice.

As usual, I am stressed about all of it. I stress over everything. I have started the pack and will get that done over the weekend. I am busy here and there tomorrow but Sunday will be clear and I don't have to be ready to go until Tuesday afternoon. I will have some hours to myself when I get in on the other end Tuesday evening. I have done some radio shows in advance for the ones I will miss and the office won't need me for some days. We have been trying to get the new Fanatic! book done and out the door. I was hoping for early July but it's not going to happen. The depression is at a manageable level and I think I can get through the next few days. Sometimes it is day to day, sometimes hour to hour. Last week was really bad, now, not as much. Heidi says I have to figure out a way to enjoy things more. I don't know how. I want to do things and work hard but I don't really enjoy any of it. I engage and then break off, no matter what the task is it seems. When I am off the road, I look forward to the weekends so I can be alone and not have to talk to anyone. It's a relief to just be here on my own, staying busy with enough time to prepare for what lies ahead.

Tomorrow I will work with Chuck Dukowski on some notes for a release he's doing of his pre-Black Flag band Würm. It ends up that all of his practice and demo tapes I copied back in the 1980's are pretty much the only recorded evidence of the band, the originals have gone missing. Months ago I transferred them all to CDR for Chuck's use. Now I am going to interview him and we will build a history of the band for a website and just to get all the facts in one place. I will do this with him for a few hours and then have a couple of hours to myself and then I will go to The Hammer Museum at UCLA to be part of the Hammer Conversations series. They describe it as: "Hammer Conversations: This ongoing series pairs creative thinkers from a range of disciplines for engaging, provocative discussions on culture, science, and the arts."

The museum asked Amanda Palmer from The Dresden Dolls to take part and she asked me to be her guest. I have never met her. My initial instinct was to not do it. I don't know why. I have nothing against her or UCLA but I said yes to it because my instincts, well, I really don't have any that can be relied upon so what I reckon is a bad idea is probably something I should consider, so that's why I am doing it.

It's getting late and I want to work more but I am trying to get myself on UK time to a certain degree so I will try to rack out as soon as I can and get up early. Fuck, I forgot to eat. Nice.

07-07-07 LA CA: 2346 hrs. I am back from the Hammer Museum thing with Amanda Palmer. She was great and it was a good time. I talked to people until they were all gone then I drove back here. I want to write more but the depression has got its teeth in my neck tonight and it's making things difficult. It has become a large factor in my life. Better luck tomorrow. 2352 hrs.

07-08-07 LA CA: 2305 hrs. I think I am good to go for the trip. The level of stuff in my bag is about three inches below the top, which is great but makes me wonder if I have left anything out. It's summer so all the clothes are thinner, that's perhaps the main difference. In the warmer months, I can get away with doing a lot more laundry in the sink which allows me to bring less.

My hotel is near the Tottenham Court tube stop. I don't know this neighborhood but I went on the Wagamama site and found one of their restaurants down the street from the hotel so I am good to go for food. It's one of my favorite restaurants in the world. I usually go to the one in Soho but I am not all that close to that one where I am staying this time.

I will get into London on Tuesday afternoon UK time. It will be tough but I will have to stay awake. Jet lag is very hard on me when I go east. At least I don't have any shows immediately. That one in Wales a few weeks ago was hard with only one day to acclimate. I should have left for England today, I don't know what I was thinking. I should be there now. Oh well, I'll just deal with it. I have a full day of press starting on Wednesday and then Thursday, I guess it's band practice. I have yet to hear from Segs and the rest as to when and where all that's going down. I hope it's near a tube stop.

Last night was bad enough, I could not write. I tried to sleep through it but only had nightmares that had me up and down until early this morning. Whenever I have dreams of talking to women, I am usually doing something stupid, humiliating or incredibly dangerous. In the dream, I am talking with a woman and then I notice I am hanging on the outside of a moving train or putting on some insanely stupid piece of clothing, or I'm in traction or tied up—that one happens a lot. I have these dreams all the time. I was telling Heidi about them the other day at the office and we laughed about it. She said they are right out of a textbook. She's right. Freud would put his hand on my shoulder and just shake his head.

Today I cleaned and packed and that's about it. I went to the office and tied up a few things there, printed out some more Ruts lyrics, practiced the songs and that's about it. I feel pretty good with the material but will feel better about the whole thing when we get into the practice room and I can hear what we sound like. They're really good songs but not all that easy to play.

I'm looking forward to wandering around London in a different neighborhood than I usually stay in. Piccadilly is too expensive and crowded this time of the year. I like to walk around in cities outside of America, I forget myself on the streets, especially at night.

I am not remembering much of the trip to DC. I go in and out with time sometimes. There are periods of time I just get through and the memory of what I did on that day or on a group of days just falls out of my memory. Last night, Amanda asked me if I ever relax and enjoy the moment at that moment and I noticed that I was sitting bolt upright with all my muscles contracted. I don't remember if I was always like this or if I have been sliding into this for some time.

Tonight was better than last night mood wise. I want to get out of town and get this next trip going. I feel like things are on hold when I am here. I only feel like I am doing something when I am out of here, on the road, and in a rented room or on an airplane. I feel like I am pushing back against something but I don't know what that is exactly. When I am here, it's just a cycle: home, office, whatever else. The radio show is good but it's only once a week and it's over so fast I am back here before I know it. I am going to try to be up in a few hours. 2348 hrs.

07-09-07 LAX: 1620 hrs. Here again. And so, another one starts. It's always interesting albeit somewhat depressing to sit here and watch people. The never ending line at the McDonald's and people sitting on chairs and on the floor, fisting that food into their mouths like there's a prize for eating it all in under two minutes. It's amazing to see these people load up on so much food and those massive buckets of soda only to cram themselves into an economy seat and go to Hawaii. I just saw a family walk by and every one of them had a McDonalds bag and a drink. This country has a lot of work to do. It's at airports, and for some reason this one especially, where I see that America is full of tired, fat people in bad health. Good grief, these people can breed. So many kids, so many cell phones. Everyone's talking, breeding and eating bad food. How long can it last? One day, all the toilets will just cough, the faucets will sigh and things will grind to a halt. The rivers of cola will dry up and all the screens will dim. People will start falling over or exploding or perhaps they'll just look at their cell phones, press madly on the keypad and then turn to stone. "I couldn't get any reception from this location, so I lost... everything." What if the southern states started to sink under the weight of their body mass index and all the crosses they bear, sorry, wear? "What the fuck happened to Arkansas?! It was here a minute ago!" What if

Florida broke loose from its borders and floated gently south, demolishing Key West and finally stopped after smashing into the coast of Cuba? "Do ya'll take Visa?" Since there are a lot of jobs that "Americans don't want to do" and a lot of workers who want to do them, how about employing them to dig a massive trench between America and Mexico and fill it with landmines like the line between North and South Korea?

07-10-07 London UK: 2122 hrs. I am near Piccadilly. I kind of know my way around and walked around as soon as I got here in an effort to stay awake and get used to the time change. I was determined not to do that three hour power nap that always screws me up later. A couple of hours ago, I did slump over in the chair here at the desk but that only lasted about 7 minutes. I feel pretty good and will try to work a little longer. I contacted both Segs and Ruffy about Thursday's practice and all is set. I will see them on that afternoon and we will hit it. Tomorrow is press all day.

I walked to the HMV near Piccadilly Circus and got the 3CD version of the <u>Colossal Youth</u> album by the Young Marble Giants. There were a lot of people outside today. It's high tourist season and it was a relatively cool day temperature wise. My room is hot, I have a window open and a fan on. I can't stay up any longer.

07-11-07 London UK: 2238 hrs. Back in the room. I had 8 hours of press today. It went very quickly somehow. I got turned loose from that around 1800 hrs. and came back here, worked on radio stuff and tried to stay awake. My neighborhood is very busy with human traffic and I couldn't come up with anywhere to go so I came back here. I have practice tomorrow. I am really looking forward to getting in there and getting a couple of hours of practice under my belt. I have been anticipating the show and really want to get this practice going. I have no idea how tomorrow will go but I can't wait to get into it. I don't know why I am stressing over things all the time but I am. Since I have been here I have been so distracted by the wait for band practice to start that I have not been able to think straight. That's all there is on my mind at the moment. I will be better tomorrow after we get in there and I can really see what I am dealing with and what is required of me.

07-12-07 London UK: 2351 hrs. Slept on and off last night. I woke up at one point with my heart pounding very hard and I was sweating. Is that an anxiety attack? I get them fairly frequently. Sometimes there's a nightmare attached to it and I wake up out of breath. This morning I thought my heart was exploding. I eventually got a little more sleep on and off until I had to go.

Today was good, though. I took the tube to Lancaster Gate and walked to the Columbia Hotel to meet Brian James of The Damned. I had never met him before but Casey from Amen connected the two of us and we set up a time to meet for a little while before band practice started. I got to the hotel a little early and was standing in the lobby and a man behind the counter asked if he could help me and I told him I was waiting for someone. He pointed into the lounge and said that I was perhaps waiting to meet the man sitting on the couch. I looked the direction he was pointing and sure enough, there was Brian James! That was pretty Damned cool, I must say. We walked down the street from the hotel and went to a pub, sat down and talked for about an hour. I asked him about how he got into music, early influences, etc. I asked him if at some point I could interview him at some length and he said that would be ok. He looks like he's been though a lot. I know that many years ago, he was pretty wild. He was very cool and it wasn't a let down at all to meet him and I hope I get to do that interview with him. Meeting Brian was one of those things I live for. Actualizing ideas will never lose its appeal to me. I want to do something or go somewhere so I plan it out and get it done. It makes life worth living. There's so much of life that is very hard to get through so I try and do stuff like this as much as I can. It's a way of living in spite of the frequent wretchedness of life.

After I met with Brian, I went back to the tube and went to the practice place. I am surprised I found it as easily as I did, I am usually bad with directions but I got off the train at Putney Bridge and followed the instructions I had written down from the practice place's site and walked right in the door. Segs and Ruffy were there. Introductions were made, hands were shook. Paul Fox, the guitarist, was feeling too bad to come in but they had a stand in player, who was due in soon. We decided to start in without him and did *Staring At The Rude Boys, In A Rut, You're Just A, Society* and *S.U.S.* It wasn't all that easy singing without guitar but it allowed me to lock in with the songs and it was great to hear what those guys are doing on their own.

Soon enough our guitar player of the day, Leigh, showed up. Great guy and knew the songs perfectly. We would listen to the recorded version of a song and then bang it out a few times and move onto the next song. We did *Shine On Me, In A Rut, Babylon's Burning, Something That I Said, You're Just A, S.U.S., Jah Wars* and *Dope For Guns.* I won't be singing *Jah Wars,* someone else will, but the band needed to hear vocals so they could get James, the sax player, in the right places in the mix. That's a hard song to sing.

After we had practiced for hours, we all went to a pub down the road and hung out for awhile. Segs and Ruffy are really great guys and suffered all my Ruts Fanatic questions very well. They were happy with the day's work and thought I had done well. It's good to have some playing under the belt. I think I can do it. I must say, I am tripping out over all of this. Singing these songs all day was a blast for the most part. Lee, not wanting to intrude upon the concentration of Segs and Ruffy, didn't play loud or do any leads, which is respectful and cool but I wanted him to really let it rip so we could have more of the live concert feel but he kept things pretty low volume so for me, it never got all the way off the ground. Still, I am much better acquainted with the songs now than I was several hours ago. All this is cool but it's a drag that we are together because Paul is dying. 0128 hrs.

07-13-07 London UK: 2352 hrs. Today will most likely end up being one of the most memorable experiences of my life. I got to band practice a little after 1215 hrs. Segs and Ruffy were working with our other stand in guitar player, named Lee, who will be working with the house band at the show on Tuesday. He is one great player. As soon as

I got there, we ran through the set and it sounded good. Lee plays really clean so it was difficult to hit it hard in some parts that need to be more distorted and crazy but it was still really good. We played everything three times. I think the three of us are good to go. We took a break to wait for Paul Fox to arrive. Paul showed up around 1500 hrs. We loaded him in and he set up his gear. I went out into the front lounge for a minute and I hear him checking out his rig and pedals, he goes into *Give Youth A Chance* and the hair on my arms stood up. It reminded me of the time I was outside the practice room door at Sabbath practice and Geezer was in there alone warming up playing *Fluff*. I come back into the room and it looks like he's ready to play. He's hopping up and down on one foot to another, really amped. He asks what song we're doing first and I point to the set list at his feet and faster than I can get to the mic, he tears into the first song on the set, *Something That I Said*, with easily two times the volume that either stand-in guitarist had used and instantaneously, the whole mood in the room changes and everything gets very intense and aggressive. It's like Paul kick starts the other two into some kind of memory of the past because all of a sudden they sound like they did on their album and the rhythm section is playing with an intensity that dwarfs what they were up to previously. It took Paul to unlock them and man did he do it. I was singing right next to him, watching what he was doing. His sound is so distinctive and he was so loud and laying into it so hard. It was incredible! I think we went into *Shine On Me* next and finally the song felt right because of what he was playing at the top. After that, we played *Staring At The Rudeboys* and that was amazing as well. There is nothing like Paul's sound. It was amazing to be in the same room with it. I had never seen the band live, all I have is the records, so to all of a sudden be getting slammed by that guitar and having it sound just like the records but even better was beyond description. It was one of the most moving experiences I have ever had playing music. We finally played *Society* today. Segs, Ruffy and I had played it on our own but we had never played it with either guitar player. We listened to the Peel version once and Paul said he could do it. We played and it sounded great. I think we finished with *Jah*

War and worked on an acapella version of a small bit of *Love In Vain* that we're going to go into after we play *Jah War* and practice was over. Paul looked at me and said, "Where were you in 1981?! You could taken over after Malcolm died!" That was pretty intense and I'll take it as a compliment. He thanked me for coming out here and I told him how happy I was to be part of the team.

As the gear was getting packed up, I got out my camera and took pictures of the guys hanging out. I figured that it would be a good thing, considering there might come a time where the three of them won't be able to be in a room together. I got some great ones of Paul and Segs having a laugh. I am so glad I had my camera with me.

Paul hung for a little while longer and then he left. The rest of us packed up all the gear and left it at the practice place and went off to the pub, as seems to be the custom. It was myself, Segs, Ruffy, Pablo, who will be looking after us at the show, Mica the soundman, Sarah the promoter and Lee the guitar player, who will also be handling the house band that will back up some of the performers who are doing 1-2 song sets like TV Smith, Eddie Tenpole and others. We went to this pub and hung out for awhile. It's a nice ritual, everyone hanging out and talking, all very civilized and they're all very cool people. I took the tube back here, got something to eat and then came back to the room. I was too tired to do anything else. I sang all those songs at least 2 to 4 times each so I am pretty beat. It was a good day and most importantly, I think I am ready for the show. I have been singing along with the songs here in the room, making notes on strange timing on some parts and am learning a lot about small bits here and there that were tripping me up before.

It's a Friday night and it's very hot out so that means the streets will be full of loud people looking for a good time, so I'll leave them to it. I'll go out tomorrow night. I have a day off tomorrow. I might get together with Segs but past that I am on my own. I don't mind. I want some time to think about all this and besides, it's the 27th anniversary of Malcolm Owen's death and I'd like to have some time to think about that. I like this room. I brought my kettle, some coffee, I have a small stereo set up, I am listening to The Damned and all is well. People are ok with me but I really like time on my own. Unwitnessed time is the best. I am not messing with anyone, I have paid for the space I am occupying and it's a fair deal. I have rented this space for a few days and will leave with all my stuff and move on. I think hotel rooms are the best deal ever. I like living in hotels. I like that I live in them all over the world. I like that they are not mine and that I don't have to carry them with me. It's out here in cities all over the world where I feel I am actually living. Life doesn't feel like a waste of time when I am living on my own out here. The appeal of this has never dipped, in fact, it gets more intense the older I get. When I am at the house in LA and it's feeling good to be there, I know it's time to go. I don't want to feel good there. I always want to feel that it's just the holding pen I live in until I can get out into the world again.

I know what I am about to write will seem lame but here it goes: I love London. I used to feel quite differently about this city but over the years I have come to the conclusion that it's one of the most amazing cities in the world. Londoners impress me. I love their vitality and how much they seem to enjoy the human crush. They seem to be having a blast even when the trains are late and the weather is sticky or raining. Everything is pricey here but people just get on with it. I see people in bars and restaurants and everyone's hanging out with other people and, I don't know, they make it seem that they have found a great way to have a good time pretty often. I am sure there are busloads of morose people here but for the most part people seem to be electrified by London, even visitors. I don't think I could ever live here for long but it would be cool to be a Londoner for a period of time. I can't think of any jobs I could do that would allow me to spend any length of time here but it would be cool to do it some time. I am probably just being naïve or perhaps it's because I am only here for short periods of time and never have to deal with the aspects of living here that really get to people. But all the same, I really like the British people and I really like this town. I feel lucky that I get to live here now and then. And if it is merely naiveté, that's fine with me. I like that I can be happy at some distant point and that more and more, no point is that distant and I am fine pretty much anywhere I

Henry Rollins

am. I hope I never get over that feeling. It's in these situations that I feel alive, finally.

I am having a hard time describing how intense all of this is. I have been listening to The Ruts band for so many years and here we are together, doing this thing. No matter what happens at the show, I will never forget this time. This is something that will be a chapter somewhere and hopefully, we will do something that is memorable in a good way. Seeing that these guys trust me with their songs is one of the highest compliments I have ever been paid. Since I left practice, I have been turning all this over in my mind and the more I think about it, the heavier it all gets. All this makes me think of DC and all the people I have met in the music scene there. This is for them too. For Ian, Alec, Eddie, Nathan, Vivien, all those DC Ruts fans. They are with me in my thoughts and part of this is for them. It's a way to say that DC is in the house. It's not me up there, we're up there. I know that sounds corny but when I think about all that, I forget to breathe.

Letters? Oh, I get them:

First let me state that this email will most likely be read by some production stooge therefore, I do not except Mr. Rollins to even see this let alone reply. I am a veteran, living in homeless shelter on Borden Ave. in Queens, N.Y.. I have had the privilege and honor to serve in Iraq both as a infantryman and as a contractor. I hold a degree in electronic engineering and have an acute sense of political philosophy that is unique amongst my peers. I want to let you know, Mr. Rollins that your opinions cannot be more inappropriate or wrong. The thing you and your millionaire music friends donnot realize that THERE IS a REAL and viable threat that the US must strive in opposition and must be victorious in. The issue of politicizing the justification foe hostilities is an insignificant point. The main issue is to do and say everything to support those who now and before us have given their lives for the availability for YOU to pursue a career in music and make movies and make LOTS of money. The activism and opinions of people with lots of opportunities should fall on the side of support and "critiquing" not contention. I feel lucky to be an American citizen and feel the threat to our country and way of life is threatened by ISLAM and ILLEGAL immigration - this is what I strive to combat. I was born and I will die an American and yet I cannot find employment, I do not eat a meal everyday, I pass my time looking for an honest day's work in my chosen profession, with none to be had - because the competition from immigration is too substantial. but all in all I feel lucky, I feel blessed to be an American because untimely this is the only country in the world where an individual can be at the bottom of the pile and rise to the cream of the crop. In closing let me say that I hope you realize how incredibly fortunate you are and to realize that this is the only country in the world where you are able to live out your pursuits with vigor and optimism and you do this on the basis of those who served and died and those who serve now peace be with you. —GC, US ARMY (ret.)

I wrote the man back and asked him if Islam was the problem, why didn't the good Texan president from New Haven, CT kill all his Muslim friends in Saudi Arabia? I also asked if it was all those pesky immigrants, legal and illegal, who were taking all the electrical engineering jobs. He got back to me and told me that Saudi Arabia should be turned into a "glass factory" and that all leading Muslim leaders want to destroy America and are encouraging their followers to do so. He didn't have anything to say about the men who sell oranges on street corners in Los Angeles and other American cities who were throwing their produce to the ground and jumping into the electrical engineering trade. Perhaps this man should get in on the ground floor. Sell oranges for awhile and get into his trade of choice that way. An Army vet shouldn't be living in a shelter and eating only now and then. It could be that there's more to his story but all the same, it's a drag.

07-14-07 London UK: 2225 hrs. Back from walking around near the hotel. I am staying near the Astoria, a venue where I have done a lot of shows. A lot of people are out for their Saturday night so people are loud and having a good time. I saw several women wearing clothes that were way too small for them, they looked a little ridiculous. It's like they bought the clothes and even though they didn't fit, they're going to wear them anyway, damn it. I stood on a corner near the Virgin Megastore and watched people for awhile. Young men stand together smoking, throwing punches at each other and laughing. A group of kids with pierced faces hang together and laugh at people who stare at them. There were a lot of tourists walking around with their luggage. Some skinheads walked by, they were speaking French. It's London on a Saturday night. Whenever I am out at night in London, I always think of Punk Rock and what the streets looked like outside some of the old Punk Rock clubs like The Roxy and The Vortex. I always think of the band Generation X when I am here, for some reason, they seem more London than most of the other Punk bands, perhaps because they always had their clothes together.

Tonight is the 27th anniversary of Malcolm Owen's death. I have been thinking about that a lot. I have not played any Ruts' music today. I needed a day off from it because emotionally it is a little wearing, seeing why we're doing this show on Monday. It's going to be a good night I think but there's a lot of sadness and stress involved with it all so it's very heavy dealing with it every day. It's been great to work with them and to meet them. I am glad they like what I have been doing vocally. I think it sounds pretty good.

I have been wondering though, if I am peering too closely at the object. You know when you pursue something to the end, you sometimes wish you had stopped a ways back. I have not felt that way with this experience but it's very intense to be so close to all of this. For the three Ruts, this is their back pages, this is history to them, it's all from so long ago. I guess it means enough to them to be doing all this. I am sure they understand they were a good band and that they still have fans to this day. I can't help but feel like a voyeur into all of this. Malcolm was their friend and bandmate, I am just a fan. For Ruffy and Segs, it must be very difficult wading back into all of this seeing the reason they are doing it and Fox, well, he's dealing with a very intense thing. It is one of the strangest situations I have ever been in.

I got word earlier today that a guy from the DC scene back in the day just drank a bunch of cleaning fluid and is all messed up now. I am hoping that the reports I am getting are exaggerated and that he was just being an idiot and trying to get some attention. He's a piece of work that guy but he's not bad. I thought about him when I was walking around earlier, Malcolm too. I never met the man of course but he's been on my mind a lot, things being what they are. Paul Fox told me it took him years to be able to deal with Malcolm's death. It's heavy to be playing these songs with the band and to hear them tell Malcolm stories.

I have been trying to push back against the anxiety and depression that has been with me since I have been here. The time waiting for the show makes me start to over think it. Our set will be over in less than 40 minutes but it's a one take. There's no warm up show, there's no nothing, just the one shot. That's the part that makes me nervous but there's nothing else to do about it but go for it.

I don't have much on tomorrow, I will be meeting Segs and his wife for lunch and then I'll be left to my own devices. For a long time now, the only way I have been able to deal with things is to be alone as much as possible. I look forward to these hours when I don't have to be anything to anyone.

I got an interesting letter from a soldier in Iraq who writes me now and then. His letters are never boring:

The DVDs finally made it here. Incredible stuff. I would curse the fates if you had ended up in any other career field. I selfishly glue my eyes to my cracked laptop screen (sharpening a KA-BAR with reckless idiot I-Can't-Believe-Its-Not-Civilian-Life abandon, whoops) and suck in every joke, jab, and name drop of Random Douche In Suit Fucking My Day Up, in the most greedy of fashion, of course. Things have been a lot better for us thank god or whoever. We tamed the shit out of this horrible shit-hole district, the supposed AL QAYDER boogeymen supposedly took off to their supposed safe haven elsewhere and supposedly had some supposed foreign bad guy peons fill in who we supposedly have to watch out for. And the sniper dickhead is supposedly killed or captured. So I supposedly still don't know shit, but everything seems moderately ok, and that's fine by me. There's this entire neighborhood of abandoned, trashed houses, and a wonderful duty came down upon us: knock down all the walls of all the courtyards (pretty much every house has those five or six foot walls around them). Now, I'm a pretty moral guy and wouldn't want to mess anyone's house up for no reason, but we justify this by the fact that they're abandoned, and it's a really dangerous area. With that in mind, you have to admit, it IS pretty fun. 50 cal machine guns softened up the tougher walls for us, to the point where five guys just had to push and the wall crumbles, big mist of dust flowing out in all directions. I had to lug around a backpack full of C4. Thirty pounds or so of explosives, on top of the body armor and all the other gear. It sucked in a most massive way that makes one want to puke blood, up until I got to use it. We rigged a stubborn wall up and leaned one of those big metal gates against it in the vain hope that it would help channel the blast against the wall. Connected the wire to the detonator, moved to cover, yanked the pins out, radioed up to warn the rest of the company that there was going to be another big boom, and finally jerked the keychain looking ring out of the plastic stick of doom. Nothing. Had to retry it a couple of times when it finally went off. My dumb ass forgot to leave my mouth open (something about the shock or some other crazy astrophysical voodoo like that), and it rang my bell. The gate was blown to bits and thrown half a football field away, pieces wrapped around trees and whatnot. Basically every young boy's fantasy, trucks and explosions. That aside, its pretty much just grinding through days. I'm trying to educate myself more on our situation and the direction the country is headed and all other things like that. Things that my generation SHOULD care a lot about, but really doesn't. But shit, where are you gonna turn to? The news? S'all for the rants for now. As always, thanks a million, and take care.

07-15-07 London UK: 2320 hrs. In the room. I had lunch with Segs and his wife today. They took me to a great Persian restaurant. They are great people and I enjoyed the time with them. They dropped me off around 1530 hrs. I came back to the room and worked on radio stuff and then hit the streets to walk around and take things in. I walked to a hotel where many years ago, on the steps in front, a woman I was going out with told me she loved me and I told her I loved her too. It was a long time ago and thinking about it now I can barely believe the exchange happened. That's so not like me now. It was a long time ago and people change. I feel embarrassed about the whole thing now. I have not been back to that spot since then. There were three drunk piss heads sitting on the steps of the hotel, they looked at me, I looked at the steps and then left. The streets were quieter tonight than last night. On my way back to the hotel, I sat outside on the steps of a closed book store and looked at the darkening sky and was happy to be alone in this city at night.

07-17-07 Heathrow Airport: 0834 hrs. I don't know if I will be able to adequately detail all the events of last night but I will try. Last night was the big show, the one we practiced and prepared for.

I left the hotel at 1300 hrs. for the underground to go to the Islington Academy at the Angel stop on the Northern line. I got there around 1400 hrs. When I got there, some of the gear was there and so were a few of the performers. I met Max Splodge, who was really cool. I used to have a few of his records, they were good, very funny. Over the next hour or so, Segs and Ruffy arrived as well as Molara, who was to sing *Jah War* with us. Segs, Molara and I went upstairs to work on vocal arrangements. I have never done so many backing vocals before. In Black Flag there was the occasional group chorus but a lot of The Ruts material has backing vocals and I ended up doing these interesting rehearsals with just vocals, singing along with Segs. Anyway, the three of us worked out our parts for the song as we were going to alter the arrangement of the original version. Molara is an amazing vocalist, she has a lot of power and it's seemingly effortless the way she can let her voice carry.

With our stand-in guitarist and house band leader, Lee, we soundchecked. We did *Staring At The Rudeboys, Jah War* twice and *Something That I Said*. After that, all there was to do was wait for the show to start.

I kept working on some of the songs I wasn't confident about. I looked at the lyrics to *S.U.S.* over and over again as each chorus is different and you just have to memorize it. It's strange doing someone else's material, you don't always know the motivation as to why something is a certain way. What's confusing to you might make perfect sense if you were there at the time of creation. I knew that I was at the point of over thinking everything and getting nerved up thinking I wouldn't be able to remember the beginnings of songs, come in after two or four, whatever. I kept playing the songs over and over on

Henry Rollins

the iPod making sure I had it together.

My over anticipating of things has become a large part of my life now. The last several days have been very hard because I couldn't get away from the fact that we were going to go onstage and play these songs, one time, one time only and there would be no way to make it right if I screwed them up. It's not like the show wasn't all that important, it's the one time The Ruts are getting together to play as The Ruts and I'm the singer, no pressure. I just want to do good and not make anyone who hired me for work feel like they made a mistake. That's one of those big ones for me, not making someone regret they asked me to do something that I agreed to do.

The UK Subs showed up for soundcheck. Nicky Garratt wasn't in the line-up this time which was kind of a drag but their other guitar player, Jet, was there and he's solid and a very cool guy. It was so great to see Charlie Harper, the band's singer. He's one of my all time favorite singers and I will listen to the UK Subs too much until I die. At one point, they were playing *Warhead* and I was standing in front. They were playing the outro, which is the sing-along chorus, and Charlie yelled out, "Come on, Henry!" and of course I started singing along. That made my day thus far. It doesn't sound like much but I am a fan and I am easily geeked. Come to think of it, there's going to be a lot of things like this as this report rolls out, I am sorry but I can't help it. These people and their music means so much to me. After the Subs finished soundchecking, Charlie and I talked for awhile. I have not seen him for some years and it was great to check in with him. The first time Black Flag went to England, The UK Subs and The Damned were the only two bands who were friendly to us.

Soon after, TV Smith arrived. It's always great to see TV. He was in a band many years ago called The Adverts. I have been listening to them steadily since I heard them in the '70s. His solo stuff is great as well and he's constantly touring and recording and keeping it real. TV was going to play two songs with the house band and then play on Tom Robinson's set.

Max Splodge, the house band and John Otway on theremin got onstage next and played a song, I think it's called *What's That Sound?*, so great. After that they played another song and included Würzel, who was in a short lived two guitar line-up of Motorhead. I was introduced to him and he was friendly but I couldn't understand a word he said.

TV soundchecked *One Chord Wonders* and it sounded great. TV and I talked for awhile and caught up on things. I was in Australia right after him, months ago. He had never played there before and said it went well. I was really tempted to fly down there and check out all the shows but I didn't have time.

It was getting close to doors so I headed down to the dressing rooms which are at the bottom of an incredible amount of stairs. There's no moving air down there and you start sweating as soon as you enter the hallway that holds three very small rooms that were to hold several bands and crew. I have never understood this about British venues. So many times I have been backstage and the air is dead and it feels like you're sitting in a damp basement. By the time all the bands arrived the place was going to be gross, so we had that to look forward to. The Reggae band Misty In Roots arrived with all their gear and crew, there were a lot of them. They go way back with The Ruts, they put out The Ruts first single on their People Unite label.

The doors opened and the place started filling immediately. It was going to be packed. Soon enough, it was time for the bands to start playing. This is one of those shows I would rather be at and not have to play because I can't watch the bands with any real enjoyment because I am getting focused on what I have to go out and do. Eddie Tenpole played with the house band and was so great. What a voice. I have one record of his, I think it's his best-of. I will have to revisit that one, it's really good but I haven't played it in a long time. He did a great version of *Swords Of A Thousand Men*.

Soon after that, The UK Subs went on and they were great. *C.I.D., Teenage, Party In Paris, Stranglehold, Warhead*—basically a set of singles. The place was now very hot and the audience were mental during the Subs set. It's so cool to see that the Subs have fans still. As I was watching them, I felt a tap on my shoulder, it was Gaye Advert, nice one!

She's always so cool to me and it's always great to see her.

I went down into the depths to the dressing room and got out my lyrics and went through everything again to make sure I was as prepared as I could be. I was getting more and more nervous and started to wonder about Paul Fox's status. I hoped he was feeling good and not in too much pain and in good shape to play.

I went back upstairs to check out Misty In Roots. What a band! Horns, two Stratocasters, keyboards, bass, vocals. The rhythm section just killed, they were so hard, so tight, great music. I have to search out some of their records now.

I went back downstairs and into the hallway where the dressing rooms were and there was Captain Sensible of The Damned. Yeah! I said hello and went back upstairs to see them play. Captain hit stage and looked up to the floor above where I was standing. I gave him the thumbs up and he gave me the two finger salute and laughed. The Damned were on fire. The set: *Love Song, Machine Gun Etiquette, Eloise, Neat Neat Neat, New Rose, Smash It Up Parts 1&2.* I sang along and had a great time and for a moment, forgot that I was about to go onstage.

After their set was over, I went back downstairs to get ready. Paul Fox had arrived and looked to be in good shape to play. We all stood around in the dressing room and waited for Pablo to bring us upstairs to hit it. Soon enough he came to get us. On our way to the service elevator we passed Dave Vanian. I said hello and we shook hands. He's always very cool to me. We take the elevator to the side of the stage right when TV Smith joins Tom Robinson onstage. They played *Thin Green Line,* which I think they played together on a TV single and then they played another song I didn't recognize, maybe one of Tom's songs, I don't know his material as well as I know TV's. Right after that, Tom introduced us and all of a sudden we were walking out onstage. I said hello to the audience as the band got themselves set up. I called the first song, *Something That I Said,* and we were off. It felt good and the audience seemed into it. We went out of that into *Staring At The Rudeboys* and it seemed like everyone was singing along. After that, we played *S.U.S.,* the one with the hard to remember choruses and I actually pulled it off. Fox was ripping it up and people

A Preferred Blur   **241**

were loving it. My heart rate had adjusted and I was feeling good up there. We went into *West One (Shine On Me)* and that sounded good. I made a small mistake on one of the lines, I sang "Here I am a traffic island castaway" instead of "Rescue me or here I stay a traffic island castaway." I was very mad about that but had to keep going. I was concentrating on getting all the backing vocals right and trying to match Segs and Ruffy. I think I pulled it off, only the tape will be able to tell. After that Molara came onstage to sing *Jah War*. I stood next to the drums and did the backing vocals as best I could with Segs and Ruffy as she performed a beautiful vocal. James and Colin provided some serious horn parts and Michael the soundman took the mix dubwise and even from the stage it sounded great. After we finished *Jah War,* we were down to the two last songs in the set, *Society* and *In A Rut.* We played *Society* well and Segs and I got through the backing vocals, they're a bit of a tongue twister but Segs and I practiced it on our own before and that paid off. After we nailed the first set, I looked over at Segs to see if he noticed and he did. Somehow, we all got through the song without screwing it up. From there we went into *In A Rut* and I called from the stage to get some of our other performers onstage to sing with us and we went into the song. Fox played it kind of like he did at practice, where he kept the verses really lowdown and then built up into the chorus, it sounded great. When we got to the outro chorus, the audience was singing along and I looked to my left to see people from the other bands out there singing on Segs' mic, Captain Sensible was out there, that was cool. I went back to singing and felt someone next to me and it was Charlie Harper. Shoulder to shoulder we sang a Ruts song. That will be one of the highpoints of my life. Finally, we came to the end of the song. I went over to Paul and hugged him and thanked him for letting me play with him. I said goodnight to the audience and we all put our arms around each other and took a bow and walked off. Captain Sensible looked at us and said, "Not bad."

1330 hrs. Paris France: On an airplane, waiting to take off. To continue the story: We took the service elevator back to the dressing rooms. The place was full of people. I met people who used to follow the band back in the day and they said very nice things to me about the performance. I went into the dressing room reserved for us and Charlie Harper came in and hung around for awhile. Around then, Paul Fox said he was leaving so I thanked him for everything and he thanked me. I knew that I would never see him again and tried to sum up all the things I felt about the band and I started getting worked up about it all and Paul stopped me and told me that I had done good and that I was the guy for the job and that we were cool. He was walking out of the room and I was trying to think of the right thing to say and all I could come up with was, "Give 'em hell!" I know that wasn't all that good. He said ok and walked out. I watched him leaving and people started to notice and were saying goodbye to him and they realized that they might not be seeing him ever again and it got a little intense. It was then that I think it hit everyone what the whole night was all about. It was very hard to be there. After he left I walked out into the hallway and there's Captain Sensible talking to Gaye Advert, this is like something out of my fan boy fantasy file. I wish I could turn a corner and see something like that all the time! I hung out with them for awhile and then a man who was filming the event asked Sensible and me to come into one of the other dressing rooms to be interviewed with Segs. We went in and Segs was sitting with Buster Bloodvessel of Bad Manners, they were being interviewed by John Robb. Buster got up to leave and on the way out, he hugged me and thanked me for the job I did. After that, Captain, Segs and I all sat down and talked about the show and The Ruts. This was great for me, I was in the Punk Rock Promised Land. I know this all sounds really lame but I can't help it, I have been listening to the music of these people over half my life and they mean a lot to me. From there I went back to our dressing room and outside the door some of the Misty members were hanging out. I told one of them that I thought the band was great and he gave me a look and told me he wasn't in the band. Ahem. Faux pas, anyone? In my defense, I couldn't really see any of the band members faces from where I was standing but all the same I felt bad about that. I asked them about their albums and they recommended some of the titles, so I'll check them out. I looked at my watch and it was getting late, I had to get up early so I reckoned I had better get on my way. We all left the venue together and walked out to the street. Segs, Ruffy, their family and friends were on their way to a pub and asked if I was coming with them. I don't know where these people get their stamina for this kind of thing. You've done the show after being there all day, it's around 0100 hrs. and you're going to the pub? They're made out of stronger stuff than I am. I told Segs and Ruffy that I really had to be on my own. I asked them if they thought we had done a good thing and if we were right in doing what we did and they thought we were. I thought so but I wanted to hear it from them. I thanked them for letting me be in their band for a minute and then I left them there, found a taxi and went back to the hotel.

So, that's the end of that I guess. When I get a chance I will write Segs and Ruffy and thank them again for letting me be part of this. It was a great time but not without cost. The reason that they needed a singer is sad and the reason they were doing the show was also sad so those were factors. Also the fact that I had to basically fill in for one of the best singers ever, you can't think you're going to do all that well. I did my best and I think I pulled it off pretty well. Segs and Ruffy told me they couldn't think of anyone else who could have done it and that's a compliment I'll carry with me always.

Sitting here now, I miss them and miss band practice and the anticipation of the show. As hard as it was on my sleep cycle and psyche, it was worth it to have played with those guys. I'll never forget it. I think everyone should have a couple of those experiences they'll always remember. I am trying to have a lot of them. It's making me a little crazy but I think I'm doing the right thing. Hell, it could be the wrong thing but I'm doing it anyway. It keeps my heart from breaking.

13. Relaxing On The Axis

07-18-07 Damascus Syria: 2046 hrs. In the hotel restaurant. I have no idea if I will get what I ordered but whatever comes, I'll eat it. After I finish eating I will go outside and walk around. It should come as no surprise that my bag went missing again. It seems to go missing at almost every airport. I found out that I will get my bag a few hours before I leave the country so I will be living in these clothes for the next few days. It's hard on the morale when my stuff is continually detained and fucked with. I guess it's harassment and it works. I would like to find a way to harass them back some time. I had a feeling this was going to happen so I brought a few key items with me but I sure wish I had brought my coffee and my kettle.

There are no white people around here. I saw one while wandering on the street last night but that has been it.

I always have work to do and got a lot done today. I worked on the Fanatic! book and sent in the edits to the office. It's very hot outside during the day so I will try just going out in the afternoons and mornings. It's really great to be here in one of the world's oldest cities.

The man who looked over my passport at the airport asked me why I came here and I told him I wanted to walk around and meet people and say hello. I told him he was the first Syrian person I had met in Syria. He didn't seem to care about that and gave me a strange look when he stamped my passport, like he was signing off on something and letting me out into general population against his better judgment. I thought that was pretty good and knew I had come to the right place.

07-19-07 Damascus Syria: 0308 hrs. Great walk tonight. I sat here and there, watched the locals. No one seemed concerned by my presence. It was great to walk around in the heat and all the noise. The kiosks were open and the streets were alive with car horns and music blaring everywhere. I walked around in it for quite some time and just took it in. I was glad to be alive and in the world so I could walk the streets alone in Syria. This is the kind of thing I want to do as often as I can until I die. This is really living. It makes everything else feel like an act.

I stood at a corner and watched a young boy walk around, he reminded me of other kids I have seen in my travels. In many places in the world people have to grow up very quickly and I have noticed that young people are tasked with very adult responsibilities and spend a lot of time on the street. By doing this, they take on the mannerisms of adults at an early age. I have seen this many times. This kid seemed like he was an adult, he just seemed to have an awareness that was beyond his years. This could be my western perception though. It could also be that in America kids are so sheltered they can be kids longer than in other places. Whenever I see a kid like this I always think of a boy I saw in an open air market in Bishkek, Kyrgyzstan years ago. He was so young and such a cocky character. I wondered what his home life was like. I remember him look at me like I was the kid.

I am in the right place. I am far away from what is familiar and I have to think for myself all the time. This is the thing for me to do as often as possible. This is real life and I see that it will be harder and harder to be off the road and back in Los Angeles. Sometimes I think I am taking in so much that my head is going to explode. I don't know what I am doing or where I am going and most of the time I want to be dead but at this moment, I feel pretty good. I work hard at getting away from myself. This is the kind of thing I have to do to stay alive. If I couldn't do things like this trip, I don't think I could stay alive for very long.

1036 hrs. I decided to hit the streets before it go too hot. The best way to see things is to get out right at dawn and then get back in the shade before the sun has a chance to find you. I asked the woman at the front desk where the souk was that Nancy Pelosi visited earlier in the year and she said it was called the Al Hamidiyeh souk and it wasn't far. It was one left out of the hotel and then a right at the big intersection close by and that was it. I went there.

I recognized it immediately from the pictures I saw in American newspapers from when Ms. Pelosi visited. The temperature inside was much cooler than outside, which even at an early hour is amazingly hot. Almost as soon as I walked in, men started pitching me their wares. They're not there for their health, they're there to sell stuff so you can't be acting like you don't want to know. I talked to them and as politely as I could, tried to convince them that I didn't want whatever it was that they were selling.

My friend! I will make you a beautiful tablecloth for your lovely wife!

I don't have a wife.

For your beautiful girlfriend!

I don't have one. I abduct women from parking lots and bring them to my compound.

I see!

It was fun and the men were very friendly. One man, named Walid, told me to come by his store later and we would have tea and talk about things. That is what I wanted. I promised him I would be back later on.

I found a nice bit of shade outside the souk in a beautiful public square. The ground is comprised of black and brick red tile and there's a fountain in the middle that doesn't look like it's been in use for awhile. Each side of the square has a street running into it. People walk quickly through the parts where the sun pounds down upon them and slow down a little when they hit the shade, it's that hot, even at this early hour. A couple of hours from now the sun will send many people off the streets where they will just wait it out.

Before I came here I walked to a mosque near the souk to take some pictures, I like their architecture. As I approached I saw a large group of people gathering very quickly at the front so I went over to get a closer look. Men and women surrounded a man who was singing through a one speaker system that another man was holding over his head. The more he sang, the more people seemed to get upset. People started crying and putting their hands up in the air towards the sky. I had my digital recorder in one hand and my camera in the other getting audio and visual. Without realizing it, I had been moving in closer and was now in the middle of the whole thing, with people wailing away all around me. Several minutes after I got there, the man stopped and gave the mic to another man who also started singing and then people really seemed to lose it. Then a cleric came out and spoke very calmly and the people seemed to settle down some. He walked away and then the doors to the mosque opened and everyone went in. Within a couple of minutes, I was almost the only one standing there. I am not sure what it was all about but I am really glad I was here for it. This is what it's all about. This is why I come up with these trips and go out and do them. This is real life.

07-20-07 Damascus Syria: 1734 hrs. The heat is incredible. I have been out walking in it as the sun slowly sets. Even the breeze is hot. The heat from the sidewalk comes up right through your shoes. It's amazing how powerful it is. It reminds me of how fragile humans are. In the many parts of the world where the sun can kill, the day's activities revolve around the sun and its position. If you are in the wrong place without cover, you could have a very bad time. Here in Damascus, it's hot as hell by 1000 hrs. and it gets more unendurable as the hours go on. After reading all the books of Ryszard Kapuscinski's reportage from Africa, I will always think of him when I'm in this kind of weather.

So, more about yesterday. I went from the mosque gathering to Walid's store and talked with him for quite awhile. I sat down with him in his shop and he asked if I wanted some tea and I said sure. He produces a box of Lipton's tea, much to my cultural heartbreak. It tasted just like Lipton's tea. The first thing I asked him was if he knew what I had seen at the mosque moments ago. He told me that the people there were from Iran. I guess they were there for some kind of pilgrimage or something. Walid's English was very good so I asked him a lot of questions. I asked him if he remembered Nancy Pelosi's visit to the souk months before. He got very enthusiastic, "Yes! The beautiful lady!" He was very into it. I asked him what he thought of president Bush. He hesitated and then answered, "bad politic." I asked him if he liked America and he said that he did very much and that he thought Americans were good people. He also added that there used to be a lot more Americans coming to Syria than there are now. I asked him what he thought the reason for that was and he said "bad politic" and we both laughed. I like that people are able to differentiate between Bush and America, there is such a huge difference between the man and his policies and many of the rest of us. He said that Syrians do not hate America but are afraid about what Americans see on television in regards to Syria. I had never thought of that before. I told him that was the reason I had come to Syria, to meet people and form my own opinions. He liked that. I met his brother, thanked Walid for his time and kindness and then left.

I walked back to the hotel. The heat was amazing. Even though it was so hot, the sidewalks were full of people and it was noisy and busy, business as usual. The sun was pounding on my head and shoulders all the way. It took me about 35 minutes to get back.

I am near the hotel, sitting on a curb under a tree. Behind me, two men sit in plastic chairs and talk. There's a large mosque in front of me, its silver dome is catching the sun. Behind the mosque is a massive mountain, it's quite a view. I wonder if the people who built the mosque had this view in mind. A while ago, I was out walking around and taking pictures of a mosque against a nice mountain backdrop but a soldier-guard told me to stop. I have an nice shot of his hand in front of the camera. I asked him why I couldn't take a picture. He didn't seem to know but the other guard told me I was taking a picture of the American embassy! That is a big no-no anywhere in the world.

So, it's just me and these two old men sitting in this incredible heat. I invented this trip. In this moment, I am as free as I am ever going to get. To me, this is what it's all about. 1801 hrs.

1925 hrs. At an outdoor restaurant. The sun is almost gone but the heat is still hitting hard. I know I am writing a lot about heat but it really is something else. I have been checking out the news in America. More death in Iraq on both sides. Pathetic. 1929 hrs.

07-21-07 Damascus Syria: 0826 hrs. Pretty silly airport. I was in line to go through the first hurdle and I heard what sounded like American voices behind me. I politely inquired if the man spoke English and he said yes and then said, "Henry Rollins, wow!" He had seen me do shows in DC. He and the female with him were both working for the embassy here. He was putting her onto a flight. They were very interesting people. They said the rotation here is about 1 to 2 years with occasional trips back to America. The man said that I shouldn't check in my bag as there's a good chance that it won't get to my destination. I told him how many times my stuff had gone missing in the last few years. The two of them were friendly but kept everything close to the vest. No names, political affiliations, etc. I could tell it was a policy thing. They were cool but oddly remote at the same time.

It's been an interesting time here. I got used to seeing Bashar al-Assad's face everywhere. He was an ophthalmologist working in the UK. His father, Hafez al-Assad, was the president but died and Bashar got tapped to take over in 2000. He's just starting his 2nd term. He got 97% of the vote, the remaining 3% went to someone Syrians call "By god I don't know." I will have to do more study on Syria, there's a lot to know. I want to learn more about their relationship with America and Lebanon and Turkey. I have done a little research on the massacre in Hama, Syria in 1982 but past that, know very little.

1046 hrs. Aman Jordan: At the same Starbucks I was at en route to Israel months ago. I have about 45 minutes before I have to board the next flight. I don't know what waits for me on the other side of the flight besides heat. I am glad to be out of Syria and onto the next thing.

1714 hrs. Beirut Lebanon: When I gave my passport to the man at the airport here, he barely looked at it and just stamped it. Nothing like the suspicion I encountered when I got into Syria. I got into the first cab I saw. I told the man where I was going and we took off. He introduced himself almost immediately. His voice was booming "I am Sami! What is your name my friend!" I told him. "Welcome to Lebanon, Henry!" We got to talking about things. I told him why I had come to the country and he thought that was great. We came to a large and busy intersection and what I saw was pretty depressing: Burger King, Baskin and Robbins, a large Calvin Klein ad, Rolex, etc. I asked Sami if he ever went into Burger King. "No! My wife cooks real food!" I said that there had to me more to Beirut than Burger King. "My friend, Beirut is very beautiful!" I made him an offer. I said that if he would pick me up and take me around and show me what he thinks I should see, I would pay for his gas, meals and whatever the fare was. We made a deal to meet up in a couple of days at noon at the hotel and go do it.

07-22-07 Beirut Lebanon: 0918 hrs. Letters, I sure do get 'em. They can't all be good. If I had my way, some men would just wake up in the morning magically neutered before anything awful like reproduction becomes an idea. Darwin cocks his brow and lifts his mug...

"But what confuses me is why you support the troops and do the whole USO thing... I used to support the troops... until Waco. After I saw WACO: The Rules of Engagement, I lost all respect for the military. The US government employs the volunteer method. That means these assholes WANT to join and go kill other people. It's all a complete mess."

Yeah. I know. He's got a point, it really IS all a complete mess, America's educational system, etc., etc. This is the same guy who told me that if gay people are allowed to get married, then all hell will break loose, bestiality will be allowed, that I am a proponent of moral decay in America and also that I have betrayed the entire "Punk Culture." I don't know how his homophobia would rock all those gay punks but he can give it a try and see where it gets him.

On the other hand, I am in Lebanon and am very happy about that. I like my small balcony overlooking the sea and the small lamp that juts out from the wall that allows me enough light to read and write. As soon as the sun goes down, things are pretty good outside but from 0900 hrs. to about 1700 hrs., the heat is tremendous. I asked Sami about the winters here and he said that it's not a whole lot cooler. It is interesting to come from such a temperate region of the world into this and realize that some people live out their whole lives in this kind of heat. The same thing occurred to me in the opposite when I was crossing Siberia a couple of Februarys ago. I would stand outside on the platforms when we would stop at a station and look at the old women selling goods to the passengers. Their faces and hands were so red and ripped from the cold. I bet many of them never lived very far from where they were when I saw them and had done at least sixty of those winters.

There were great moments of heat and solitude today as I walked. There were moments when pretty much the only thing I could hear was the sound of my breathing as I dealt with the heat. There wasn't a great deal of shade on today's route and after awhile, the heat began to affect my thoughts. I kept seeing myself in my thoughts from a vantage point distant and at great altitude but the sound of my breathing was turned up. I thought about an insect in a sealed jar that was left in the sun. The insect doesn't know it's never getting out and the ever increasing heat just becomes a fact to where it isn't even noticed, just endured, until life stops. 0933 hrs.

07-23-07 Beirut Lebanon: 2224 hrs. Today was good. I called Sami the taxi driver I met the other day. He took me to Jbeil and Jeita. Jbeil has some great Roman ruins. I was walking up the stairs of one of the structures and a mosque located several feet away started the afternoon prayer. I recorded it with my digital voice recorder and it sounds great. Jbeil, otherwise known as Byblos, has some serious history. It is said to be the oldest inhabited city in the world. It's where the alphabet comes from. Thanks! Jbeil has a history that dates back over 7000 years. I guess if you are a creationist, Jbeil doesn't exist. Maybe I wasn't there at all. When we were there, the sun was pounding and there was no one around the ruins and so I had the place to myself. It was amazing to stand there and think that people had stood right where I was centuries ago, thinking in a different language with thoughts undisturbed by motors and airplanes overhead. When I am in places like this, it's almost impossible to believe that these structures were built by people. In Dubai, the towering state of the art buildings seem to go for miles and none of it strikes me as amazing but standing in

Roman ruins in Lebanon, that just goes right over my head.

Sami and I drove along the ocean and we stopped at a small fish market and Sami ordered up some fresh scallops. Fresh like you see them getting scraped off the shell. The guy washed them off, put some lemon juice on them and gave them to us. Damn, they tasted good.

We went up into the mountains towards Jeita to check out the scene there and he told me he lived near by and asked if I wanted to meet his family. I said sure and we drove over there. I met one of his sons and his daughter and his wife. She rocked us on the Lebanese coffee. That's some great stuff. A little bit goes a long way. She also brought out some cantaloupe and cherries, it all tasted great. She didn't speak any English and spoke French to Sami and the kids. I drank a lot of the coffee and I think I made Sami's family very nervous. At one point, I just took off down the hallway to have a look at their house and part way down the hallway, the entire family kind of ran after me and steered me back to the living room. I sat back in my seat that I had now started visibly ass sweating in and we watched television, a Bruce Willis film with subtitles. Sami's wife couldn't speak to me directly because she only spoke French. The room got very quiet and they all seemed to just watch me twitch, my blood rich with sugar and caffeine. Finally Sami's wife whispered in his ear and that's when I knew I was getting kicked out of the house for being too weird. He came over to me and told me that his wife thinks I am very interesting and would I please stay for dinner. I passed as it was going to be hours from then and I couldn't see sitting there for hours and then eating. Sami was a little disappointed but I did him a favor. He took me back to the hotel and I kept his phone number. I hope our paths cross again. 2307 hrs.

07-24-07 Beirut Lebanon: 1905 hrs. I am at a coffee place near the Palace of the Martyrs. I took a taxi here from the hotel and I have been walking around for a couple of hours. It's cooling off some but it's still hot as hell and I am soaked and people are looking at me. I guess I look funny to the people here. I am the only one dressed low rent. I think I am in a designer neighborhood. All around me are new buildings built in an Italian style with exteriors artificially distressed to make them look old. All the streets around me are blocked off so you can't drive on them, they are made of black cobblestone. The first floor of all the buildings are stores and restaurants: Adidas, Telio, Diamony and such. The people walking by are young, well dressed and good looking. I could be in Century City.

It took me awhile to find an actual neighborhood to wander around in. For a long time, I walked endless blocks of massive construction projects. Guards were everywhere. It looks like they are trying to build a small city all at once. All the buildings looked basically of the same theme as the ones that are around me now, shops on the ground floor and condominiums above. Some of the buildings had large murals on them of what it all will look like when it's done. I looked closely at the people depicted and all of them were white and black. I wonder where all this money is coming from. It seems to me that there's a lot of money coming into Lebanon.

Finally, I found a small neighborhood to walk around in. All the houses were dwarfed by the tall, unfinished buildings rising dozens of floors into the evening sky. The small buildings being steadily encroached upon by the oncoming future skyline. I walked through there for some time. People checked me out but no one seemed all that curious and many people waved and I waved back. I really like it when things like that happen. It's a push back against all the artificial tension that governments instill in the citizenry. Walking around places like this is why I travel the way I do, this is what it's all about. 1941 hrs.

07-25-07 Beirut Lebanon: 0748 hrs. Sitting on the plane, waiting for take off. Waiting. Did a lot of that this morning. This is one slow and cautious airport, reminds me of the airport in Istanbul, Turkey. Multiple security checkpoints and careful viewing of travel documents. I think my passport was checked at least four times. There is always a knock against countries like Lebanon in that someone will insist that it's total mayhem all the time and there's no order when often, quite the opposite is true. Things really blow up here. They're

Henry Rollins

not kidding around with security, they really do have to deal with the fact that you might be up to something. This airport is state of the art, extremely clean and efficient. It's a hell of a lot easier to deal with than the very hellish London Heathrow Airport where, unfortunately, I have to catch my next flight. The shuttle, the walking, the long lines, the lack of moving air, this is just to get to the next plane. The more they build on at Heathrow, the worse it seems to get. I am there all the time and it is always a pain in the neck to deal with. The only thing I can hope is that since it's the middle of the week, it's not a heavy travel day.

So, that was Lebanon. I have to come back and see more of it. I barely got my feet wet and I didn't see nearly all the things I wanted to. I need someone on the ground here who can take me to the places I really want to see, like a journalist. Perhaps I can set that up for next time. I can always tack on a few days here after a European tour. I also have to get back to Jordan and go to Petra. When I was there months ago, all I saw was rain.

What I can't get over is the amount of American and European products and advertising I saw in Lebanon. It was hard to find any Lebanese anything on the billboards. The massive Western infusion of products and culture must be a desired presence. I didn't see any of the signs vandalized and people were all decked out in those awful clothes so they must be into it. I guess this makes Thomas Friedman's case for globalization. He could probably gather countless groups of people from all age groups who would testify that they love their iPods and their Hummers—many I saw here. And perhaps it is just some colonial / imperialist echo in my mind that makes me think that a Burger King is ugly and crass when situated on the street in Beirut, that perhaps I wanted to see an environment that was reminiscent of a Discovery Channel documentary. I don't think any country should be stuck in the past but what I saw on the streets here felt like the place got sold a bill of goods by men who slapped each other on the back and laughed their asses off on the way back to the airport. "McDonald's? Oh, it horrible food, just horrible! I don't eat that shit, I just sell it." In the long term globalization will "win" and almost everywhere will remind a traveler of America or their own country, which will also be a lot like America. America seems to be a default. When you don't really care about how a house looks, build it like an American one. If you don't really don't care about what you put in your body, go to an American fast food restaurant. When you're in a hurry and you don't want to sweat the details, America is your go-to disposable culture, ready-to-buy, good to go. No money? No problem—we'll catch up later. It makes me wonder what these places were like when travelers moved through these cities way back in... the 1970's.

I will end this chapter when I put my bag down on the floor of the house and that's still days away. Today after I get on the next plane and away from the never fun London Heathrow Airport, I will land in San Francisco, where originally I was supposed to have a night off. Not surprisingly, my schedule changed. I was asked to moderate a panel on Thursday at Comic-Con and I said I would so I will now go onto another flight to SD and get in there late tonight. In the morning I do the panel and then go back to the airport and back up to San Francisco for two nights of Grinderman, Nick Cave's stripped down badass rock outfit. The record is great. They are doing five shows in America and two of them are in SF so I am going to both. I don't get to see the man play nearly as often as I would like. How many times have I seen Nick onstage? 1983 with the Birthday Party and with the Bad Seeds, 1984 in England, 1985 in LA, 1986 in LA and England, then it gets slightly hazy, 1987 in Germany, 1988 or 1989 we opened for them in London, 1990 we were on a festival with them in Belgium, in 1992 I saw them in Detroit, after that I am not remembering any other shows until Paris in 1997. After that, let's see, LA at the Wiltern 2004 or something, then there was the two nights I saw them in 2006 in Sydney. There might be another show or two in there that I can't source at the moment. For the most part, the man and the band have always delivered. The LA 1986 show was a little off, Nick seemed to be more interested in where his cigarettes were than singing the songs but it was still a good show.

I first met Nick in 1983, the night after the Birthday Party played

Henry Rollins

in LA. I saw him at a Minutemen show. I walked over to his table, introduced myself and pestered him for much too long. I think about it now and wince, the poor guy probably wanted nothing more than to be left alone. I was 22 and very curious and besides that, The Birthday Party was my favorite band. He suffered my fanboy inquisition with patience, well-mannered man that he is. Since then, we have published his written work in America for well over a decade. I am very proud of that. He's a good guy and an astoundingly consistent artist. The last Bad Seeds album, the double album <u>Blues Abattoir/The Lyre Of Orpheus</u>, is fantastic and this Grinderman album gets better and better the more I play it. I am hurrying back to America just for these shows, otherwise I would have stayed out here a little longer. It's always good to see Nick but I won't try to contact him while he's in SF, I'll just go to the shows and let it be. When in doubt, I leave people alone, it's usually better that way.

After the Grinderman shows I go back down to San Diego for Comic-Con, to shoot a promo thing for <u>Wrong Turn 2</u>, do a booth appearance for the film and then go to the IFC booth and hang out there for an hour. After that, I fly to LA and arrive late Saturday night. Sunday I have a radio interview on a station that's located down the street from where I work at Indie 103 but the rest of the day is mine. I have a lot to do on that day and the rest of the week is pretty nonstop. I have the radio show, perhaps IFC show stuff and I go to NYC for meetings on Wednesday and Thursday. I'll have a night off in NYC, I can walk around. I love that city at night.

Perhaps it's poor planning or cowardice on my part but I honestly don't know what else to do with this life I am stuck with. I don't see myself as actually in it, I always feel next to life, like it's a compulsory exercise. That's why I try and take it places. It's like weekends with my father many years ago, it was easy to tell he had no fucking idea what to do with a kid. We would go to the same places over and over, you could tell he would rather be doing something else. He gave it a shot, I must say, but it was easy to see he was saddled with me two days a week. His two days off, I felt bad about that. Hell, it was my two days off too. I started working on the weekends and the visits started

A Preferred Blur

to trail off so that was good. That's what I do with my body, I take it places. I put it here for awhile, there for awhile, and then somewhere else. I don't know if I really enjoy any of this, it's just what I'm doing as I wait for the clock to run out. I don't want to start a family, I don't want to matter to anyone. I don't want to have context in another person's life. I don't want to have kids so I can eventually resent them and fuck them up. Spare me, spare them—spare everybody! This is better, being on my own, traveling on my own. Living alone in rented rooms is one of my favorite activities. I think the whole thing is just perfect. I close the door, I sit in the room and do time, unwitnessed and unburdened. When I am alone I can be myself. It's a relief. I like people just fine but more often than not, they upset me so I don't get too close to them. I get too upset when they die or something bad happens to them and besides, there's too much compromise in constant companionship. And if you're fucked, it will never work out for you.

London Heathrow Airport: 1421 hrs. It's a perfect UK day, overcast and slightly cool. I'm not trying to be funny, I like London on a day off when the weather is like this. I wonder what the guys in the Ruts are doing right now. It's been 9 days since the show, feels like a lot longer. It was great being in a band again, even if it was only for a little while and under such strained circumstances. I have spent so much time in England that I really have come to like it here. I wouldn't mind spending a couple of days here but I have a lot of memories that come out when I am here and I have a lot to do in America so it's good that I'm moving on.

San Francisco CA SFO: 1910 hrs. Interesting thing happened when I got out of the flight. I picked up my bag and went to hand in my customs declaration. A man took the declaration, put it in a blue folder and pointed me over to a counter. A man took the folder and asked for my passport. Another man came over, recognized me and asked me where I had just been. I told him. He remarked, in a Boston accent, "Syria, that place is hot." I told him it was one of the hottest place I had ever been. He said, "Well, the government says that Syria is..." I cut him off and asked him if he was going to say "dangerous" and then asked him if he knew what our government does all over the world. He said, "I'm not trying to get into a political discussion with you, I just..." I cut him off again and told him he was getting political merely by using the word government in his question. He said, "I'm a fan of yours, I just need to ask you some questions, I'm not trying to argue with you." I said, "Ask away! I believe in complete transparency!" He said, "My opinion of Syria..." I cut him off, "Is of absolutely no interest to me! You can have any opinion you want. The fact is that one can obtain a visa to travel there, you'll find one in my passport!" The other agent immediately went through all the pages looking for it. The young man said, "I'm not trying to make you mad." I said, "That's it, I'm writing a letter." His eyes went wide, "You're going to write a letter?! To who?!" It occurred to me that these guys actually do get written up. I told him I was going to write Oprah Winfrey about all this and then he knew I was joking. Then the guy asked me, "What was the high point of your trip?" I told them that I am a curious man. They put my customs declaration in a nice blue folder and sent me to a special desk and this is all they can come up with? I said, "Come on you guys, ask me some questions, don't you want to search my bags and my person?" One of them asked if I had any questions for them so I asked them how long this was going to take. They said they had asked all the questions they needed to and I could go. That's homeland security?

07-27-07 San Francisco CA: 1221 hrs. Sitting in the hotel room. Went to see Grinderman last night. I walked from here to the venue and met up with Dawn Holliday who books the Great American Music Hall and Slim's. I have known her many years, she's one of the great ones. She walked me into the venue and got me my pass and all the rest. I went up to the balcony level and got my seat.

Around 2215 hrs., the band hit stage and went right into the song *Grinderman*. Such a great song. The band is Warren Ellis on guitars, other stringed instruments and percussion, Jim Sclavunos on drums,

Martyn Casey on bass, and Nick Cave on vocals, organ/keyboard and guitar(!). The band was amazing! The Bad Seeds are a fantastic band but this is a different thing. It's so great to see Nick just cut loose like he does with this line up. The album is great but live, it's a whole other thing. The song *No Pussy Blues* is hilarious. Nick is a very funny man and I love it when that comes out onstage. *Go Tell The Women* was great live as well with a sense of humor that the album version only hints at. Warren Ellis is one of the most dynamic live performers ever. What a great night, complete with Bad Seeds songs for the encore. I went backstage after the show and told the lads that I had flown all the way from Lebanon for the show. I think they liked that, I think Nick thought I was nuts. Hey, I'm a fan! Totally worth making the trip to see them.

07-31-07 LA CA: 0803 hrs. Traveling is getting interesting. Since I went to Syria, every flight I go to now has me screened by special security. The other day at SFO was interesting to say the least. Again, my ticket for this flight was tagged for special security as it was at Heathrow so they put me through a machine that blasts bursts of air all over your clothes and skin, knocking particles off. The particles are vacuumed up into a computer to see if any of them hate America. This is the new wave of technology to keep us all safe from American foreign policy. All my particles seem to love America and I was allowed to pass. Perhaps now that my passport has all those cool visas from "hot" places, I will get to do even more interesting security exercises. I feel safer already.

I think I just figured out how America will justify their invasion of Iran. Condoleezza Rice is on tour in the Middle East right now, throwing billions of dollars at nations that don't like Iran. America is planning on doing a 20 billion dollar arms sales deal with Saudi Arabia that includes sales of the Joint Direct Attack Munition also known as the JDAM. Nice. You might remember Saudi Arabia, that's the country where most of the 9-11 attackers came from. Best to sell them a bunch of weapons. Egypt will get to be in on the fun with a 13 billion dollar deal. Israel will no doubt be really upset by this so I am sure we will sell them more shit too. Iran, not getting any love from this plan, will perhaps want to keep up with the rest but will have to get their stash from somewhere else. When they do, if they do, that's it. They will be considered an imminent threat and will be bombed into extinction. Meanwhile, we sell more arms and the world becomes less planet and more suicide machine. This has to pass through Congress and if it does, then fuck Nancy Pelosi and all the rest of them. It's incredible. We are going to destroy the world. It's happening right in front of me and there's nothing I can do.

The next night of Grinderman was as great as the night before. I was watching the show from the side of the stage and when it was time for the encore, Nick told the crowd that they were going to play *Deanna,* a great Bad Seeds song. Then he said that I would sing it with him. That's great. There's no way I can sing but there was nothing I could do to get out of it. He started laughing when he saw the look on my face. Then he said, "Jello Biafra will also sing!" Jello was standing next to me and told me he didn't know the words. I told him to just repeat "Deanna" a lot and watch my mouth. I figured the soundman could turn our mics down enough that we wouldn't ruin the song too badly. It was probably more fun to do than to listen to. It's not great to be back. 0854 hrs.

14. Life On The Fringe

08-15-07 LAX: 1653 hrs. Here again. Extremely uncrowded here. Usually this area, gates 74 & 75, is packed with humanity, eating fast food while they chatter away on cell phones but today, it's very sparsely populated. What's the matter, don't want to go somewhere? Off to Europe again, some shows to do.

08-16-07 Heathrow: 1326 hrs. One more flight to go. I have been thinking that I need to get more done on tours now. This time around, I want to get more writing and reading done. Will do research during the day to add to the show at night. I should try to get to sleep fairly early after shows. Fitness will be a big part of the tour. I have to step it up. Diet and fitness are how I battle depression. I have a long way to go before the year is over. I have to concentrate. These shows coming up won't be easy. Doing talking shows in the festival environment is not the ideal situation but it's a show and I'll take it. I must never lose that.

08-18-07 Brussels Belgium: 1029 hrs. Enjoy this day. Enjoy it. I have been sitting here for the last few minutes thinking how much I want to die. To take myself out would take some time. I would give myself as much time as I needed to get affairs squared away so I could exit and benefit the right people and not inconvenience anyone I work with. There would be time spent boxing up things and making sure the items get to the right people as best I could. Perhaps I would get a storage space and tag all the boxes and then when I was gone, the UPS truck could come and take all the boxes away. I can see myself now, waving goodbye to the truck. It would take awhile with all the books, records, letters and all the other things I have accumulated over the years. It might be an interesting way to go out, running through the memories as the things were boxed up. I am not in a good mood today and don't see the point of living. I get this way. I don't want to love anyone and I don't want anyone to love me. I don't want to be close to anyone and I don't want anyone to be close to me. It's better this way. What holds me together and makes it possible for me to deal with myself and have a shred of self respect is that I do not grovel in the pit of humiliation in an attempt to be loved. Many years ago it was what I wanted but now, I am embarrassed to even think of the concept. Stay alone and be polite, it makes things go quicker, less friction. At this point, I am all about the paths of least existence. 1103 hrs.

08-20-07 Edinburgh Scotland: 0248 hrs. The regular weight of depression has lifted and I am feeling pretty good. It's been an interesting few hours feeling so light. I like it and hope it lasts awhile. The only downside of the show is that I only get 75 minutes. It was hard to get offstage tonight, I was having such a great time. The audience was fantastic and I am still buzzing from the whole thing. This is when I am at my happiest, when I am onstage at night and doing my thing. I have four shows here. I wish I was more popular here and they wanted me to do more because I think it would be amazing to do a couple of weeks here. If I could have an audience like tonight's every night, I would be happy to be onstage for weeks here.

One of the things I know I am going to enjoy over the next three nights is the walk back to the hotel. I got out of the building after talking to some people, all very friendly, and started back here and had to stop for a moment to take in the scene before me. It was past midnight and the area around the venue was packed with people. Colored lights were everywhere and the temperature was such that I could see my breath. If someone had told me it was October, I would have believed them. So, I just stood outside the venue and took it all in, breathing the air and feeling the elation that surges through me whenever I am in fall weather. I walked at a slow pace back here because everything looked so great at night. All the buildings, old ones next to new ones, looked like a dream when lit by the street lamps. Places were open and people were hanging out, there was the sound of voices, laughter and for a moment, it occurred to me that these people had figured out something great. This was a great way to spend time. It can be more than schedule and place and time. Sometimes you can just hang out and live. As I walked, I inhaled the air, it was cold and crisp. Seagulls flew silently overhead and I watched them as they orbited around the traffic intersections. As I got closer to the hotel the human traffic thinned out and within a couple of blocks I was pretty much on my own walking through Edinburgh. At that moment, I was happy to be alive and alone. I was happy that I live all over the world and this kind of life has not lost a bit of appeal to me in over 25 years.

Behind the hotel there is a massive area where a few buildings come together. I sat on a bench on the edge of it, just looking at the night and watching women clean offices in the building opposite to where I was sitting. I don't know how to describe it but there's a look to streets in the UK at night that I have never seen anywhere else. Some of the buildings are so old and when they are lit, they look like art. It's like walking through an artscape painted by night and street lamp. At Bread Street and Laurinston, there are several old row houses and I saw one apartment with all the lights on, the windows open and heard music coming out. The music filled the air and I just had to stand there and take it in for a few minutes. Tomorrow I will walk back from the venue slowly and perhaps stay out for awhile. The way the streets looked and the way the coolness and dampness of the air registered to me made me want to read Thomas Wolfe, from Of Time And The River specifically. I don't know why just the look of a city at night and the temperature of the air can have such an effect on me but it does. I wish I was still out there but I have to get some sleep soon. I have two meetings tomorrow afternoon.

For the next few days I guess I will be living in a strange rhythm of getting up in the late afternoon and heading to the venue late at night. It's strange going on at 2315 hrs. but that's what I was given and I'll take it. The one hour stage time will be a struggle but I'll do the best I can. I really wish I had more time up there. I have so much I want to say when I am up there. What the hell is that about?

2158 hrs. At the venue, backstage. Slept on and off today. Meetings and obligations precluded me from getting all I needed. I am here and looking for the angle by which to enter into the stream of thought for tonight's show. I could do last night's basic set, lose the Ruts story and go right into travel stuff. I would like to start with a thing about why I think these festivals are so important. It's a time when people of a certain stripe should be getting together and exchanging ideas, reading lists, site addresses, etc. It's a time for information to go back and forth and spread and for momentum to build. To me this is as important as anything that happens on the stage. I want to tell them that the walk back to the hotel makes me think of Thomas Wolfe and F. Scott Fitzgerald. From there I could talk about my America and why I leave and return all the time. Then some travel stories and something about Mother Nature's jihad on mankind. That should be the show. I will get here earlier tomorrow so I can write more. I have to get the thing going now. 2222 hrs.

08-21-07 Edinburgh Scotland: 0338 hrs. Slept a good part of yesterday afternoon. Vampire hours is what I'm keeping. Show tonight really fun. Weather having major effect on me. It's like October here. Walked out of the venue tonight and it was beautiful outside, lights on, cold air, lots of people walking around, good mood. Made me feel happy, which is strange for me but I didn't mind. I walked back here very slowly, enjoying the night air, the street lamps, the sounds of the people walking around. It was a good night on earth, all you can want at that moment, really, as good as it gets.

Tonight I will walk even more slowly from the venue back here and take in the air. It's like a gift, the night making me think that October is here. When I was walking back last night, I sat on a bench behind the hotel and wondered what it would be like to feel that good more often, is it possible? 0346 hrs.

2155 hrs. Adjustments, that's what it's all about. Tonight will be better than last night. I have to get on a better time schedule. I guess it's too late now. I will try and tough it out tomorrow and get out of there. I have to see what I can do sleep-wise tonight. What did I do today? As far as sleep goes, basically I went to sleep in the morning. That's no good. Tomorrow I want to be up at noon, see a show called Truth In Translation and then see what else is happening. Perhaps I can stay up and then knock out for an hour in the afternoon and then stagger down here. After my show is over, I have to be up and out at 0400 hrs. I will fly from here to the awful Heathrow Airport and then back to LA. I will have the weekend coming up when I get there which will give me a little time to re-set and get ready for what happens next. It's no big deal only 50 more shows. 2235 hrs.

08-22-07 Edinburgh Scotland: 0711 hrs. It's been a strange few days here. I am only sleeping here and there and it's been impossible to get on track. I have done three of the four shows and am already starting to miss it here. I am having a really good time onstage night after night. I liked last night's show the most of the three so far. I have one last one tonight and then I am out of here. It's hard to believe that it's August. I like September through November so much that I start pretending it's September in August. This weather is really doing a number on me. I got back here last night around 0130 hrs. and did my best to get my head down as soon as I could, managed to sleep for a few hours and then got up again around 0515 hrs.

15. Provoked

09-14-07 Flagstaff AZ: 1746 hrs. On the bus. We took off out of LA very early this morning. I got on the bus at 0200 hrs. and we went from my place and picked up Ward and Angel and headed out. I slept all the way here. I sleep very well on busses. I remember pulling in and that's about it. I got out of my bunk hours later.

1842 hrs. Now backstage listening to music. I walked around a bit near the venue to have a look. I got a new watchband for my watch and went from there to the bookstore across the street. I met a woman inside who had a picture of Mark Knopfler of Dire Straits on her phone and asked if I had ever met him. I have not but I was able to suggest a song he did with Phil Lynott of Thin Lizzy called *The King's Call,* she had never heard of it.

The weather outside is surprisingly cool and crisp. What I saw of Flagstaff has been very beautiful. Seems like a good place to be. I don't know if I have ever played here. It's not in my memory.

The bus is good, Ward and Angel will be easy to tour with. They are smart and professional. Ward knows a lot about music and is a serious record collector which will make things interesting.

Flagstaff reminds me of how American towns looked in the '80s. I am not able to really elaborate on that observation. I guess it's because there's not a corporate outlet every ten feet here and it reminds me of towns in the Midwest. The bookstore had really well chosen books and it was easy to tell the owner loves literature and art. I found two books, one a study of Celine called Celine And The Politics Of Difference by Rosemarie Scullion, Philip H. Solomon and Thomas C. Spear, which I have never seen before but figured I better check out and also a hardcover edition of the new Mark Harman translation of Kafka's The Castle, which I really enjoyed and would like to read again. If I can find the right price, I like to switch out my paperbacks for hardcover editions. I do this thinking of the next person who will be reading these books. I think of my stuff going to the kids of some of the people I know from my old neighborhood and perhaps it would be a good thing to have some hardcover books on the shelves. Does that make any sense? On my way out of the store, I happened to notice a used copy of Wolfe's Of Time And The River on the shelf behind the young man who rung me up. I took it down and put a bookmark at my favorite part of the book and told the guy that if he had a moment, he should check out the 12 pages or so past the bookmark as it is some of my favorite work in American literature. Who knows what he'll do with that information. That book knocked me out. It was Thomas Wolfe's 2nd novel and it seems to me that he realized his peak moments as a writer. It's hard to say, he died so young but the book has such force and strength and beauty. I know that Wolfe knew how good he was. Certain writers know what they have at the moment they have it and they don't waste it. The same thing could be said about Capote when he was writing In Cold Blood. He knew he was a great. What am I, some kind of critic?!

Soundcheck is done and I am looking forward to the show tonight. Tomorrow's venue is in the middle of nowhere and a pretty tough room but a good audience, same goes for the venue in Albuquerque, NM. I don't mind, I am happy for the shows. When I am on tour, I always feel that I am doing the right thing. The stage is the place to make good, to fulfill the promise made and to honor the trust of the people who paid to see you. I like that kind of pressure and I like the chance to deliver.

I like the confines of touring. I have the bus, the backstage and towns I don't come from. I have a show at night and work to do beforehand. In those confines, I get definition and direction. I also like the fact that we're moving all the time. That's the first thing that I liked about touring. The constant movement allows me to get past my depression and anxiety. The last period back in LA was hard on me and it's good to be back out here again. I hope this tour can go well into next year. I don't have much else in my life to do but this. 1918 hrs.

09-15-07 Tempe AZ: 1802 hrs. In the venue. I ate lunch with my old pal Staci earlier today. I met her in 1984 when she lived down the street from Black Flag. She would run the book company, as small as it was, while I was on tour in 1984 and 1985. Whenever I am out here we always have lunch. We went to a record store down the street from here and I found a copy of the new High On Fire album, <u>Death Is The Communion</u>, a week before it was supposed to come out. Listening to it now, liking it.

The Marquee, where I am tonight, was the 2nd to last stop on the band tour last year and one of the two shows we did without X. This show and the one after it in LA were my two favorite shows of that tour. While I am a fan of X, I didn't enjoy touring with them and didn't like having to go on before such a half-into it band. It was great to be able to play a full set on the two non-X nights.

Not a lot happened today. Before Staci arrived, I read a good way into Chalmers Johnson's book <u>Nemesis</u>. So far, it's not a lot different than a book I read of Morris Berman's called <u>Dark Ages America</u>. It's a downer but I am learning a lot and that's what it's all about. Both books are short histories of America and the Military Industrial Complex and how America conducts business all over the world. I learned some interesting things in the pages I read today. It made me think a lot. What I didn't know was how many countries we have a Military presence in. In addition, there are bases whose locations are classified so we'll probably never know how many countries we are in. Johnson talks about the violence that occurs in local bars perpetrated by US forces as well as accusations of rape, hit and run accidents, pollution and other things that would make for great resentment from the locals. He also noted that there's not any bases with the Military forces of other countries in America. I had never thought of that before and wonder how we Americans would deal with a foreign Military presence in any American town or city. Personally, I don't think it would go down so well, that is to say, it wouldn't be casualty free. I don't know if many people here ever consider what our actions abroad engender in these places. It's obvious that the White House and their supporters don't. The way they framed the 9-11 attacks, it was if they came out of nowhere for no reason. Even suggesting that the attacks could possibly be in response to something gets you called all kinds of names. For these people, it's better to go along with the incredibly hard to believe notion that Osama Bin Laden and company got a wild idea one day and went ahead with it or that Islam is an anti-American entity that is out to kill us all. Anything short of that is treason. It's so frustrating to listen to grown men who know better say this stuff.

Tonight, if I can remember, I want to talk about the first time I saw a woman in a burqua and what I thought about it then and what I think about it now. I also want to talk about Senator Larry Craig and his antics in the men's room the other day and perhaps raise a point that doesn't get mentioned enough. The point is that, if he is gay, then it's too bad he's been living a lie all these years by being married and legislating to limit rights for gay people. It's the lie that leads to all the bad stuff. Perhaps he comes from a time when you really had to sneak around and meet in toilets and other places to be yourself. Nothing good comes of it. I guess Craig will just attempt to carry on until his term runs out or something. Republicans march bravely onward! 1930 hrs.

09-16-07 Albuquerque NM: 1720 hrs. On the bus, waiting for soundcheck. Not a lot to do in town on a Sunday. This is always a tough show. The theater is not all that good for the audience, it's a dingy old thing and the backstage area is lame and I rarely use it. I usually just camp out on the bus and hang out until the show. The audience is fine though and I am looking forward to the show.

Last night was a great time. There was a lot of people there, more than I expected and they were great to be in front of. It's always a great audience there. Sometimes I am at the Celebrity Theater in Phoenix, I really like that place but I am probably, at this point, too small a draw to get booked there again. It's too bad, I think the audience really likes that place as far as a place to sit and check out a show.

In August, I started thinking about September because I prefer the fall months to late summer and it alleviates depression to a certain degree. August went by so fast and now September is almost over and

Henry Rollins

again, I don't know where the time goes. I am usually so busy trying to get onto the next thing in order to keep myself distracted from my mind—that's where it goes. It's just wasted on bad sleep and anxiety. I don't know what to do in order to slow time down. I have been told that I don't live in the present, that I am stuck in the past or anticipating the future a lot of the time. I think to a great degree that is true. The 8 pm stage time is what the whole tour is about for me. It's all about that show and doing a good one. I gotta walk around more before shows, get out into the world more before soundcheck, that might help.

Touring is time outside of time for me. I could live on this bus, traveling from city to city for months, maybe years. I guess it's a way to not have to be "responsible" for a lot of things. I would rather live this way than live "at home." I'd rather keep moving and not be such an easy target for so many things. Anything can become a rut I guess but I like this one the best. Living on a bus is like living on a ship. The roads are rivers and when we pull into a town, it's no different than casting the anchor. We buy provisions, load them onto the bus and head out, it's the best. I will be getting on and off this bus for the next two months. I wish we were out for much longer. I don't miss anyone and no one misses me, it's the only way to go long. That's what it's all about for me, going long.

1828 hrs. Back from soundcheck and hanging out on the bus. Weather outside very nice and cooling off nicely. Listening to a Mark Stewart album called <u>As The Veneer Of Democracy Starts To Fade</u> before that, I checked out the <u>White Pepper</u> album by Ween. I have not played that one in a long time. I'll stay here until show time, the backstage area at the venue isn't all that great. We have a long drive tonight and a day off tomorrow in Dallas. I will do laundry and try to find a gym. Last night I started watching a film called <u>The Lives Of Others</u>. I guess it came out some time ago. I usually just wait and see things on DVD. I will finish it tonight after the show. What I saw was really great. I just looked out the window of the bus, there is a line of people outside the venue that goes down the block and around the corner. It's a hell of a thing to see. 1906 hrs.

09-17-07 Dallas TX: 2117 hrs. Sitting on the bus as this day off nears its end. I woke up on the bus many hours ago as driver and crew were leaving, crew visiting friends and driver visiting bed after a long drive that was difficult for him due to high wind.

Last night I finished watching <u>The Lives Of Others</u>. I thought it was great. After that, I had the TV on and happened to catch a PSA for an organization called 4Parents.gov. The last part of the ad, which seemed to be about what to teach your child about sex, said something about waiting until marriage before having sex, which I thought was out of line for a federally funded PSA. I looked them up and found many articles slamming 4Parents.gov for giving out wrong or misleading information and promoting abstinence only sex ed. I have a lot of reading to do, I dragged off a lot of articles about them. Last night was the first I had heard of them. The National Physicians Center for Family Resources was asked to put together 4Parents.gov by the Department of Health and Human Services. The 07-14-05 article in the Washington Post by Ceci Connolly states that the NPCFR at one time promoted a study done by board member Joel Brind linking breast cancer and abortion. That an organization like this gets federal funding should not be a surprise at this point. I wonder if Bush even knows of the existence of this site and what's on it. I bet his daughters never had to deal with something as stupid as abstinence only sex ed. or creationism or even going to church. Bush could be considered a hypocrite if he preached one thing and did another but he does neither. I get the feeling that he's a man in way over his head. That's why I don't hate him. I pity him and feel bad for all the people who have to suffer for his inability to do the job. I don't think I have ever taken any one leader or otherwise "important" person with less seriousness than Bush. I pay attention to what he says because he is causing great disaster in America but I don't take him seriously as a man or a leader. It's a waste of time taking him seriously. As far as this whacky and dangerous website, I'll know more when I get a chance to read more. Apparently, it's been going for years, who knows how much it costs America a year to keep the site going? Does anyone keep track of any of this stuff?

09-18-07 Dallas TX: 1840 hrs. Backstage. Listening to Men Of Porn's <u>Porn American Style</u> album, what's there not to like about this album? Before that, I checked out PIL's <u>Flowers Of Romance</u>. The CD edition has as an extra track from a single called *Another,* which is basically *Graveyard,* an instrumental from *Second Edition* with vocals. The Wobble bass line is so great.

09-20-07 Houston TX: 1935 hrs. Backstage. I have been to this venue at least twice before. The band was here last year with X and I was here the year before on the last talking tour. I am listening to the new High On Fire album <u>Death Is This Communion</u>, it's brutal. They are playing here on the 28th. Nothing much happened today. I listened to Bush catch himself up, nothing new there but it was a pretty good one. He said, "Part of the reason why there is not this instant democracy in Iraq is because people are still recovering from Saddam Hussein's brutal rule. I thought an interesting comment was made, when somebody said to me, I heard somebody say, now where's Mandela? Well, Mandela's dead, because Saddam Hussein killed all the Mandelas. He was a brutal tyrant that divided people up and split families, and people are recovering from this. So there's a psychological recovery that is taking place. And it's hard work for them. And I understand it's hard work for them. Having said that, I'm not going the give them a pass when it comes to the central government's reconciliation efforts."

It's bad enough when you read it but the real gaffe becomes evident when you hear the audio version. After he declares Mandela dead, he stops for a second, realizing that Mandela is alive. (He's alive I tell you! Alive! Alive!) Bush then tries to drag the sentence out of the fire although it's fairly burnt to a crisp by informing us that Saddam Hussein killed all the figurative Mandelas of the world, that is to say, all those who are Mandela-esque, all those who possess Mandelatude, are dead. Saddam, he killed them. He killed them all. Hello? Brain matter needed, stat! I read postings back and forth underneath the article and there were people defending Bush, saying that we are not to take his statement literally but that we should try to understand what the man really meant. Ok, I'll try. I am trying to think of all the world leaders, statesmen or Africans that Saddam Hussein killed. I'll keep working on that. What a fuckin' sad clown this guy is. Anyone who can still carry the water for Bush has strong arms. It doesn't really matter at this point. He's gone soon.

Last night in Austin was really cool. That town has been getting better and better for me over the years. It's such a cool, switched on group of people I get there these days. For many tours, Austin wasn't on the list, there was this several year absence and then I started seeing Austin back on the itinerary. I don't know why things like that happen but I am glad to be doing shows there more often.

I talked to management earlier today, 2008 is already looking to be very busy. Usually by every February, I pretty much know what the rest of the year holds for me. Now we are working even more in advance. I am going to try and keep up this rate of work for as long as I can. I don't know how long I can keep it up but I am going to try. I am hoping that this tour I am starting now can go all the way through next year on and off. It would be great to be able to go out for at least a month next fall. I wish I was more popular and could do more shows in more places. Living on the bus and touring all the time would suit me fine. The older I get, the more I like it. It's also possible that I see there is really nothing else for me to do or nothing that keeps myself distracted from myself.

2022 hrs. now, need to get ready. It's a 2100 hrs. stage time, I don't know why they want the show so late but it's Houston rules tonight. It's a gig and I'll take it.

09-21-07 New Orleans LA: 1918 hrs. Backstage. I got in a good workout today. That helped somewhat. I did phone press and one of the guys didn't know a single thing about me, which isn't important but he didn't really have anything to ask me. At one point I asked him, although I already knew what the answer would be, if he had heard the radio show, seen the IFC show, heard or seen any of the talking show stuff and he said, "No. I am a novice." I said, "Flying blind, no preparation for the interview that's fine, I'll just interview myself." We didn't get too much further past that and I went on to the next one. Hacks are a dime a dozen.

After that I spoke to a small group of students that wanted to meet me, their instructor asked me via e-mail weeks ago and I said sure. That went fine. Past that, let's see, oh yeah, Dave Chandler, guitarist of Saint Vitus, came by the bus to say hello. He's living here now and will be at the show tonight. I have not seen Dave in at least 15 years. We are much grayer than we used to be. He looks good and it was great to see him. I did a lot of shows with Vitus back in the day, they were an awesome band and I had some good times at their shows.

I have an 2015 hrs. set time tonight. It's an interesting place to do a talking show, seeing that The Jena Six are stirring up the news a little. A woman was wearing a Jena Six shirt outside the venue today, that's so cool. Yesterday's Bush quote will be fun to chew on for a few minutes and also the local news station's weather report I saw on television today at the gym. It was at least ten minutes long and was so detailed that it was like watching The Weather Channel. I guess they take their inclement weather here very seriously. And why wouldn't they? It was really something to listen to the weather man tell the viewers over and over again not to get upset, that the storm pattern was nothing like Katrina and that there was no reason to be frightened. It's time to start getting ready for the show. 1937 hrs.

09-23-07 Orlando FL: 0259 hrs. Sitting on the bus even though I have a hotel room. I would rather be in here, the light is better and there's a better work area here. I got in a good workout earlier and got a lot of radio work done as well, I just finished that for the night. I am listening to PIL's Second Edition album at the moment. There's really nowhere to go around the hotel area so I just stuck around here and walked around a little and dug the moisture and overcast skies.

I also worked on liner notes for a DVD that we might release one day. It's scenes of Heidi and I fighting in the office. She told me to write up the liner notes, even though we have not decided whether to release anything or not. She likes to be prepared. This is what I wrote: *A Survivor's Notes: At some point, Heidi felt compelled to make a home movie of her life at my company 2-13-61 Publications where she has worked for over a decade. In this time, I have done everything possible to make her a better person and less of a threat to the general public. I figured it was the least I could do. I have learned that you can't win them all. From this brief but very telling exposure to her conduct, it is easy to see how unruly, volatile and potentially dangerous she can be. Viewers of this DVD will witness the constant challenges and abuse I face in controlling Heidi and trying to maintain an orderly place of business. The first person who watched this said to me at its conclusion, "Good grief man, get out while you still can!" Some may view this work as a "mockumentary" and even feel some sympathy for Heidi but they should not waste their time. She is stronger than all of us and one day, all of this will be hers. Thank you. –Henry Rollins*

Well, I just heard back from Heidi and these notes will not do. I have been instructed to start over again. I just wrote this and sent it to her: *Still Alive Somehow: It was a long, brutal and hellish experience. A recurring nightmare if you will, seeing Heidi walk into my office with her camera attached to her beady little eye, day after agonizing day. When she came in, all work ceased and it was all about her home movie and the slow, methodical dismantling of my mind. I was her subject, in various states of willingness, for endless hours of inquisition and withering attacks on my person and psyche. After what seemed like a journey only Dante could have envisioned, it was finally over and Directress Heidi disappeared into the edit bay and came back with the DVD you now hold in your hand. There is no hiding from this woman, she has a way of wearing one down to nothing but the truth and desperation. So here I am, flayed open and exposed in all my mortal wretchedness by Heidi May. Welcome to Hell. Do with it what you will. –Henry Rollins*

I did an e-mail interview that was boring and tested my patience but I got through it. Every other question started with, "What was behind..." like what was behind the idea for your IFC show, etc. There's no behind to it. The guy meant well and I answered every single question he had. Past that, the night off is over and nothing happened. I should have been onstage but we couldn't find anything for this night I guess. I have ten straight or something starting tonight.

It's all the same to me. I don't look forward to nights off. I would rather be onstage. I used to look forward to nights off when I was younger but not so much now. I won't be minding the night off in DC coming up though, that will be great.

My mood is pretty good at the moment, perhaps because the shows have been going well and I got in two good workouts the last two days. I'll find a place to go if I can before I hit stage tonight. Workouts are very important for me out here. It's a good way to keep the depression at bay. It's a constant struggle but I have found that I can stay pretty even if I expend myself physically several days a week. It's not always easy to find the gym in town and get there and back but it's a lot harder feeling bad with a show looming. 0345 hrs.

09-24-07 Tampa FL: 1857 hrs. Backstage at the venue. This is at least my 4th time in this place. It's a beautiful venue and I always have a good time here. I have to strip the set down a little, it's going long every night and while no one seems to mind, I think it needs to be less to be more. I don't think I am wasting words or time up there but perhaps I am trying to achieve too much. The shows have been coming in at about the 3 hour mark, it's too long for people to sit but there's so much I want to tell them that I will have to make up my mind as to what to say. I will make some slight adjustments to the set tonight and not try to cover as much stuff as last night. It's an early set tonight so I will get ready to go out there and do it and then get back at this when I am back on the bus. 1900 hrs.

09-25-07 West Palm Bch. FL: 1857 hrs. Literally 24 hours later. Sitting on the bus. Backstage is a little hard to access. It's been interesting to hear the fallout from Ahmadinejad's visit to America. He spoke at Columbia the other day and proclaimed that there's no homosexuals in Iran. Sure. Duncan Hunter, psycho from Orange County, CA said he wants to "...initiate legislation, and try to get as many people as can see it my way, to cut off funds to Columbia University." Why, just because a man spoke to some students at a university? Aren't they there to learn? What a coward Hunter is. What a bunch of cowards Republicans are. Let me look into my crystal ball... nope, Hunter won't be president. I have spoken. I just wrote to his site and told them I have seen the future and he's not going to win. He's kidding, right? No, he's not. I wish I could have been there to see Ahmadinejad speak. I think that would have been interesting. He's nuts, of course, but it would have been interesting to see the whole thing go down.

Last night's show was good but I still have to pull things out of the set or rotate some things because it's going too long up there. I asked people afterwards if they thought the show went too long and none of them thought so but I don't know if the post-show crowd are the ones to ask. It's a 2000 hrs. show tonight so it's time for me to get ready to go out there. I am doing two nights here. There's not much to write about today. I spent the earlier part of the day working on radio stuff and will work out post show. 1928 hrs.

09-26-07 West Palm Bch. FL: 1817 hrs. Ok. Wow. A man who works here just talked to me for several minutes about the classes he has taken with Dr. Moorehouse and how he is now able to bi-locate. He told me about being on the deck of the Titanic when it was sinking and also added that he has coached Tony Robbins. It was intense to listen to this guy but he was very interesting.

I liked last night's show ok but want to do better tonight. I will make some adjustments. The venue is difficult. It's small and not really built for shows and the acoustics are strange onstage.

After the show last night, I was talking to people by the bus and a man came up with at least 10 photos of me he wanted me to sign. It's an old racket, they are sold at conventions and whatnot. I don't think you would get much money for my signature. No matter how politely I try and get these guys to cop to the fact that they're making money off this, they always insist the photos are for all their friends who couldn't make it that night. I wonder if the guy will be back tonight to try his luck again. This happens in West Palm every time I'm here. Sometimes there's two guys together who have multiples of the same photo and insist they are for their friends. They have a lot of friends.

I couldn't sleep last night for some reason. I was tired but I couldn't get my mind to stop and whenever I would doze off, I would wake up out of some work dream. Finally I gave up and just started the day. I have been up ever since. One of the thoughts I had before I turned off the light a few hours ago was about getting shot. I thought about what it would be like to be lying on the ground bleeding out and having full knowledge that you were going to die. I wondered if those minutes or seconds were some of the only ones you would have in your life where you were truly free because you were no longer in a position where you would be judged, held accountable or in any way had to be responsible for anything except existing for a few seconds more before it was all over. It made me wonder if people who are dying and know they have a limited amount of time just want to be left alone to sum it all up one more time before they check out. One last chance to check in with yourself before you're gone for good. I think that's what I would want if I was in a position to choose, just a chance to walk through a few memories and see a few faces one more time. Could it be that in those moments, those memories are more powerful and poignant than the event that created the memory? The event is one thing, your memory of it, that's all yours. Your thoughts are the only thing that are really yours, I can understand why someone who is dying would want a lot of time alone to go through those file cabinets and pull some folders out one last time. It was a long shift in the bunk last night. 1841 hrs.

09-27-07 Atlanta GA: 1905 hrs. Great unsigned e-mail today with funny typo: *"I do not understand what your problem is. What did Anne Coulter ever do to you? You sound like a fread who hates the USA and to think I liked your music."* Well, there you go. I am backstage at The Roxy. I don't remember when I was here last. It's been awhile. I was here last summer with the band but I am unable to remember a damn thing about the show. So much of that tour is blocked out of my mind. I thought the playing was good but the overall was depressing and I regret that we did it. I should have not fallen for the romance of being back with the band. They are great people who I like a lot and that's what screwed me in the end as far as that experience goes. At least now I know.

I went with Ward into town and checked out two record stores and a bookstore but couldn't find anything. I got started on this a little late and should get ready for the show now. It's usually a great audience here. You never know, it could all go horribly wrong at any moment. 1925 hrs.

09-28-07 Charlotte NC: 1857 hrs. Backstage. Damned's <u>Machine Gun Etiquette</u> playing as I so often start the weekend with this one. I got a good letter from Ian today, he's back in DC from his week of songwriting with Amy and he said that they got some good work done. It will be good to see him in a few days. Speaking of Ian, I have been asked to do an interview for NBC for a series they want to do about people who shaped culture, etc. and they have asked me to be part of it. The interview is basically the demo for the show to put on the boss's desk. I said I would do the interview, sure. I don't know how much impact I have had on culture but I am interested to hear what the line of questioning will be. This will take place on the afternoon of the first show at the Birchmere in VA. It's impossible for me to do this interview and not think they are missing the boat by not interviewing Ian. I am going to tell them that when I meet up with them on Monday. If there is one person I know who has had a definite impact on people of my age group and otherwise, it's Ian. It certainly isn't me.

The show last night was pretty good. I went on way too long but will work on some kind of edit tonight. I have so much on my mind when I am up there. I need to leave some things out unless I am going to do three hour shows every night and that's just not going to work. It's not that I mind being up there but you can't hold people in seats for that long, it's indulgent and asks too much of an audience. It's up to me to tighten the damn thing up and make it hit hard.

After the show last night I met a lot of people and they were all really great except for one couple who were pretty intense. They were somewhat intoxicated. The woman told me that the last time we met she asked to kiss my cheek and that I had not been all that into it. She asked if she could do it this time and being put on the spot, I said ok. She kissed me on the cheek and when that was over with she asked for a photo, which her husband took. She started kissing my face and neck and I tried to joke my way out of it by reminding her that she was a married woman. She kept at it and I was able to artfully extract myself from her embrace. Many years ago I stopped asking myself what the hell is up with people. The worst part of all of it only occurred to me this morning. The two of them eventually left walking crookedly into the night, presumably to a car. If the husband was planning on driving, well, I hope no one got killed.

And then one day, there is change. Today is the first day on this tour where the weather feels remotely like autumn. I noticed it when I was walking to the gym earlier today. I sat outside this evening and took it in for awhile. North Carolina is a beautiful part of America, it's always great to be here. Usually, I am at the Tremont but tonight I am in a place called Amos' and I go on at 2100 hrs. That should be interesting, one more hour for the audience to get all liquored up. That's just great. Should be a loud one.

Van Halen launched their tour last night here in Charlotte. I read some online reviews and saw some photos and apparently it went off very well. The band looked great. The only one who looked out of shape was Eddie Van Halen's son. David Lee Roth looked like he had been training his ass off for this, good for him, I know he's wanted this one for so long. I remember hanging out with him over a decade ago and we talked about it quite a bit and now there they are selling out shows weeks in advance. I hope they can maintain and get through all the dates. Dave put me on the list for the LA show. I am looking forward to that one.

Another night and another show, I am into it. 1946 hrs.

09-29-07 Richmond VA: 1741 hrs. Sitting in the bus outside the venue. The backstage area is a hike and not really worth it but I'll get a shower in there before show time nonetheless.

A Preferred Blur

Last night's show was good, the audience was fantastic and really into it. I managed to bring the set in under three hours but still make the points I wanted to and not shortchange the stories I told. I will work on it some more tonight. From the look of the venue set up, which is a bar-tavern type thing, I think it will be important to keep it streamlined.

1806 hrs. Sitting backstage now. Listening to a mix I made many months ago called DC Car Music #1 which I have on CD and play when I have a rental car in DC. It's just old music from back when I was young. I am on at 1900 hrs. and we have a short drive tonight. I am behind on radio work, although it is a little difficult to put shows together from out here. I have been annotating new songs I am getting familiar with so the shows will be interesting at the end of the year with a lot of new releases and interesting re-releases. Looking forward to hearing a lot of Krautrock bands I have never heard before, which is most of them. I have a lot of the CDs on order and hopefully I will have a chance to get them into the iPod on my day off in LA in a couple of weeks.

I will be flying back to LA for a day in a couple of weeks to do some office stuff and check on things. I will have a few hours there and then go back to the airport and return to the tour in Minneapolis at some awful hour of the morning, sleep it off and get back to work. I don't look forward to the trip as there is nothing I miss in LA but it will be good to swing by the office and do whatever needs to be done. It will also be good to be able to get some new music so I can work on the November and December shows from the road. I also need to resume work on the 1st draft of the next Fanatic! book. I don't know if anyone will really care about that book being out but I want to do it. So much of the stuff I do doesn't matter at all if it reaches completion. It's just this stuff that I am doing and I am into it. I give it all I have and it takes up a lot of my time and in that I hope it has some worth but past that, I don't know if it's legitimate. At least no one is forced to check out the books or whatever else. That's the bottom line, it's all an elective and you have a choice. I have made good use of that over the years. Instead of railing on some band I don't like or whatev-

Henry Rollins

er, I just check out what I am into. Too much time is wasted defining yourself by what you hate, I think that's called "negative identity," and it's a waste of time to me at this point. Life isn't all that short, but it's definitely too short for that.

I am to the point of distraction with the Bethesda Medical visit I will do on Tuesday. I hate doing those visits. Don't get me wrong, I like the wounded soldiers but it's one hard day seeing these guys so mutilated, one after another. I am glad that I can provide momentary distraction for them but it's a tough visit, that's all I'm saying. I have done it a few times now and it doesn't get any easier but I know it's the right thing to do. 1836 hrs.

09-30-07 Near Norfolk VA: 0247 hrs. Sitting at a rest stop near the venue. It's not worth it to take the bus into town. A lot of times the venues are in a tough part of town and when we arrive at the next venue while it's still dark out, it's a smart idea to stay out of town and wait it out at a rest stop or a truck stop. The show was good tonight, I am getting the set more under control, getting more out of the stories night after night. The shows have been going by fast.

It takes awhile for the tour to find itself. The first few shows are a combination of getting used to the material, how it sounds and feels onstage, what the bus ritual is, what the crew is like and what the overall thing of it all is. We're at least two weeks into it now and it's feeling good. I always wish these tours could go longer. I prefer life out on the road than one off it. I guess one of the things I like about it is that there's less to think about and there's less of everything. I have some music, a few books and some clothes and that's it. I am left to my own devices a good amount of the time and am allowed to be onstage and to pull my weight in the world. Being off the road is a drag, I feel time go by and it's depressing. Out here, not as much. Ever since I started touring, I have never gotten over how great it is to be constantly moving. I should get to my bunk, even though I would like to stay up longer. I should have started writing earlier tonight. 0314 hrs.

10-01-07 Washington DC: 0347 hrs. It is the start of the month of months. October is here. The bus just dropped us off and I am in the hotel at Wisconsin & Calvert. I am in the sadness room. It's the same room I was in last July and the same room I was in when Ginger MacKaye was passing away.

It is the 1st of October and I am here. I am tired but not tired. I want to walk around until the coffee place on the corner opens up but I should try to get some sleep.

As we drove into town, I stood at the front of the bus and noted the changes to Wisconsin Avenue. It's always changing. New buildings, big chain stores replacing the older smaller stores, removing the personality of the avenue forever and putting the familiar and anonymous in its place. The more it belongs to everyone, the more it belongs to no one now. These big stores inspire no sense of community, just consumer familiarity and easy access. A lot of what I remember being on this avenue is gone so my memories will have to suffice.

For October, the most beautiful of all months, perhaps I can forget momentarily all the things that cause distraction and pain, like the fake war, the real deaths and the endless waste of everything good. It's been so long since I was able to think of things without "the war" bleaching my thoughts until they dissolve.

It would be something to just think about these streets and the coolness of the air, the leaves turning color, the end of summer, long afternoons outside, walks at night. It's the simplicity of all that which amazes me the most, that all I need to be happy to be alive is to be outside in this weather, walking through the old neighborhood. It makes me think of those who are no longer here and remembering back when I walked on these streets as a younger person, relatively unscarred and undestroyed. Now my walk is slower and some have passed away but I am still here to walk and remember. Well, then, well then. 0413 hrs.

1338 hrs. Sitting on the avenue, taking things in. I slept on and off, felt bad for sleeping and wanted to get up and get out to the street. I could still be sleeping now but I'm glad I got up and out. There's a new structure being built next to Pearson's Liquor Store. The new building will be modern and generic. Soon, almost all of the old buildings on this stretch of Wisconsin Avenue from Calvert to Hall will be gone. As I sit here, I try to remember what it was like when I used to live around here. In the late '70s, it was a fairly sketchy bit but not really dangerous. Now it's very expensive. There are lots of young couples, many of them with children. At least the sidewalks and enough of the storefronts are the same for now so when I walk around here I can get a sense of how it used to be. I come back here when I can so I can get some reference.

You can go far enough and live in such a manner that your body becomes a temporary historical object. When I am sitting here, I think of all the places I have been and all the things I have put my body through. I am a human souvenir, someone should collect me. Sitting here also makes me think of where I am now and where I am going. I'm just in motion, trying my best to keep things happening. The less people and things I attach to, the easier it is to concentrate on the work of doing a show every night and moving all the time. I like being back in the old neighborhood but I don't feel any connection to it anymore. It's a reference point and a welcome sight but just a place I'm passing through, like everywhere else I go.

10-04-07 Sayreville NJ: 1847 hrs. Backstage at the venue. Bus broke down today which threw things off slightly but it got fixed and all is well in that department for now. I have been away from this journal for a couple of days.

Yesterday was my yearly October day off in DC. It was a great one. I met up with Ian at 1130 hrs. and we went to the Adams Morgan district and walked around for awhile until 1230 hrs. when we met up with Eddie Janney, Guy Picciotto, Mark Sullivan and Alec MacKaye. We got lunch and took it out to the park down the street from Eddie's work. Ian Svenonius joined us there and we hung out under a tree for a good while. It was great seeing all these people. I got some great photos. I have known some of these people 30 years or more so it was great to spend time with them and not have to think about soundcheck and a show that evening. We left the park and went to Red

Onion, a record store, and from there, people started going back to work and wherever else they had to go. Ian and I were back on our own. We went to Crooked Beat, another record store, and looked around there. We went from there back to the old neighborhood and visited Alec's place. I visited with his wife and played with his kids, who are a blast. They have two daughters, the older one is very funny and we always have a good time. We went from there to visit with Ian's father, always great. From there we picked up Amy Evens and we all went to eat at a place near the Calvert Street Bridge. We went from there to Ian's house and from there Ian and I drove back to the hotel. We parked the car and went for one of our epic walks all through the old neighborhood. We have been doing this since we were very young. We walked all over the place. The street lights illuminate the trees and the leaves look amazing. The air was cool and still and while it didn't exactly feel like fall weather, it was still great. I was hoping for cooler weather but that's DC for you. It relinquishes the last bit of summer with great resistance sometimes. As always, it was great to talk to Ian and hear what he has to say. We walked back to his car and he drove to my hotel. We sat in the lobby and talked a while longer. Spending time with Ian is always great. I am very lucky that we are friends. We left the hotel around 0230 hrs. and I woke up this morning to find out the bus was broken down, parked in a car lot. So, that's the last several hours.

1912 hrs. So, that was that and now I am here in NJ. I am really looking forward to the show tonight. I have not had the chance to think about the great day I had yesterday. I will try and get some writing done tonight when I get back on the bus. I am usually more emotionally charged when I am there, walking around on the streets, seeing places I used to live and work. This time around, being on tour and all, I really didn't think very hard about any of that. I didn't have the time. Usually I walk around a lot on my own when I am there for a few days but this time around, I only had the one day off and I spent it with people all day and into the night, which was really great but kept me busy and away from the amount of introspection I am afforded when I am on my own. If I had yesterday on my own, I wouldn't have done much with it so I am glad Ian was in town and that he and everyone else had the time to spend. It is a hell of a thing that all those people took some time out of their day. It's such a blast seeing all of them. It reads lame when I write it out, I know, but it's so great to be with them. I don't know many people even though I meet so many. The people I saw yesterday are the ones I think about. I like them, their spouses, their kids. I don't see them all that often so it's a big deal when I do. I think Ian knows this and that's why he sets up opportunities for all of us to get together whenever possible. It is 1931 hrs. and I have to get changed up to get out there. I am so glad there's a show tonight. I had a great time yesterday but one day off is all I can handle. I need to get back out onstage and get back into harness.

10-05-07 Albany NY: 1808 hrs. I am now backstage at The Egg, also known as The Hart Theater. I always have a good night in this place. The fellow operating the elevator said that the show is sold out. I'll take it. I didn't get much done today and that makes me a little angry. I will get a good workout in tomorrow and get some radio work done as well. It's a bit difficult to get that happening out here with the limited amount of music I have with me. I am tempted to bring out one of my 500 gig hard drives that has all my music files on it so I could sit here and really knock out some work. I will have to look at the schedule and see if it's really worth it to lug that damn thing all the way back out to the tour. If I made an effort backstage every day to get it set up, it would be worth it I think.

About last night. It was great to be back onstage, even though I had only been away from it one night. I felt at points that my voice was a little scratchy and I think that was due to the night off. Having time in DC was worth it of course but I am very happy that I have one show under my belt and I am again back in the teeth of the tour. For me, the only way to really make these shows hit is to do it every night.

For the last few days, much has been made of what Rush Limbaugh said about soldiers who are against the invasion and occupation of Iraq. He called them "phony soldiers." So, people have been rolling out the ancient and useless talking point about Rush Limbaugh and his pilonidal cyst that he claims precluded him from service to America in its war on the spread of communism in Vietnam. I don't know if there is anything illegal about how he achieved the 1Y status that excused him from service but that it's apparent that this medical condition is treatable, rarely fatal and that he never went for a Military check-up makes his defense up for discussion at the very least. That he perhaps did whatever he could to get out of going into that very awful mistake of a war doesn't bother me. I can't blame a guy for doing whatever he could to get out of it. It's the gusto that he attacks those who go and those who have served and are critical about the invasion and occupation of Iraq that is irritating. But then again, it's Rush Limbaugh. He's the Paris Hilton of talk radio like Fox News is the Mohammed Saeed al-Sahaaf for the Bush administration. Neither can be taken seriously. Rush is not the only tough guy who didn't go to the hoedown in Vietnam. He's joined by Dick Cheney, Newt Gingrich, Ken Starr and Pat Buchanan to name a few. President Bush? Texas Air National Guard? Mission accomplished, indeed. So, what's the point of mentioning any of this? In my opinion, it's a good thing none of these men went to Vietnam. America and the men and women who went and came back alive were all the better for the fact that these men were not there. Their absence could have very well saved lives. Think about it, would you like to be in combat and have to depend on Rush Limbaugh or Newt Gingrich to back you up? Guys like that get you killed. Also, it is better for Rush and co. that they stayed behind as men like that were ripe for fragging and would have made an already bad situation even more unendurable. All in all, everything worked out for the better. Phony soldiers? No. Rush is just a show pony. Poor Rush, he knows what he is. He knows it's too late to turn back and make something of himself. All he can do is count the money and go to the office, he gets no real respect.

I watched a bit of news earlier today and the weather for the east coast is anything but October like. This is a drag. It's a good way into the month and I have yet to get a real fall day. There have been hints of it but not the real thing. I sat outside the hotel after the first

Birchmere show in DC the other night and it was pretty good but still not cold enough to kick in the mindset that I usually have when I am there. It sounds lame but when the temperature is right when I am visiting DC, I think in a way that I just don't at any other time. I think it's an echo from October of 1980 before I left DC. I remember that particular October very well and it has stayed with me all these years. 1913 hrs.

10-06-07 Philadelphia PA: 1908 hrs. Backstage at the very nice Keswick Theater. The bus has broken down again so we are living in a van and hotels and hustling to shows as best we can. It's no big deal, just a hassle and a distraction. We are hoping that we will be back to normal in Boston on Monday. It's a day off for driver and crew. I have voice over and on camera stuff to do. It's for the Hendrix At Monterey DVD. I have not looked it all over yet, I will do so when we get to the venue tomorrow. I want to get this show going and not think about all the hassle that tomorrow will bring. The bus has blown out twice in the past few days. That's the road. It can't be looked at until Monday so I don't think we'll be seeing it for awhile. We'll get by.

Last night's show was good but maybe a little too long at 3+ hours. I will trim it tonight. Last night was the first night I talked about my visit to Bethesda Medical and it took a little while. It is hard stuff to get through as far as describing what I saw. I have not written about it here either. I will perhaps get a chance post show. We have hotel rooms tonight so I will have a room that sits still in which to write after I am done tonight. I am looking forward to getting onstage and forgetting the hassle of today and the hassle of tomorrow. 1918 hrs.

10-07-07 Boston MA: 1755 hrs. Long day in the van. Now backstage. Sound and lights are good and I am on at 1930 hrs. I hope Mitch Bury knows about the show and comes tonight. I have not seen him in awhile. Mitch was Black Flag's road manager and a very long standing pal from 1981 to now. He was a very good friend of Joe Cole's. I have a great picture of the two of them that's hard to look at.

Tomorrow morning, on the day off, I will go to a studio somewhere in the Boston area and do some voice over and on camera stuff for the <u>Hendrix At Monterey</u> DVD/CD that's coming out next week. I think I am doing some stuff for an online version of the DVD. I'll know more when I get there in the morning.

2354 hrs. In a hotel. I just got the script for the work tomorrow. I could have used several days of prep for this one and I don't know how I am going to do.

Mitch Bury Of Adams Mass. showed up to the show. Always great to see him. I have known Mitch for 26 years. The show was good tonight. I love that venue and the audience here is always great. I was out to top the show I did last time I was here which I didn't like at all that much. I am hard on myself but that's the only way to be. I have a lot of work to get through before sundown tomorrow so I better try and get some sleep. 2358 hrs.

10-08-07 Boston MA: 2315 hrs. In a hotel room, waiting on the bus. We will hopefully be getting on the road somewhere around 0600 hrs. tomorrow. It's not our bus but one that they are lending us for a few days. We don't get our bus back until we hit Ohio. It's a pain in the ass and it throws me off my game a little hustling around and loading in and out of hotels. One of the things that I benefit from by having a bus on these tours is the restorative sleep and a place to go post show where I can repair and prepare. The last couple of days have been aggravating but that's life.

The studio work today was so-so. I got the script post show last night and hardly had any time to look over the 3000+ word thing before I got into the studio today. I didn't get much sleep for the last two nights and my voice was killing me when I was trying to get it done. I got some of the voice over work done and will have to finish the rest on an upcoming day off in Chicago. I got all the on-camera stuff done and they seemed to be happy with that. It's great to be part of Hendrix projects. I do voice over stuff for them now and then, it's always cool.

After the session was over Road Manager Ward and I ate dinner and came back here. I have been in the room ever since. There's nowhere to go outside so I am good to go here. I talked to Ian for awhile tonight. It was great to see him when I was in DC. I have not had time to think about the visit to DC since I was there because of the shows and all the moving around we have been doing. Being there and being glad to see those people reminds me that there are still some normal aspects to my life. Ian said that he checked in with some of the people we hung out with the other day and they thought it was great. It's a hell of a thing to know someone for as long as I have known those guys. When I see Eddie, I realize that's the same guy I went to all those shows with back in the day. He was there then and he's still here now. I know that's not much of a statement but seeing him or Mark Sullivan, Alec MacKaye or any of the others trips me out. We're still here and after all the things that have happened in the world and in our lives, we can still find some time to be in one place at the same time.

I have always been somewhat unsure about the idea of pride. Proud to be an American or black or white seems irrational. I am trying understand what it is I feel when I see these people or think of them. Even though I only see them now and then, I think of them quite a bit and have a lot of photos of them. I guess I am grateful to know them and grateful that I can spend time with them. Perhaps when you see someone you have known for so long, you see yourself in them, or part of your life, an investment of time and effort. It was a great day off and thanks to Ian for arranging it all on that day. I thanked him for that tonight, for arranging all those people to be in one place. That was all Ian's doing, even though he's busy, he took the time out to get all that together. Walking the streets of the neighborhood as we did the other night, as we have for decades, the same streets, that's the best.

I think I have figured out the thing. When I see those people and know I have seen them all these years, I realize we have made a history over all the years. When Ian and I walk on the streets, someone passing by us would only see two men walking but it's a lot more than that to us. It's only sidewalks and streets and trees and streetlights but it's so much more than that. It's everything. It's what it's all about and it's as good as anything I have ever experienced. Perhaps better. 0013 hrs.

10-09-07 Buffalo NY: 1744 hrs. At the venue. This is the 2nd time I have been here in this venue. I have done a lot shows with Artie, the promoter. He's a good guy and it's always good to see him. He had to split because he has to go to Rochester to take care of his Dylan / Costello bill happening there tonight. Wow, what a show! Those are some happy ticket holders for sure.

We got picked up by another bus around 0630 hrs. and came here. Hopefully we will get our bus back tomorrow in Ohio. It's a pain in the neck but at least we have a ride to the next show and we're out of the van / hotel cycle. I would rather be on a bus any time. The backstage area here is a drag but it's ok. It's an old venue and a little dank but it's a good place and the audience here is always good and I am happy to be able to work with Artie again. I basically woke up at the venue and so far, there's nothing to report on.

1825 hrs. We went down the street to the market and got some provisions for post show. There's nothing on that bus and since we didn't have our bus in Boston, I was unable to take advantage of the Trader Joe's that was across the street from the venue. I was hoping to pick up some frozen food. I think there is a TJ's in Cleveland that we're going to, that'll do the trick. One of the things about being out here is that small things take on a larger meaning.

I got a letter from management, there was an audition for me to do voice over work for the ARMY. It was 100 grand if I got the job. I passed on the audition. What if I got the job? I would be taking tax money and helping to get more kids into Iraq. I didn't want any part of that. The pay would have been pretty good but I can't make money that way. 1858 hrs.

10-11-07 Cleveland OH: 1858 hrs. Backstage at the House Of Blues Cleveland. We got here many hours ago. I went to a Trader Joe's nearby with the nice runner lady and got a few things to throw in the freezer for when we get our bus back a few days from now. It has broken down three times and hopefully this time it's fixed. It's been a pain in the neck dealing with it, shipping stuff to meet us at shows, etc. That's the road.

Show was good last night. The venue, not the usual one, was a little stiff in that it was a theater and nothing like Bogart's, the place I have been doing shows at for quite some time but at least people were more comfortable this time around I think. I always feel bad for the audience when they are seated at Bogart's.

Before soundcheck, a guy named Billy took Ward and me to Shake It, a record store he works at. It's a great place. I found a few things but Ward found a lot of really cool Jazz stuff, original Impulse! stuff, very nice.

Damn, it was sad to see how beat up parts of Cincinnati are. There are some really rough patches we drove through to get to the record store. Stores closed, more boarded up, people hanging outside of bars and on corners, waiting for nothing as Tom Kromer used to say. It's the America that no one writes about, it's the America that I want to show to the rest of America. This is the America that doesn't vote, trade stocks, have a voice, or matter no matter what they do. It's the silent America. They just die off year after year and no one seems to know or care. It's amazing that you can drive across an American city and see stuff like this. I know it shouldn't surprise me at this point but still, I can't get over it.

Sometimes I think I can't have my eyes opened any wider in America and then I turn around. Sometimes it's hard to see the good parts when it seems that the country is so set on self-destruct. From the average America diet to the media content to the policies to the debt, personal and otherwise, it seems we have voluntarily pulled our own kill switch. 1919 hrs.

10-12-07 Toronto Canada: 1523 hrs. Sitting on the bus outside the venue. I have to get out and walk around more than I have been. I have been in a rut the last few days, basically dealing with the schedule and the transportation aggravation. It's kind of a drag to walk around in Ohio. I am not putting the place down but there's nothing I want to see out there without a film crew in tow. So, I have been staying inside for the most part. Usually, October is a month I enjoy and it makes me think back to my past. Not as much as it used to though. When I was younger I used to space out a lot in October, listen to music I was checking out in my 20's and think about when I lived in DC before I moved away. Now I don't as much. Perhaps I burned out on those memories or perhaps it's so far in the past, it has lost some of its hold on me. Still, it was great to see those people in DC the other day. I have written Ian a couple of times since, thanking him for setting everything up, especially on his schedule.

For the most part, I have just been thinking about the shows and trying to be clear onstage every night. That's the goal, clarity and impact. Every night is a chance to sharpen it more, give the points more punch, lose excess words and say more with less. I like doing that. It's waiting for the shows that gets tedious sometimes.

I will be in LA on Sunday to check in on stuff and will bring out one of my larger hard drives that has a lot of music on it. I will then be able to work on radio shows out here. It would be great to get at least 3-4 for November and December done before the tour is over, or at least get them mostly done and add new release stuff the week of the show to make it up to date. That will be good for the afternoons to make them productive. Also, after getting back on our real bus with all of our stuff I can resume a more normal workout schedule. If I don't do things all the time, it gets very hard for me out here. It's always been a matter of keeping myself distracted.

I saw a thing on the news a few hours ago about the increased rate of Americans retiring or buying second homes in other countries. The reporter said these people were still retaining their American citizenship but were choosing places like Costa Rica to go to. I often think about where I would go if I had to leave America. Sometimes I want to leave and never come back. I get so sick of what's happening here and what America is doing all over the world, I don't want to be on the team anymore. Also, when it seems that a majority of Americans don't want anything to change, it makes for a pretty dark picture of what might be up the road. I think that anywhere you are in the world you will have to deal with America so it probably doesn't matter where one lives. 1630 hrs.

1711 hrs. I just spent a few minutes looking at two pictures I have stored on my computer, they are both images of the same thing, Ian's parent's living room. One is from February of 2002 and the other is from January of 2007. In the first picture, Ian's mother is in the picture along with Ian's father and two of his sisters. The 2nd picture has no people in it, just the room. In the time between when the two pictures were taken, Ian's mother passed away. I remember the moment I took the picture in 2002. I was on my way out the door and was saying goodbye and wanted to capture the moment. The room is different now with her gone. It's dimmer somehow. I know that is a somewhat spiritual sentiment and I am not a spiritual person. I guess I don't see many people sitting in that room anymore where I used to see so many. I think her passing might be one of the reasons that I don't think of DC in the same way I used to. Usually the first thing I did when I got there was walk from the hotel over to her house and visit. I have done that so many times in the past and now I don't. Things change. It's a bad idea to hold onto that kind of thing, it only makes the present hurt when it doesn't have to. People are painful, it's risky to get close to them. It's worth it sometimes though. 1731 hrs.

10-13-07 Ann Arbor MI: 1900 hrs. Backstage. I walked around quite a bit today as I always do when I am here. The weather was great, cold but not too much. We got the bus back and we are all aboard so all is well there. That was a strange week.

Walking around here was not as easy as it has been other times. A lot of people talked to me and that made looking at books and stuff a little difficult. I don't want to talk to someone and then have to talk to their friend on the phone, that's a bit much. These people don't mean any harm and they're cool so I deal with it as best I can. At one point, I was walking up the stairs to what I thought was a record store and looked up when I smelled incense and figured it was not a record store. I heard a man behind me on the stairs tell his friend that I was ahead of them. It gets to me when people talk about me like I am not there. I didn't want to get trapped in the place with these guys so

A Preferred Blur   **303**

turned to bolt and they were looking at me so I asked them what they were looking at. They were cool but it was a little much. I shook their hands and got out of there. I walked around a little more and then went back to the bus after getting a book that had been suggested to me called <u>On Killing</u>. It's a book on the psychological effects of killing in the time of war. I think I can learn something there. I want to know, if it's possible at all to get it from a book, what these young people back from Iraq are going through. I have a feeling that a book just won't get it but I am willing to read it and see what I can learn. The men who have killed people in Iraq and Afghanistan, those who will make comment on it, are not ok with it. I wonder if some of these people carry around the kills with them for the rest of their lives. So many times I have heard people say that their father was in Vietnam and never spoke about it. Hopefully I can pick up some insight from this book.

Let's see, what else. I got a letter from a guy who hated the show and said his ticket cost 60 dollars. I don't know who sold him that ticket but I hope that's not true. He said the story I told about The Ruts was 90 minutes long and he was bored as was all the audience. I don't remember anyone being bored, that's the story I get the most mail about. I guess he won't be coming to the next show. All I can do is go out there and give it my best. I imagine there will be less and less people showing up at these tours as they go. They've been going really well for years but that can't last. It's a tough business. 1924 hrs.

10-16-07 Milwaukee WI: 1832 hrs. Backstage. The backstage area here at The Rave is all low lights, candles and cloth covered walls. It's a "vibe" thing I guess. I know they mean well but it's just a pain in the ass because it's so dark back here you can't see anything. I have stationed myself at the front door of the area where there is a real light and where the mood, or vibe if you will, is for people who need to see.

I did the show in Minneapolis last night. I thought it went pretty well. It's a strange venue to do a show in, high stage, built for music. This place is the same pretty much. What saves it is the audiences in both places are really great so it's always a good time. The material I am doing this time around is not easy to work with so it makes for a challenging night of balancing the amount of time I spend on any topic.

It was a relief to be back on the bus and for there to be a show that evening. The 14th was a day off so I flew to LA to check on some things and to update one of my hard drives. It was strange to be there and to be back in the office knowing I had a show the next night in Minneapolis. Almost every time I go back to LA it's the same story, nothing has changed and after a few hours there it doesn't feel like I was on tour anymore. The place seems to swallow things. I drove to the grocery store to get some things for the bus and it felt like any other night driving to the grocery store. My life is much better out here. I did get a lot of things done and I am glad I went and all but having a show at night is the best thing for me. I am so happy to be here and to have a show in less than two hours.

Today was pretty useless from my end. I had to get up early for a radio interview and it was hard to get back to sleep and it screwed up my sleep cycle. I got up and did more press and then came in here and shot an interview with a camera crew who are putting together a thing for a William Shatner DVD. They asked me questions about working with Bill on the song *I Can't Get Behind That* and what I thought of him, etc. That took an hour and then we did soundcheck and here I am. We have a short drive to Madison, WI tonight.

I am looking forward to the show tonight. I need to get more done during the day and hopefully, now that I have a hard drive with a lot music out with me, I can work on November and December radio shows. If I keep doing the show next year, I will have to get a lot of shows ready now as I will be out a lot of January and February. Next year will be busy, it's getting booked up pretty quickly. I don't know what else to do with the time. I don't know if it's a matter of really liking what I do or just not having anything else to do with my time. I guess it's a bit of both. Here I am again backstage in this building about to go out on that stage again. I have done so many shows here. I was here last year with the band but I don't remember what the show was like. It's strange that I don't remember much of that tour. It's like a lot of experiences with that band, I don't remember much of any of it, or perhaps I have walled it off somewhere. I am listening to this amazing CD by a man named Omar Souleyman called <u>Highway To Hassake</u>, incredible stuff from Syria. I have been listening to it for two days now. Guy Picciotto recommended it to me. Anything he suggests I check out immediately. 1907 hrs.

10-19-07 Chicago IL: 0137 hrs. In a hotel room. Yesterday was a day off. We got in here around 0330 hrs. yesterday. Ward and I went to a couple of record stores during the day and found out that Van Halen was playing. We made some calls to management and we were given tickets for the show. So, we went.

At 1945 hrs. we took a taxi to the arena and got in line at will call for tickets. As we walked to the ticket booth to pick up the passes, I started getting recognized and people started coming over. It was a different experience than getting recognized on the street. Several of these people were drunk and were calling out my name really loud which made other people look and come over and it got a little crazy. They were all friendly enough but it was a little much. Finally, we got the passes and went in. As we were going to our seats, more people called out my name and shook my hand. Do these people come to my shows? I have no idea. We were sliding by people to get to our seats and met David Lee's bus driver and I asked him to give my regards to Dave. We were in our seats at 2022 hrs. and the band hit stage at 2029 hrs. They opened with *You Really Got Me* and it was pretty cool to see them out there. I was happy for Dave, he's wanted this for so long. People were into it and the place looked sold out at around 18,000 people. Dave was in shape for the show, he was lean and fit. He didn't sing hard, more phrased and talked through the songs, pacing himself. It sounded good out front. It was loud as hell, my ears are still coming back from it. They played pretty much the entire first album and songs that everyone knew. Every one in the band took solos. The son bass player did a very short one, which was a good thing. Alex's drum solo was good but pretty uneventful. Dave came out with an acoustic guitar and told a story about hanging out with his friends back in the old days and then went into *Ice Cream Man* and was joined by rest of the band. Eddie's solo didn't start out with a great deal of direction but ended very well. There is nothing like that guy, his tone was really amazing. His playing fell apart a little by the end of the show but he kept it together rather well overall.

I just went to their site. They seemed to be playing every other night and the show we saw was #11 of the tour. It looks like they will do 29 shows and end on 12-30-07 in Las Vegas. A lot of the shows are sold out. I hope it works out for them and they pull the shows off. I don't have any idea how far they plan on taking the tour. They played well and it wasn't a bad show at all but while watching them I felt depressed. It was three people trying to recapture what cannot be recaptured, to repeat what cannot be repeated, just emulated. The audience was there for the ride.

Ward and I got a taxi back to the hotel and I am back in my room. I wrote a letter to Dave's manager and thanked her for the tickets. The hotel has a 24 hour gym so I went down there and worked out for a good while and managed to shake off some of the depression I felt. 0220 hrs.

1814 hrs. backstage at the Vic. I have done a lot of shows in this place, with and without the band. We pulled up a few hours ago and the venue said that the show was sold out. I didn't sell it out the last time so that's kind of cool. I try not to think about the numbers too much. They are a factor and they do matter but it's the endless comparison of the time before. How's it looking? Are there more than last time, less? Oh no, losing traction. There's nothing steady about this line of work. It's approval based and never a sure thing. There are small moments of relief when you know, or at least have convinced yourself, that you're doing a good job out there. Yesterday's day off wasn't much, just running around town for a few hours and then to the show. I couldn't miss seeing VH, but I was also looking forward to a chance to get some other stuff done that I needed to do. We will be in St. Louis tomorrow and I will get some radio work done. I have to finish notes for next week's broadcast. I will get on some of that tonight. I will take advantage of the early stage time to get more done on the bus post show.

A Preferred Blur   **307**

I listened to a little bit of talk radio today before my phone press stuff started and it was mainly about California Congressman Peter Stark and what he said about Bush. The quote:

You don't have money to fund the war or children but you're going to spend it to blow up innocent people if we can get enough kids to grow old enough for you to send to Iraq to get their heads blown off for the President's amusement.

I don't know if Stark meant what he said as far as the president getting amusement from the deaths of soldiers but from his quote, it would seem that he does. I don't agree. I don't think Bush rejoices that Americans are getting killed at all. I think he truly believes that he's doing the right thing. I think that's how lost he is. I bet a lot of his supporters feel the same way. I don't think any neocon or anyone else gets any amusement or good feeling by the awful information that comes in daily. It is interesting to me that when someone wants to provide health insurance for children, as with the State Children's Health Insurance Program (SCHIP), that anyone would have a problem with that or call it more of that liberal spending. Damn man, you gotta spend some money on some things besides the war. It can't be that the people who voted against the increase in S-CHIP spending hate kids, I don't think that's it. If nothing else, isn't the health of all those kids an investment in America's future? Aren't these young ones the next crop of soldiers? Time to get ready to hit it. 1850 hrs.

10-21-07 Lawrence KS: 1638 hrs. Sitting on the bus. I got this letter today:

PAUL FOX OF THE RUTS DIES AGED 56

Legendary guitarist, Paul Fox, died at home in Uxbridge at 3AM this morning.

Over the years Paul has performed and recorded with many of the worlds greatest musicians but he will mainly be remembered for his revolutionary punk/dub reggae fusion guitar playing with influential punk band The Ruts.

Paul had been in semi retirement for several years but went back out on the road again in 2006 playing the Ruts music with Foxys Ruts which featured his son Lawrence Fox on drums. The band were well received, both in the UK and Europe.

Following his diagnosis with cancer at the end of May 2007 a benefit gig was organised featuring many of the musicians that Paul had worked with or alongside over the years. There was no doubt about the high esteem in which Paul was held by his fellow musicians as the line up read like a who's who of the UK punk scene with performances by The Damned, Misty in Roots, the UK Subs, Tom Robinson, John Otway, Splodge, TV Smith and many more. For the first time in 27 years the surviving members of the Ruts took to the stage together with Henry Rollins standing in for the late Malcolm Owen who died of a drugs overdose in 1980.

The night was a fitting tribute to one of our much under rated and unsung guitar heros.

Paul leaves behind his sons Lawrence and William and his wife, Sharon.

He will be dearly missed.

So I guess he expired when I hit stage last night in St. Louis. I sent the press release on to Ian, Andrew The Canadian Fanatic, Heidi and Engineer X. He hung on for a long time. Apparently, the last few weeks had been very hard on him and he was in a lot of pain. I found out that just a few weeks ago, Paul went to see the Rolling Stones and he hung out with Keith Richards, that's great. I am glad we got to do that show for him. It was a hell of a thing to be a part of. I have been walking around today thinking about Paul and trying to get my head around his death. It's not surprising news. He was in rough shape when I met him but it's sad that it's over for him. I got a letter from Dave Ruffy but nothing from Segs. I think Segs is in Egypt. I believe he went to see Paul before he left, which is good. I don't know much more than what was sent to me. I was asked if I wanted to add anything to the press release but I passed, I don't know what else there is to say.

It's Sunday here and things are moving slowly around Lawrence. I like the area around the venue, I have been here many times. It's a perfect October day here. Whenever I am here, I always wonder if I could live here. It seems like a place that wouldn't drive you nuts after awhile. 1655 hrs.

1905 hrs. Backstage. I am getting letters with links to all the different sites passing on word of Paul's death. This kind of news travels quickly. 1906 hrs.

10-23-07 Denver CO: 0158 hrs. It's the end of the day off. I am in a hotel room. Train horns are blasting outside. It's kind of cool but also fairly loud. I went to see a film today called <u>Michael Clayton</u>. I thought it was good. I got in a workout and worked on radio stuff and then swatted down some mail. A lot of letters on this tour, more mail than I have ever received before. I am doing the best I can to answer it all.

I am feeling pretty good but kind of dragged that October is going by so quickly. I was hoping it would give me more to think about but I have been all about the shows every night and that's about it. It's one of the harder tours as the information I am trying to impart up there takes a lot of aim to pitch just right and I feel, perhaps wrongly, I have so much to say that it becomes hard to edit while I am onstage. I wish I could have one more hour up there but you can't do that to people.

Past that, I am just on tour. I am 30+ shows in all of a sudden. It's been good. It's been a lot of work but I look forward to being out there every night so that's a good thing. It's easy for me to stay out for weeks like this. There's no one I think of and no one I miss. I don't miss anything I have back in LA, I am fine with what I've got out here. My phone rarely rings and most of the time I can't find it anyway. I guess it's a ritual in a way but it's a life I like. Being all over the place, being nowhere, always moving, not mattering to anyone and not having to be responsible for anyone but myself is the best way for me. I like giving the audience my best. It's a level of duty I aspire to every night when I walk out there. I don't know if I am lonely or not. I really don't remember what that's like and it's been so long since I was close to a female, the idea of it is unfamiliar. That kind of relationship is nothing I could sustain anyway.

I need urgency and distraction in my life to keep me away from myself. I don't know what else to do. I don't know if I am lost or what but I am so glad for all the work and the chance to be onstage being live one take. The more I think about seeing Van Halen the other night, the sadder the event seems. When I am on the bus in the back of a venue I imagine what it would be like if I was there with the band that night. I don't want it. It seems sad to be my age and going out to play rock music. That's just me though. When in doubt, go on to the next thing, whatever it is.

10-24-07 Wyoming: 0225 hrs. On the bus, on the way to Salt Lake City, UT. The Denver show was, strangely enough, perhaps the best time I have ever had in that town. I didn't get in all the things I wanted to say but I thought the show went pretty well. I am used to a rougher ride from that audience. I talked to a lot of them post show and they were great.

Earlier in the day I did some on camera and voice over stuff for a NASCAR event that will be on ESPN. I have done a lot of race stuff for them over the years. It's cool work and I enjoy it. I can always use the work, I rarely say no. I have to survive America so I have to keep working and saving. Knowing what a racket America is keeps me working all the time. The shows are for the sake of doing them but stuff like the NASCAR thing, that's employment, and I'll take all I can get.

The full moon is coming and I am getting more and more depressed. It's always the two days before the full moon that are the worst for me. I don't know why but it's a sure thing that gets me almost every time. Sometimes, I won't even notice the moon at all and I'll be feeling really bad, like I can't move and I'll look and sure enough, the moon is almost full. Sometimes it's very bad, sometimes not.

It's really cold outside. We were just at a truck stop and I went outside to check things out. Shapeless men in their layers of clothing service their trucks while others wander in and out of the store. Inside, men watch television and talk on the phone. It's a small world that many never see. It's an island in the middle of nowhere that people of the road know well. I like being out here. I feel like myself when I am out here. Sitting here now, with the road rumbling under the wheels, I feel like I am doing something with my life. By staying on the move I can keep a grip on life. I get lonely sometimes but it doesn't last long, too much to do and think about. There's no way I would be able to trust a woman enough to get to know her. It's not that I have anything against women, I just can't get close to them. A female masseuse handed me her card earlier and told me and our crew to check her out when we were back in the area. I told her that I would never allow anyone to touch me. I don't know why I felt the need to tell her that. I know she meant well. 0255 hrs.

1814 hrs. Salt Lake City UT. I am in the backstage area underneath the ground. I remember this place from last year when we played here with X. I don't remember how that show went, that tour is walled off in some distant corner of my mind. It's interesting that I can't remember much about any of the shows, not even the last one.

I didn't get much done today besides press and some thinking. It was hard to sleep last night with the mountainous roads. I did get out and walk around some earlier. The weather is really great out here.

10-26-07 Bellingham WA: 0025 hrs. The day off is over with and tonight starts 16 shows straight. I am sitting on the bus, waiting to get tired. I worked out hard in the gym next to where we're parked a few hours ago and feel pretty good. The workouts combat the depression. I have been feeling pretty bad for a couple of days now. I am hoping it will lift soon. I need to be sharp for all these shows coming up. It's not like I need a night off. I am good to go for a show a night. I really like being up there with that audience in front of me. The older I get, or the farther along the road I get, the more I like doing these shows and living on the road.

Finally some real fall weather. The air here is so clean and smells so great. I walked around a little after the workout just to be out in it. It's one of the only nights this month where it's actually felt like October. I got some work done on an upcoming broadcast for November. I will annotate all the songs for the radio show as I have been doing until the end of this year and then that's it. I can't give that much time to it next year. I like writing about music but it takes up a lot of time and I don't think anyone needs any more of that kind of writing from me. I have a few more broadcasts to write up and then I'm done. I'll miss that writing but I just can't sustain it. I could if it was all I did. It's a nice way to get lost for awhile, just writing about good songs. 0055 hrs.

0205 hrs. I went out for a walk. It's amazing outside. It feels like the first real day of October. I know it sounds stupid but when I walked around tonight, I pretended I was in DC and was walking from my old job back to my apartment across Key Bridge. It was the kind of weather I remember from when I used to live there. I might have to go out there one more time. This is a good indicator of my depression, when I start thinking of being back in DC. When I start thinking of my youth and simplicity of how things were then, that's when I know I am having a bad time. I don't get lonely much but there are times that push me into my mind more than others. It's one of the reasons I don't like nights off. When I get off this tour I will have enough time to work on radio stuff in the early morning and then work on mail order during business hours at the office, that will keep me busy. I do think of women and that it might be something to be around one but all that feels so foreign to me at this point, I don't even remember how I was in that situation. Just thinking about it now makes me embarrassed. I'm going outside again. This last run of shows will be intense. I have been coming up with some new ideas for stuff that I will start working into the shows. Looking forward to that. 0225 hrs.

Letter Of The Week:

hi henry! Lately (please undertand my english) you are my only ear! ja! pathetic, don´t you think! what ever!

But in my darkest dreams i am lost, seekeing for the end of human life, i don´t know anything, but i know i hate my race(again, forgot my english), this race is human, dont you think that the world will be better without us? Think about that!

Sorry if i scare you, but try to live in my mind, is near the apokalipse (double again, forget my english) JA JA JA JA JA JA!

PS: Please don´t listen to me, i´m talking bullshit(for the common peo-

ple, JA JA JA)

PS2: i´m writing drunk every sense, but i´m realy me!

PS3: if you fell that this is rare, tell me and i stop send you e-mails!(again x 3, forget my english!!!!!!!!!!!!)

My best, C_____! I hope i stole you a laugh!

10-28-07 Calgary Canada: 1838 hrs. Backstage at this very nice theater. It's a sold out show which is pretty good for a Sunday night. It took a long time to get here, we have been on the road since about midnight last night and only got here a couple of hours ago. I will be onstage for a 2015 hrs. start. Last night's show was pretty good, some drunks made things a test but all in all it was a good time and I hope I get back up there soon.

I have been talking about veterans coming back from Iraq with mental trauma like PTSD and other problems that don't necessarily exhibit themselves externally. I have been telling audiences that sometimes when these men and women seek help from Veterans Affairs, they are turned away and have no other resources to deal with their condition. It's happening a lot and it's a big problem. It's no surprise that it's not on the news more. It's too much truth for the press to deal with. I think it's very important to talk about it because it looks to me like it will be the private sector raising the money to help these men and women out and we need to get on it and stay on it. So, I have been talking about it and every few nights, an Iraq veteran comes up to me after the show and thanks me for bringing it up onstage. Two have cried in front of me. I got a letter today from a disabled Iraq vet single parent of two:

The purpose of this writing is to express my gratitude. When one does something to support the Iraq/Afghanistan troops, then quite simply one has done a great favor for myself. For the troops are my companions and I know first-hand what it means to have the level of support that you have given. You cannot imagine the importance of the gift of your time with the troops, and the words that you say for the public at-large. It's incredible that you have the courage of your conviction to speak clearly and intelligently about the war and the current state-of-the-union. Not only are you speaking to your conviction about the war, but supporting those of us who had/have been sent into the Iraq mess to come out in pieces; physically or otherwise. I thank you sir, and I applaud you.

Well then. I think I am doing the right thing. This war is breaking people. It is breaking them into pieces and they are unable to get themselves back together again. They will hit the streets and live in parks, shelters and who knows where else. Last night after the show, someone told me about their friend who returned from Iraq and killed himself recently. They will move to places like Oregon and Washington state where it's wide open and quiet. They will drift and subsist and die off quietly.

The other side of the argument is that liberals are using PTSD reports to demoralize the troops. Meanwhile, these people are coming back to America damaged and they need help. What more could possibly be expected of these people is beyond me. The withdrawal = defeat equation will do nothing but keep American forces in Iraq and increase the rate and severity of PTSD cases. There is no victory in staying. 1915 hrs.

10-31-07 Seattle WA: 1812 hrs. Backstage at the Moore Theater. I like doing shows in this place. Last few days of shows have been in Canada, the one last night was in Vancouver. The audience was, for the most part, fine. A few drunks made the last few minutes distracting. It's nothing that angers me really. It's more the audience's problem than mine in that it's for them to police themselves. It's not like I can climb down there and quiet the man. Last night was the Vancouver that I remember from so many times before. I think the next time, to have fun, I will pick the smallest place possible to do a show and let people deal with that. Better than leaving them off the tour altogether.

The last few days have been good shows and bad everything else. Depression is a large part of my life and when it bites down on tour, it's hard to carry it. The audiences make me feel good though, getting out there in front of them every night is a great thing and I enjoy talking to them after the show so that's cool. Past that, I have been keeping to myself, working on the radio show and trying to keep the shows happening every night. I guess I am also suffering from some strain of loneliness but there's nothing to do about that. When I was younger I felt lonely on tour but now when the feeling comes it's much more faint and I have no one to assign the emotion to. I really don't know anyone who I would talk to, in fact the very idea of that repels me. I think, for me at least, it's something that I need to be able to ignore to keep moving. I always feel that I have compromised myself when I spilled over the side to someone, although I can't remember the last time I did it. Oh, I remember, it was about five years ago when I was going out with a woman. Wasn't worth it.

It's the last night of October. I can't think of this night without thinking of that photo I have taken 10-31-80. It's in the front of the Get In The Van book. In earlier versions of the book, I had the photographer's name wrong and he was really mad about it. Understandable. We got it right eventually. It's a photo of a bunch of us outside a Teen Idles show. A lot of the people in the picture were in bands. There are Teen Idles and future members of Minor Threat and many others. It's the last Halloween before I joined Black Flag and the last night of the last October I spent in DC. I always think fondly of that month and of those times. Things have not been the same since. I don't have a very accurate memory of those times. I have probably enhanced them to a great degree and left out all the parts I didn't like, of which there were many I'm sure. It's what one does. I always have high hopes for October, that some kind of epiphany will come to me. I really don't know what that would be but it never happens. Recently, we had a night off in Bellingham, WA and the weather was very cool and the air smelled great. I walked for a long time pretending I was walking back from my old job I had 26 years ago. In October I listen to a lot of old music that I used to listen to back then and it makes me feel pretty good. I am listening to some of it right now, some old UK Subs.

In October of 1982, I went back to DC to visit for a week. Black Flag was off the road and I had some time. I went out there and stayed for about five days. It was very intense as I only had been gone for a little over a year and it was like stepping back into a time machine. Since I had been gone my life had changed so radically that I felt like I was on the outside of things yet at the same time, I felt so familiar with it all, like I could have just gone back to my old job and resumed my old life and the past several months would have been like some strange dream. 1917 hrs.

11-01-07 Portland OR: 1840 hrs. I am backstage at the Aladdin Theater. I have done a lot of shows here and really like this place. I have actually done a lot of writing here in this room. I am listening to the <u>Perfect Teeth</u> album by Unrest. It's one of my tour favorites.

I met a very interesting woman the other night. We spoke briefly and have exchanged a few letters since. I am rarely interested in knowing someone but when I met her, I was immediately curious. She wrote me a day later and we went back and forth a few times. The correspondence is nothing I can sustain and I am very sure she has her hands full with all the things happening in her life so today I thanked her for the letters and told her that I can't write her anymore. It's not like she isn't busy enough anyway. For me, it's not a good idea to keep in touch with many people. The less, the better. I talk to office staff and management all the time, Ian fairly often. Past that, I answer the letters people send and hope it doesn't turn into one of those endless back and forth bouts of correspondence as I don't have the time or capacity. I can't be looking forward to hearing from someone, can't depend on someone, can't want or rely on anything more than myself sitting here right now. I can't but sometimes I want to. Sometimes I want a woman's hands on my face but that's not happening, all that does is weaken resolve and fill me with self disgust.

This room, this table, the fact that in less than an hour I will be out in front of those people doing the show, that's what's happening, that is real. All the other stuff, pack it, it's no good out here.

I am in this room on almost every tour. Whenever I am here, I imagine that I live here. It's basically an upstairs apartment, this place. I pretend that I have sold off most of my belongings except for a few photographs and some necessary items and I just live here in this very small and simple space. Sometimes, that's all I want. A small room with very little in it. Things are pain. People are pain. It's that kind of pain that I can't stand. I don't hate people, it's just that they are painful to be around. Things are painful to have. I have some photos on the wall at the office and I like them but they bring me pain sometimes when I look at them. I can't take them down even though they make me think of times and places that are behind me. Like that photo taken on 10-31-80, I always think of it on October 31. I have it framed and on the wall and don't want to take it down but it hurts sometimes to think of those times. It's all very confusing to me at times and trying to think through it doesn't seem to do any good so I try to leave the thoughts alone so perhaps they will leave me alone. I do the same thing with people, I leave them alone and perhaps the pain of them will leave me alone. Does that make any sense or is this just stupid? I don't know but it's on my mind a lot. I guess writing that woman made me think of it.

I read some bad news concerning Mandy Stein, whose father is Seymour Stein, the man who signed The Ramones. From what I read online, Mandy went to her mother's apartment yesterday and found her dead in a pool of blood. I feel bad for Mandy, that must have been horrible. Mandy's a really good person, she is the one who directed Too Tough To Die, the documentary about the Johnny Ramone cancer benefit. 1928 hrs.

11-02-07 Reno NV: 1753 hrs. Backstage at the venue. It's not the place I'm usually at which is fine for me. The regular place is a bit too much for me, a very corporate place, not bad but this place seems more appropriate for the show. The venue is called Stoney's and I have no idea how this will go. Nevada is a strange place to do shows. I have put Reno into the tour on the last few occasions and it's worked out to be a good stop. I always do a show in Las Vegas as well and that always seems to be ok but it's a House Of Blues and I can never really tell how those shows go or why people are there.

Heidi wrote me today and directed me to something on the internet that was of some interest. It was an article in The Miami Herald, written by Diana Moskovitz about Dennis Cole, father of Joe Cole. Dennis, awful man of all time, was arrested for obstruction of justice when the police came to serve him a domestic-violence injunction. Dennis locked himself in a room in his dwelling and the cops had to force the door to get him out. What a pro! He's getting divorced from at least wife #3 and I guess he's been knocking her around. He's a class act. I wouldn't be so hard on the guy, seeing what he lost in his life, but the fact that he's been such an asshole to me forbids me to have any mercy whatsoever. At one point, he was accusing me of having something to do with Joe's murder and telling the police and media that I wasn't telling all I knew. He's such a piece of shit. I am only sorry that Joe had to endure him as a father for so many years. He always told me he loved his father but that he was a fuck up. Apparently, Dennis and his soon to be ex wife were real estate brokers for Celebrity Realty. I guess Dennis lives in Florida now. His mug shot looked sad, he looks fat and tired. He's had a fucked up life but he brought it all on himself.

Last night's show was a good time, it's always a good one there. I talked to a lot of people after the show and they were very friendly. Soon after, we were off for Reno. This was the last of the long drives, from here to the end it's all pretty easy travel. I have a challenging patch soon when I leave the bus from San Francisco and fly to Missouri to speak at a university and then fly to San Diego the next day for the show that night. It will be ok, I'll get enough sleep in the afternoon to pull the show off that night in SD. The flight to MO will be a little rough but past that, I should be ok if I can get a couple of hours sleep on the other end.

I have to start rehearsing a lot of voice over material I will be doing when I get off this tour for two National Geographic documentaries. I just got the print outs and the shows today. I will get into them tomorrow and start getting my head around them so by the time I have to hit it I will be familiar with the material. I don't think I have ever done anything for National Geographic. I think it's really cool that I got the shot, I don't want to screw it up.

I have been looking over what the upcoming schedule will be for the next several months and it's going to be really busy. This tour won't be half over when this leg is done. There's still Europe, a trip to South Africa, five more weeks in America, back to Europe and then to Australia. All that should take me about five months into next year to get done. I'm not complaining. It's what I want. If I just stay on my own and keep it together, I will be good to go. The only time I fail is when I allow myself to lose focus like if I get distracted by a woman. If you want to not accomplish the goal, that's how you do it. Women aren't bad but you can't do all this and be with one without something failing so why compromise? Exactly. 1847 hrs.

1931 hrs. Usually at this time, I am getting ready to go out there but it's a 2100 hrs. stage time tonight. I think they will probably be fairly drunk by the time I get out there. This room is poorly lit, it's cold and the lighting onstage is not all that good. It's one of those autumn evenings I have to get through. I am looking forward to the show though. I remember in the early days of the band we used to have a lot of nights like this in America and Europe, cold outside, cold inside and not well lit. Tonight reminds me of a show we were doing in the middle of NY state. I just looked on my show files and found it, 10-29-90 in Leitham, NY. It was one of those freezing rock halls that I had never been to before or since but know all too well. It was one of those hard nights out there. I think I wrote about it in one of the old books. That's kind of what tonight is reminding me of. There is a lot of alone out here. It's all how you deal with it. For many years, I have been curious about people who live in solitary or have been isolated for long periods. This life is hardly like that, there are a ton of people around all the time but I operate from my head quite a bit out here. The way I was raised made this kind of life not so hard to adjust to. When I was younger, I was more susceptible to the downs of these kind of places but now, I don't care, I am fine here. As the years pass I have toughened and hardened myself to everything from fucked venues to hatred from hecklers, media and anywhere else. It's all the same, it's all stuff coming at you, adulation, hatred, it's all just the proverbial slings and arrows. I read the excerpt from that 10-29-90 journal entry and it's somewhat emotional. I seem now to be mostly

Henry Rollins

drained of all that. I take things for what they are these days. It's a place, you do your show and are grateful for what you have in front of you. I used to look at the walls of these places and read all the stuff people would leave and have feelings about it but now, I don't care. I remember when I used to want to be somewhere else, like a different room or something but now, I am good to be out here for as long as possible. Also, it must be said that it's a lot, and I mean a lot, easier to deal with the road with the way I travel these days. Those days would have been very different with a tour bus instead of a rental van with everyone all smashed in together, very aware of each other and no room to be on your own. All that was definitely factors on the overall stress level.

Being in a band was really great back then. I was young and we were out there knocking it out every night. I think of what it would be like right now with all the guys in the band back here, getting ready to go out and play in front of a few hundred people. I don't think it would be all that good. Judging from last year and how burned out everyone got so quickly on the tour, it was like touring with a bunch of fucking hacks. I can't imagine months of that again. The other night when I was watching Van Halen, it was cool to see them play and I felt good for Dave to be getting out there again in front of all those people but at the same time, it was incredibly depressing like they had nothing else to do but be rockstars. I know that is a really fucked up thing to say but it looked at times, very much less than a party onstage even though everyone played really well and everyone in the audience were obviously getting off on the whole thing big time. There's nothing for them to achieve out there though. There's no new frontier to be explored. It's a tried and true thing and in many ways, a ceremonial event at best. I think it would be really depressing to be out there doing music at this point as tempting as it is at times. I really liked being in a band but last year when the old line up got back together and hit the road, it was so depressing and poisonous. Thankfully, the shows were good but the times between the shows were very hard to deal with. When in doubt, move onto the next thing.

11-03-07 Chico CA: 1853 hrs. Tonight's backstage is the venue's office. Not so bad. It's a theater and it's not really built for a live show, the stage is basically the area in front of the screen. I have been on stages like this before. It's more like a plank than anything but it's ok. The lights are from far away so I am basically in darkness and it's a drag but that is what I've got tonight. The venue in Sacramento is equally as depressing but that's how that is. The audiences here are really great so we'll have a good time anyway.

Last night's show was good. I prefer Stoney's to the place I am usually in, the Hilton. I was talking to people after the show and there was a drunk woman who was ok at first but as drunks are want to do, she stuck around for too long and restarted her story that she told before. It's a fucking drag to have to sit through the bullshit of a drunk person. Then I met her husband who seemed pretty cool and we did photos and just when I thought the thing was over she came back again and started in with more bullshit, this time sexually oriented. It was so fucked because her husband was there and I had to be polite when I wanted to tell the fuckin' guy to take his fucked up wife out of my face. My inclination is to just punch the guy in his head for having to endure his wife but I just stood there wanting to be somewhere else. She finally left and then came back and told me how she was embarrassing her husband with all the previous bullshit and then went back into it. I offered that she was now embarrassing me and she should stop. What the fuck is with people? I try to be as cool as I can but sometimes people really make it hard. I guess it could be a lot worse. I have a very low threshold for drunks. They never know when it's enough, they are always on their own time.

You really know you're in California here in Chico. It's very student / hippie oriented. A lot of arts and crafts all around, the place reminds me of Santa Cruz. It's no bad place to be but the tie dye thing gets to me after awhile. It's depressing to be back in California. It's not really America to me, it's its own thing and never been a place I liked. I appreciate the opportunity to perform but it's a drag to be back here. It just occurs to me that nothing one says means much out here. Almost every interviewer from CA is obtuse, distant and uninvolved when talking to me. There seems to be a film over their minds. This really isn't much of a dressing room with all these people going in and out of it all the time, I will get out of here and leave them to it. Amateur hour. 1927 hrs.

11-04-07 Sacramento CA: 1821 hrs. Backstage at one of the most challenging shows I do on every tour. The very dark, cavernous and almost impossible to deal with Crest Theater. The venue is beautiful but not really suited for this kind of thing. It would be much better if they could light it a little differently but they won't because they won't and that's that. I always feel like I am talking to no one when I am up there. Last night was a good warm up for this place.

Last night's show was the low ebb of the tour. The stage was basically the small space in front of the movie screen curtain. I had a narrow plank to work on. The lights were a mile away and all night long people would move around, throwing me off whatever topic I was clinging to with all the concentration I could muster. At one point, in mid-sentence, some guy walked up and asked me to sign his book like there was only the two of us there. It would be great if the floor could just open and swallow up people like that. After the idiot came up, I struggled the rest of the night. I got my points across and delivered but it was all I could do with what I had and it was a drag to be up there dealing with the bullshit all night. I talked to people after the show and they all seemed to dig the show fine so I don't know, perhaps it was ok. Tonight has to be better. It will be. I am looking forward to the show even though it's a frustrating stage to be on but I will blast through that as best I can and keep it happening. Doing shows in CA is always strange. I never know if I am getting through. San Francisco is good but the rest of it, I don't know. I always take the show if I can get it, it's what you do.

Not much happened today. It was hard for me to get to sleep last night so I ended up working on radio show stuff until almost dawn. I got up here around noon. I didn't walk around, Sacramento is depressing to me. It's the state's capital but it looks almost abandoned in parts. The neighborhood the theater is in is broke and there's homeless folks wandering all around.

I watched that <u>To Catch A Predator</u> show last night as we drove down here. What an insane program that is. It shows these men, responding to the e-mail of what they think is a 13 year-old girl they are going to have sex with, go to a house to meet the girl not knowing there is a television crew there with police standing by to make the arrest. Some of these guys send photos of themselves naked to what they think is a young girl. It's really brutal when you find out that some of these men are cops, parents, teachers. One guy brought his kid when he came to the house. I get letters from girls telling me they are 16 and even if it's a simple question about a book or whatever, I just delete the letter or answer in the most bland and general possible terms. It's not like I have to fight the desire to be with an underage girl but it's better to not answer the letter at all. You never know what's on the other end of something like that. People are fucked! Danger! 1854 hrs.

11-05-07 Santa Cruz CA: 1802 hrs. Backstage in the "cry room," a room off to the side of the projectionist's booth where mothers could deal with their kids who were howling during the film. I am sure the projectionist was so happy about that. I used to work in a theater many years ago so it was an interesting piece of trivia. Our theater did not have a cry room.

Last night's show was good even though that stage is a hard one to deal with. The audience in Sacramento is always great so that's a big help, of course. I went on and really went for it hard right at the top to get myself past any difficulties I thought I might have and I ended up having a good time up there. So much of these shows is all about how much the audience allows you to do. If their cell phones ring or if they are talking, like they will no doubt be in Las Vegas at the House Of Blues show there, then it's a limited experience. I can do so much and then it's up to people allowing me to do my thing or not. Last night they were all about letting me go for it and it was great. I met a lot of people after the show and they were all really cool. For the most part I get a very cool audience, now and then there's some duds but they're mostly drunk or not aware of what they're in for and leave soon enough.

So, what else? We're almost at the end of this leg of the tour. Including tonight, there's six shows until the end. I feel pretty good although I see that my face is very tired. It's been a long year packed with a lot of stuff and I have not slowed down at all for a couple of years now. Usually in November it all starts to catch up with me. I still have a lot of work to do in November and December but it will be mainly office stuff and I will be able to be on my own a lot which is how I recover and prepare for the next thing. 2008 is going to be very hard. I am still into the shows and am looking forward to tonight and all the other shows this week. By Sunday morning I will be back in LA and getting myself squared away for Monday. I always try to finish a tour on a Saturday and be back in LA on Sunday so I can have a day to get myself together and be at the office by Monday morning and get onto the next thing. I try to disengage from a tour as quickly as possible, get everything back in its place and get moving onwards. It's how I keep the depression at a manageable level. There is a lot of it at the end of a tour. 1824 hrs.

11-07-07 Columbia MO: 1923 hrs. I am backstage, waiting to go out and do it. I was on three flights to get here today. I am feeling a little punchy but ok. I got some sleep here and there on the flights and a nap at the hotel. Last night's show in San Francisco was good, always a great audience there, and that venue seems to be very comfortable for the audience so that's good. I am going to work on the set now and get the ideas together. I have to go back to the airport at 0445 hrs. Later on. It's going to be another long day getting back to the tour. 1937 hrs.

11-08-07 San Diego CA: 1920 hrs. Backstage at the venue. Today was long. I didn't sleep post show last night. At 0445 hrs. I went to the airport in Columbia, MO and from there went to Kansas City, KS and then to Phoenix, AZ and then landed here. I don't remember the cab ride. I got to the bus and hit my bunk for about four hours and then got up for soundcheck and chow. I am feeling ok. I have only slept about 8 hours over the last two days but I'll be ok once I get out there. I will get some good sleep post show on the way to Las Vegas tonight. It's always this way when I get to shows via airplane. It's hard on the sleep, all the hustle to get to the shows. It was perhaps not the best idea to fly out for that show but the smart money is on taking the work when you can get it and avoid nights of inactivity. When I get tired at the end of a tour, I think of the line I am walking on. It is a line, a forged point of view, a thing that I am committed to in more ways than just doing a bunch of shows. It's a degree of compression that I am existing in that I have chosen and architected. It's not there to be betrayed by exhaustion or stupid ideas or illusions of need and vulnerability. When working at this level, I can maintain as long as I remember the line and never to break it. Sex with a female is ok but the desire for something more than the interaction is out of the question. That kind of thing is a line breaker. I keep to myself and stay on the line. This is not a job, this is a self-created reality that I am existing in. It's better than having a boss or some other factor to determine actions and outcomes. To betray the line is to disrespect the stage, the audience, myself—all of it. 1933 hrs.

11-09-07 Las Vegas NV: 1916 hrs. At the good old House Of Blues again. It's one of the more challenging rooms I deal with. The stage left wall is a long bar and there are a lot of people who are there just drinking and talking all night. They are not antagonistic but they are a dull roar that I have to tune out for the entire time I am onstage. All in all, it's a good group of people. I don't know how many of them are tourists and how many of them are locals.

For the last hour I have been working on radio broadcasts for next year. Last night I looked over the calendar and saw how long I was going to be out on the road and I will need to have a lot of pre-taped shows prepared. Engineer X and I will have to start on them immediately to get some stored up.

I had an interesting conversation after the show last night with a man who told me he was god. That's how he introduced himself. He sent a letter backstage as way of introduction, here it is transcribed from the handwritten:

Dear Henry Rollins, I am God, The father of Heaven, The Angel of the Lord, The Lion of the Tribe of Judah, Jah, The Angel of the Church of Philadelphia, God Almighty. I ask for your help. In the bible I spoke "Ask, and you shall receive," so I ask. I ask you to help me get enough money to open a mine and refinery. The mine includes Water Rights that I can sell to the California Water Companies. It is rich in sands that carry Platinum Group Metals like Rhodium. I am almost King of Israel, so it will be nice to have the extra money. I am a little poor, and that needs to change.

In favor of you, I would like to coach you to turn to a more rewarding seminar, by telling you to not force blashemy. As you can see, it hurts! I am here to help. Jesus loves you allot, and I do also. I thank you for your extra care for people in your writing, speach, and life. Please help, and please collaborate to that you can help, in the sense as if you did not kow I was making my presence known.

I thank you, and would like to see you to help and have a bond servant and apostle, if that's the right word. Please make sure to keep my information private to prevent criminal behavior.

I can share allot and I would like to, including travel, so that I can get together in person to discuss with you about mine conditions, coaching, money, and a contract. Please help!

He elaborated on his need for funds for the mine. I told him I didn't believe in him. That made him frustrated. Then I told him I was god, that seemed to frustrate him more. I asked if he had ever been to a doctor. He said that he wasn't crazy. I told him I meant a doctor you go to when you're sick or have a broken bone. He said yes. I asked him if he had ever said to a doctor, "I am god and I have the flu." He told me he had. I will have to continue this later, I have to get ready to get out there. 1931 hrs.

11-11-07 LA CA: 0403 hrs. Back at the house with the Santa Barbara show behind me. We arrived from Las Vegas yesterday morning around 0447 hrs. We unpacked the bus in front of the office and the bus and crew took off. I humped all the stuff up the driveway and into the house. It was a lot of work but I got through it pretty quickly. I got back to the house eventually and tried to get some sleep but couldn't get more than a couple of hours so I stayed up and tried to get things done. I did laundry and got some groceries. I figured I wouldn't be good for much later today. I got things organized at the office as best I could and then at 1700 hrs. we drove up to Santa Barbara and I hit stage at 2200 hrs. which was a bit tough at first because I was really tired but I got it together and got it out there. This was the venue I started the 2005 tour in. It's a nice place but the monitors leave a lot to be desired, it's hard to hear what's going on. It was a good show and people seemed into it. We got back on the road in the road manager's car and headed back to LA. At around 0311 hrs. I got dropped off at the office, got my car and went back home. So, that's the end of the tour.

It's now very late and I don't want to sleep. I am very depressed that the tour is over and want nothing more than to get back in the bus and head back out on the road. I know that sounds a little nuts but it's true. As soon as tours are over, I miss being on the road. Today will be hard.

I am very underweight and very exhausted so like it or not, I really need some time off to get myself ready for the next leg of the tour. I got a lot of good food at the store earlier, carrot juice and stuff like that. I have to put some weight on and rebuild myself. These tours take it out of me and the end of the year shows on my face. I get asked every night if I am ok. I guess I look pretty ugly or something. I am glad I am alone and will have a couple of days to even out before I have to go anywhere or do anything. Later on today, I am going to start preparing the office for the November / December mail order and start getting the 2008 radio broadcasts together. If only I could get to sleep now. Perhaps I can fool myself into taking a nap and get up in a couple of hours and that will do it. I don't want to sleep. When I am depressed, like I am now, I want to stay awake. November and December are hard months for me, perhaps the hardest of the year.

So, the tour is over. In a way, it feels like I have not done many shows or really done anything at all and then I think that I just did

Henry Rollins

50 shows in 58 days. I could have done a few more in that time. There were a couple of weekend nights that were nights off and that's really a sin on tour. I have only been out for two months, that's really nothing. I shouldn't feel like I have been out on anything all that substantial. Next year will be a lot of shows. I am going to try and stay out most of the year next year. I have nothing else to do. If I stop moving, I don't know what I'll do.

November and December are the two hardest months of the year for me. I am usually off the road and my thoughts catch up to me. It's a long walk down a dark hallway. I think of Joe Cole getting killed and other people who are dead. I feel more isolated and fucked than ever. This time of the year beats on me pretty hard. I don't want to spend time with anyone, alone is fine. Sometimes I think that it would be cool to hang out with a female but that feeling doesn't last long. It's never worth it. Alone is better. It is the only thing that makes sense at times like this. I should try to get some sleep so I can get it over with. 0442 hrs.

16. Lost Without You

11-12-07 LA CA: 0244 hrs. I am tired but my depression is fighting my urge to sleep. I think my mind is trying to wait out sleep so I can get onto the next day. Right after Joe was killed I started having insomnia. It kicks in really hard around this time of the year.

Yesterday was pretty good. I worked at the house and office, mostly organizing and working on radio stuff. I stayed busy as I could but I was feeling pretty bad about being off the road. I'll do the best I can but I can already feel this wave of depression is going to be very difficult to deal with. Things will get better when mail order picks up and I'm busy. I have to get my head down now. Perhaps I can take a nap and that will be enough sleep and then I can go to the office and get some things done there. 0301 hrs.

11-18-07 LA CA: 0502 hrs. I can't sleep. I have been off the tour for a week and it's been very hard adjusting to being back here. I have been battling the usual depression but along with that I have had trouble controlling the surges of anxiety that are coursing through me.

On Wednesday and Thursday of last week I had some voice over work. I narrated two documentaries for National Geographic. It was a big deal for me. As always, I wanted to do as best as I could. I read through the material many times before I went in to do it. Even as prepared as I was, it was hard to sleep the night before the first session. I did ok the first day, we got all of the script done in the allotted time, actually less than the session time scheduled. The producers seemed to like my work ok. Whenever I am doing voice over work, I reckon they are not going to use my voice after hearing it but are going through with the session anyway. I felt a little better after the first one was completed but the rest of the day and into the night, all I could think about was the next one and how was I going to get through it. I did get through it and actually knocked over half an hour off the day's previous time even though that copy had more words. I felt pretty good about that. It didn't used to be this bad.

I just signed on to a film with Cuba Gooding and Ray Winstone. It looks pretty cool and it's work so I'll take it. I don't think it's a good idea to say no to work. I will start prepping myself later on. I have to get some sleep at some point, I have not slept yet. I am not tired at all. In fact, now I am getting distracted thinking about the film. I have some time, right? They're not going to start it before Thanksgiving so I have some time to get my head around it. That's what I'll do, I'll get some sleep and then I'll start working on prep for the film. The longer out I get the lines under my belt, the less I'll stress about it.

Last night was pretty cool. A woman I know named Jennifer works at EMI, she is in the press department and works with some really great talent. She is very good at her job, I have known her many years. Anyway, she asked if I wanted to go to a dinner event for Brian Wilson. He's about to go to Washington DC to be given a lifetime achievement award at the Kennedy Center. Capitol Records and his family wanted to have a west coast celebration for him. She had a +1 and asked me if I wanted to go. I did. The thing was at the Bel-Air Hotel. I got there before she did and pulled my car in right behind Rodney Bingenheimer. It was good to see him, he's an amazing guy. Eventually she got there and I met some of her co-workers and she introduced me to Brian Wilson, that was pretty cool. It was time to be seated and as I walking to the table I saw Van Dyke Parks. I really wanted to shake the man's hand. I walked up to him and said, "Van Dyke Parks!" and he said, "Henry Rollins!" We talked for a second and then I went and sat down. After we ate, people started speaking from a small stage in front. Brian Wilson's wife spoke, his daughters, people from the record company and others. Of all of them, it was Van Dyke Parks who was the best. He spoke about working with Brian Wilson and what it was like to collaborate with him. He was so eloquent, he has such a grip on language. He was truly remarkable. Eventually, Wilson's band got onstage and they all made dedications to him and then Wilson got onstage and they did a short set of songs.

Brian Wilson sang really well and his band, damn, they are SO good. There was 8 of them I think and they all sang and it was so damn good. They did *Good Vibrations, California Girls, God Only Knows, Love And Mercy,* a new one that I don't know the title of and at least three more. It was a great time. I talked to Carny Wilson and her husband for awhile. I told her that I used to live in Redondo Beach when I was in Black Flag and saw some of the early Beach Boys landmarks. She asked me if I had ever read the book <u>The Nearest Faraway Place</u>. I had. The thing went on past midnight but it was worth it to see the band play and to meet Wilson and Parks. That was a great night. Jennifer was so cool to invite me. She probably knows that stuff like this isn't lost on me. It's not. I got back here very late and eventually fell out around 0130 hrs. and didn't get up until 1430 hrs. I must have needed the sleep.

I spent most of the day working on radio stuff. In 2008, I won't be annotating the songs anymore. I wish it didn't take up as much time as it does but it does so I can't do it next year. I am finishing up the work on the rest of the broadcasts for this year and starting up broadcasts for next year for pre-taping because I won't be here much for the first few months. I have a lot of work to do on the radio show still. Engineer X and I are going to try to pre-tape two shows a week until I leave. It's a lot but if he's willing to do it, I gotta be ready.

So much of the work I do is to keep myself away from myself, especially around this time of the year. November is hard and so is December. I start thinking about the night Joe Cole got killed and it makes me very agitated. I don't like the thoughts I think, the conclusions I come to, the truths I know. That's why I stay alone as much as I can. It doesn't hurt as badly when I am alone, being around people gives me a reference point and it makes me feel worse. It's lights out. 0612 hrs.

11-22-07 LA CA: 0126 hrs. Just got back from the office. I spent the evening going through boxes of mail and whatever else has piled up over the last several months. I get a lot of books and records sent to me, many include letters asking me to check out the work when I get a chance and get back to the person with how I liked whatever was sent. It's not an easy position to be put in. I know these people mean well but it's a lot to expect that someone you don't really know will drop everything, read the book you sent and get back to you. I found letters from 2006 and earlier. I answered them on the backs of postcards. I went through those boxes for almost three hours.

I save handwriting of people I know, I have always thought handwriting was very interesting. I have hundreds of pages of handwriting samples, everything from small notes written on post-its to letters, postcards, faxes, you name it. It has always fascinated me that when someone dies their written words stay on the piece of paper. After Joe was killed, I was kind of surprised that his handwriting didn't disappear off his old cassettes. I have been saving people's handwriting for decades. I think it nails down a time and place as well or sometimes better than a photograph. I have some books signed by Henry Miller and some by other writers I never met and what makes it so cool to me is that the writer actually had to handle the book to write his or her name in it. I think that is so great. Any handwritten letter took the time of the person writing it, they had to apply themselves to the actual writing of the words and just knowing they did it in real time makes it very special to me.

I have some pieces of paper written on by the great artist Raymond Pettibon. Many years ago I lived in back of his house. I would hang out in the living room and watch him work. Sometimes I would sit out there and write just so I could say that I was working in the same room as he was. He would do drawing after drawing, like a machine. Almost every single one had a line of writing at the bottom. Once I asked him about that and he told me he came up with the line first and the image afterwards. I saw that he had these pieces of paper with hundreds of lines written on them. When he would get to the bottom, he would throw them out. I retrieved them and held onto them as I thought they were amazing. He spent more time on one of those pieces of paper than he did on the art and that made them very special to me. I still have them.

I have saved a lot of letters over the decades. I think they are important. For a few years, I would devote many days over the Christmas holiday season to going to the office supply store and buying those massive three ring binders, acid free page protectors and sorting out letters and pieces of paper and getting them organized and preserved. I have been working on that for years and am making some headway but there's still a lot more to go.

I made some interesting finds tonight. I found some handwriting of Ian MacKaye's that I had not yet put away. I have almost every bit of his handwriting he's given me over the years since we were teenagers. Tonight I found some address stickers and some odd bits he had sent me over the last couple of years.

When people ask me for my autograph, I never mind doing it. Sometimes people show up with several of the same photograph of me that they want me to sign, I know it's for resale. I always sign one or two but leave the rest alone. I tell the guy that no one will want to buy them anyway and that he just wasted a lot of money at the copy place.

The best find of 2007 happened several weeks ago. For a few years, I had been searching all over for a single, small piece of paper that I was sure I still had but try as I might could not locate. Years ago, I was on tour with the band and we were in Italy. My good friend, the late great Mick Geyer, was in living in Switzerland at the time working for the UN. He took the train to our show and after it was over we resumed the conversation that we started in 1989, as we usually do. Upon parting, he wrote down an author's name that he wanted me to check out. Ryszard Kapuscinski. Of course, I went online and got all of his books immediately and read them one after another. To this day, they are some of the finest books I have ever read. Anyway, that was the piece of paper I was looking for. Right before the last tour started, I was cleaning out an old drawer that was full of everything from power cords to receipts and at one point, a piece of paper fell out of my hand and hit the floor next to a pile of stuff destined for the bin and by chance, I turned it over and there was Mick's handwriting. It made me happy that I recovered the piece of paper but it also made me remember that he's gone now. I put the piece of paper in a hard back edition of my favorite Kapuscinski book, <u>Imperium</u>.

I am going to get a few hours sleep and resume writing of some kind. The more depressed I am, the more I write so I think it's going to be a very productive few days. I got a great letter today:

This is the time to require & ask for the American and the Jewish vote.

To elected RUDOLPH W. GIULIANI. He is going to be the best president ever for USA & Israel.

The Jewish have to elect Republicans as a gesture to the policy of the president George .W. Bush & his staff. This message has to go all over the country and especially in synagogues.

This is the time to put on the car & out of doors the American flag proudly outside the hose to supporting our services troops. However the USA at war with the terrorist every day & everywhere in the world Thanks to the US Troops soldiers & President George W .Bush we have a freedom a liberty & plenty of rope to live good & vintage in the USA.

Where is the UN? The UN needs to fight the war against the terror & not the USA. We must bomb the terror facilities instantly at once & for allLet them-terrorist be dread from the USAonce and for all. Every now and then we see the terrorist in the TV in their marches & camps why we do not destroyed them in Iran & Syria.

Take the fighting to them and do not hesitate! Where is all the association of human rights for the lost of the innocent people that died from terrorists?

This is the time that Europe & the UN should close or shut down the mosques in response to the Terrorism. In addition to lower the voice of the prayer of the Mosques in Europe there is now religion that is so noisy for the public such as the Arabians.

Enough we do not need to be dread from them.

We have to make a stop to their lunatics & to their terrorism.

Aren't adults a scream? 0302 hrs.

12-09-07 LA CA: 0045 hrs. In my room. For the last hour or so, I've been outside pacing the walkway in front of the house, pretending I'm going somewhere. I worked on radio stuff most of the day. I have to get a lot of shows pre-taped for next year. I don't know my shoot schedule for Tuesday. I will probably be ok to make the broadcast but I might not be able to get there early enough to do the pre-tapes. I'll have to work that out later today.

Depression was on me pretty hard tonight but at a level that I can deal with. It is with me on such a regular basis that I just factor it in and keep moving. To a certain level, it feels "normal" and I can function pretty well.

Tonight as I stood outside, I thought about my old neighborhood in DC and felt very homesick. I wanted to be there and be able to walk around. Sometimes that's all I want, just to be able to be back on those streets and have things in my life be more simple.

In the days when I lived back there, I had less on my mind and had seen less things and didn't know what I know now. I guess that's what I miss. Perhaps that's what feeling nostalgic or sentimental is all about—the desire to be in a less complicated time. That's a big part of it for me. At least a time that isn't as ruined as things seem to be now. That's one of the main reasons I keep to myself, it makes things less complicated. Sometimes, it's hard enough making it through the day, people make it more challenging. For the last several years, I have become more and more isolated from people. It's what makes sense to me. If you're going to be nuts, you should not put other people through it. 0129 hrs.

12-10-07 LA CA: 2210 hrs. I shouldn't be up this late. I will go over my lines for tomorrow and try to knock out. I don't know if I will get off work in time to get to the station for the show tomorrow and of course I am thinking about it too much. I am in the last shot of the day so I bet that will make me late. There's nothing I can do about it so I shouldn't worry about it now.

I got a letter from a soldier tonight. I wrote the guy back and forwarded the letter on to Paul Rieckhoff at the Iraq and Afghanistan Veterans of America to see if he could help the guy out. Paul got right back to me and told me he was going to help the guy if he could.

Here's the letter:

I only write this because I know Henry is a supporter of our troops, and works with USO tours. My hope is something positive can come from my loss.

This past March I was forced to leave the Army, the one place I've ever felt at home, on a medical discharge after tearing up both of my knees in a training accident. I will require complete replacement for both knees within the next ten years or face a life confined to a wheelchair. Up until last weekend I had never even taken off my dog tags. I still wore my combat boots as a daily reminder of the pride I took in joining our nations military in a time of war to fight with fellow soldiers.

My injuries got me a 20% disability rating from the VA, and free medical coverage for any injuries I got while on active duty. After months at home, never getting responses to inquiries about my medical coverage I got the letter I am attaching to this email. It states that my 20% disability pay has been restructured and that my country is willing to pay me exactly $0.00 a month for the rest of my life for any and all medical coverage related to my injuries. (I have almost no cartilage in my knees and can not even sleep through the night because of the pain.) That wasn't a typo... The US government has told me that they will pay me "nothing" for the rest of my life, to compensate me for my service to my country and the injuries I sustained as a result.

Pride? There is none left. How could I feel pride for serving in an army which marches us off to war with promises of taking care of us if we're hurt and then sends home letters telling us that we're worthless.

I support the troops in every way. They are my brothers and sisters. They are why I need help. I am a big boy and can find my own way of dealing with my problems, but if I keep silent and allow this to happen to my brothers and sisters who may not be able to take care of themselves, I would never forgive myself.

Henry, I need advice. How can one soldier help all of his fellow soldiers? How can I make sure the army and the VA pay the people they promised to take care of. They're out there fighting a war and will soon come home to realize that not only the citizens don't care about them, our government doesn't either.

I think there's going to be a lot of situations like this and that's why this will be a multi-trillion dollar war, say nothing of the men and women who gave their best and got something like this as a thank you. The soldiers can't get what they need to get fixed up and the president is cutting taxes. Fantastic. The soldier sent me a jpg of the actual letter, the rigid formality and impersonal nature of it makes it all the more insulting and injurious. I am glad to be able to contact Paul about this stuff. He's as solid as they come and I look forward to working with him in 2008.

It was a short day for me on the film set. I was only in one scene. I am not really in the film much, no surprise there but it's a cool part and I get to be intense, which I like. I like being in films where I can really let it rip.

The weekend ended too quickly for me. I don't know what I wanted and even though I spoke to no one but the man at the grocery store and to management's son for literally 20 seconds, I still feel I need a break from humanity. 2244 hrs.

12-12-07 LA CA: 2316 hrs. I shouldn't be up still but I am. Been up since 0530 hrs. Worked on the film today. I think I am pulling it off. Whenever we move onto another shot, I always ask the director if he's sure he's happy with what we got and he always says he is. I didn't drop any lines during takes today. I always drop them in rehearsal but when it's time to hit it for real, I always seem to be able to do it. Cuba thought we did good work today. It's a good group of people on the set, actors and crew alike. I stay quiet and keep to myself for the most part as the other actors are in a group, shooting together every day and I don't want to get in the way of their momentum and the thing they have built up for themselves. There's not one scene in the film where I am not extremely intense, so to keep that happening I have to stay to myself and not talk if I don't have to. I try and stay in character the entire time I am on the set. If I am going to be off set for more than an hour, I will pull it down a little bit but for the most part, I stay in it. It's what I think is the right thing to do. I am not an actor so I have to try extra hard just not to hold up the show. I never want to have confidence onstage or in films. I want be nervous and reaching for it, always. I never want to come to the conclusion that I am any good because I am not and also because it keeps me trying to be better. At this point, that's my test, to try and do my best.

I was reminded earlier today that I am not dead yet even though I feel that way a lot. I got off the set around noon and went to the office. I went through mail and opened a letter with no return address. It was from a female that I had quite a lot of affection for years ago. I am ashamed to admit that but it's true. I had not thought about her in a long time. Her perfume was in the letter and it made a lot of memories come back very vividly. I felt very weak and confused by it all. She said she still thought of me. I threw the letter out but it slowed me down for the rest of the afternoon and I didn't get much done, or at least not as much as I would have liked. I should have never gotten involved with her. I deserve everything I got from that one. I was and still am disgusted with myself for feeling the way I did about her years ago and how quickly it all came back when I opened her letter today. I have done my best to starve that need, that weakness, to death but it seems that it is still there. I think it is bad strategy to need or think you need companionship of that kind. It's fine for someone else, it's not my problem what other people do but for me, it's just a downside, a vulnerability I cannot afford. The last couple of times I have liked a female, it always felt like I was trying to sell myself something I really didn't want or need. I am better off with some cold weather gear and a place to head out to. I don't want to care about someone, miss someone or have to matter to someone. That's perhaps the main thing, I don't want someone, anyone, wondering when I'll be back or how I'm doing. Well, sometimes I do but I know it's not a good thing and I keep away. When in doubt, stay away. Alone is truth. 2359 hrs.

12-14-07 LA CA: 2217 hrs. Did phone press today and then worked on mail order stuff with Heidi. I got an interesting letter from a soldier who is currently stationed in Iraq. I hear what he's saying but it's time for the bullshit to cease. His point is pointless and tired. It's time to get out of Iraq but, of course, that's not on the schedule. America will never get out of Iraq. I don't care what this guy says next, if he chooses to answer, I just hope he gets back to America in one piece.

Sir, I am a current Active Duty Soldier in the U.S.Army. I have been an enlisted soldier now for almost 12 years. First of all, I want to let you know that I may not be as articulate and well educated as yourself, however I will do my best to explain myself. I have been a long time fan of your music and your spoken word comedy. I just watched the show where you hosted Iraq War veterans. I myself am a 3rd tour Vet. In fact I was just asked to go for a short deployment in the beginning of the new year which would be my 4th. I must tell you that my occourances there are not the same as the nature of the deployments of the Infantry Soldiers. I am fortunate that my deployments have been short, no longer than 8 months each. However due to the nature of my team's mission, we travel extensively throughtout Iraq during our deployment. As you may know, any travel outside the "wire" increases any risk of injury. I have been missioned out to as many as 9 Forward Operating Bases(FOB) with in 3 consequetive days. My team travels alot. We, a team of only 3 personnel, are tasked with providing electronic repair support for a specific and unique type of equipment that is not common Army equipment. This puts my team and consequtive teams into very dangerous positions with having to travel from the most Northern most FOB in Iraq to the most Southern FOB as well as the Western corridor and eastern with all areas in between. My point being, I and my team have seen all parts of Iraq. I will testify over the last 3 years I have been to almost every FOB in Iraq. With that being said, I want to let you know that for the most part the Iraqi civilans want us there and are pleased with what we, the U.S. have done. Media however almost never reports the positive. I have seen many times flying over the farmers fields and watching them come outside their homes into their fields just to wave and give a thumbs up. I have seen Herdsman wave and smile as we pass over. In fact once, due to the low flying helicopter, that it unfortunately made the animals spook but the pilot helped the farmer corral his herd back in to a more managable form using the helicopter. My major point is that I want to put forward that I have witnessed alot of support for the U.S. while being deployed. I personnaly think that we are doing the right thing by being there in Iraq. I won't get into too much personal opinion here so as not to discredit my report to you. I will appreciate any feedback that you may send me and I welcome any discus-

sion. Stay safe, stay free, God bless our troops and keep up the support.
—Name withheld for privacy purposes and nature of my current position

I wrote him back:

Name Withheld, I know that American Forces do good things all over all the time and that some people are glad for it. That's not really the point though, is it? It's a corporate war for dominance in the region. Saddam killed himself when he switched the food for oil program from the dollar to the euro. You can get all the waves and smiles you want, it's still time to leave Iraq. The welfare of thousands of Iraqis is nothing compared to the death or injury of one American soldier. You can dress it up with the bullshit but it's still what it is. It's an invasion and an occupation and the locals will resist it to the last man. Just as every American would resist occupation by any invader at any time. There's not one thing I have said here that is wrong. Our soldiers are great. The mission however, is screwed and below the dignity of America and its Military. I only hope you and your guys get out of there in one piece. I visit the men in the hospitals. Brains blown out of their heads, skulls missing, legs, arms gone, families destroyed. For what? So some fuckin' farmer can wave at you? FUCK THAT. —Henry Rollins

Well, fuck it then, if he's happy where he is, then have a great fucking war. America is in a sad place.

Tonight, I listened to music, worked on the last of the broadcast notes for 2007 and basically stayed alone. It's the only thing that makes me feel better or at least normal. 2241 hrs.

12-15-07 LA CA: 2211 hrs. Today I went to the radio station to work on pre-tapes for the many weeks I'll be away. Engineer X and I managed to pull off three of the four I had hoped to get in the can. Getting to the station late did not help things. After that was done, I met up with Heidi and we went to see <u>No Country For Old Men</u> which I thought was fantastic. After the film was over I came back here and went over my lines for the film work which resumes on Monday. Right now, I am listening to the Air Miami album <u>Fourteen Songs</u>. I am listening to it on a small system that holds an iPod. It is a great invention for me.

Right now, I am in unwitnessed time. I am alone in a room. This is a truth I understand and draw a great deal of relief from. I will spend a great deal of what life I have left in this manner—alone in a room somewhere. I like it. I believe it. Being with people is always a bit of a put on.

Yesterday I spent a few hours with a woman I have worked with in the past. She contacted me recently to ask if I would write a thing for her nephew who has a school project that requires people to write a page or two in a notebook that is passed around. She and I met at a gallery she works at and I wrote a thing in the notebook about how actions speaking louder than words and other things I wished an older male had told me at age ten. She and I got to talking and she expressed concern that I am not getting out enough and hoped that I would meet a nice woman sooner rather than later. I thanked her for the concern, it was sincere and well meant. I think about all that but not all that often. No woman would be better off by getting to know me, I know that much. Life is fucked. Why anyone would want to tie their life to another's is beyond me. I know couples who are great together but I don't see myself in that position. When I was younger I used to think about all that stuff but now, fuck it. I don't care. I see relationships of that kind more of a liability and a hindrance than anything else. That's just me though, who cares what I think? I wrote the woman a thank you letter earlier and told her that none of what she said was wasted on me and that I appreciated the time and good intentions. That's partially true. I do appreciate the concern but it really was wasted on me because it didn't change my mind one bit.

It's time to get back out on the road. I'll be leaving town in less than a week. It's better that I go. When I am moving I don't feel as bad, when I am still it's very difficult. That's why I try to do interesting and fucked up things as often as I can. I fuckin' hate life most of the time. I don't hate myself, I hate being stuck here to wait it out. 2252 hrs.

12-16-07 LA CA: 2312 hrs. Sitting in bed. I have been going over my lines for the work ahead. I had a bad day and as the day went on, I sunk lower and lower. I think it's going to be a bad week. I wish the weekend was starting again so I could have another 48 hours of nothing. This is a very hard time of the year for me.

Ian called me today, so great to talk to him. That was the best part of the day. I wrote him a brief thank you letter last night. I was just checking in and recommended that remixed version of Led Zeppelin's The Song Remains The Same. We both like that album a lot. It's always good to hear his voice, he's the best.

I wrap out of this film on Thursday and will be at the airport the next evening. I am well over half way packed. I'll have that bag zipped and good to go before Friday. One less thing to think about. My destination has me a bit distracted. I don't know exactly why I feel the need to go these great distances but I do. I guess it's the only way I learn. I have to go. I can't get it from a book. Also, I have to maintain and strengthen my resolve and my alone. If I hang around with people too much, I get softened up. I can't have that. Spending those minutes talking with that woman a couple of days ago was a confusing experience that weakened me somewhat. I'll get past it.

I need missions. I need goals. I need to keep hitting it. Not having a band and that whole thing has knocked my compass off a great deal. I really wanted that tour in 2006 to be the start of something. For a minute there, I thought we were onto something but soon enough I saw that it was not going to be more than some shows. It broke my heart pretty bad and also made me really angry that the band members said yes to the shows when not all of them were into it. That was fucking weak and I am done with them. I should have known, my fault.

I have been warned that where I'm going on Friday is not a good place to spend time in. I'm not looking for trouble but I'm sure looking for a break from this shit. I come up with ideas and I make them happen. I can't think of anything else to do with life. Fuck it. 2341 hrs.

12-18-07 LA CA: 2234 hrs. This is the 2nd worst day of the year. In a few hours, less actually, it will be 16 years since Joe Cole was killed in the early hours of 12-19-91. I usually stay up and think about the whole awful event.

Today I was on the set for over 12 hours. Today was all my big lines and I think I did pretty good. I am holding my own with the actors and not slowing down the production. I have to be up at 0600 hrs. tomorrow so I can't stay up and sit with the memory. I feel that I am not respecting the whole thing by not staying up and thinking about Joe but I am so damned tired and I have to sleep.

I'm getting tensed up with this being the night, the film not done and being so tired. I feel pretty bad. I am mad that I can't stay up for Joe. 2301 hrs.

12-19-07 LA CA: 0820 hrs. In the trailer, waiting to be told when to go in to see hair and make-up. I didn't sleep much last night. I woke up a few minutes after midnight. I don't remember how long it took to get back to sleep. I walked around the house a little and thought about Joe's father Dennis and the pitiful ruin of his life. His recent mug shot flashed in my mind and I wondered what he was thinking about at that moment. 0825 hrs.

0940 hrs. Out of make-up. I think they have switched the order of the scenes and if that's the case, I am probably here all day and into the night. I have to make a final to-do list so I can get it all done before I leave. I have a few hours on Friday. If I can wrench myself out of bed early enough I can get it all done before noon Friday. I am usually up against a brisk schedule. I like a schedule that's hard to deal with. It keeps me honest.

1035 hrs. Back from rehearsal for some scenes at the top of the page so maybe we are shooting in order.

I am going to finish packing tonight. It's only Wednesday so I have some time before Friday night. I know I think about this stuff too much.

I have been thinking of 12-19-91 since I got up this morning. I have gone over all the moments of the incident but at this point, it's not the part that I dwell on the most. It's the futility of every aspect of Joe's murder that really gets to me. He's dead, his family is gutted and the shooter has now transformed himself into a murderer, perpet-uating the cycle of abuse. The list of downsides goes on and on. All the sorrow and crushing misery that it engenders just thinking about it, while sincere, is empty and leads nowhere. It's not as if you ever feel better about any of this stuff, you just learn to deal with the dis-ability of it. You are now challenged, damaged. What was taken is irre-placeable and the act itself is the very definition of needless. There is nothing to do about it at this point. The shooter, who was never caught, could have walked by me ten times over the years and I wouldn't have recognized him. It's years ago but the pain stays.

12-20-07 LA CA: 1752 hrs. Sitting in the trailer, waiting to finish this thing. I have to run down a hallway, I have been waiting for quite awhile to do this. I think all my speaking parts are done. I have made a list of all the things I want to get done tonight. I think I can do it. I am aiming for a couple of hours where I don't have to do much so I can catch my breath. I am happy to have done this work and to have a part in the film and to have remained employed until almost the end of the year but I am getting nerved up about the trip. I know why I do this stuff, why I go at this pace. I believe that if I relax too much or go without a challenge for too long I will get soft. I know this is true, I will get softened by leisure, by money, by thinking that I am good or that I have accomplished anything. I have to keep reaching for it or I shouldn't be around. I want to check out most of the time, a lot of life is a waste of time to me. There's so much waiting around, expectation, humiliation, etc. I know there are good things happen-ing in life but they're not the moments I remember, it's the bad and barely endurable that stays with me. I reckon I should just keep going until I can't go on anymore and if that leads to an "early" death, so be it. If you live to be 80, then perhaps you didn't have the guts to push it hard enough. Ever think about it that way? Sitting still is depressing and fills me with too much anxiety. If I am on the move or in unfamiliar surroundings, it keeps me distracted from myself. I am looking forward to heading out but on the other hand, I don't want to go anywhere or do anything.

Henry Rollins

This film has been hassle free and everyone's been cool but I want to wrap out and get some work done tonight. I want to rack out early and get up as early as I can tomorrow. I have felt depression filtering into my thoughts since about noon today. It comes more often, hits harder and stays longer.

America Inc. killed Joe. Crime is great for business. The beast gnashes its teeth and screams for more, always more. 1825 hrs.

2355 hrs. Back at the house. The film wrapped around 2100 hrs. There were two last shots I had to do, just running down a hallway and that was it. The actors were jumping up and down, very happy. I found the director, thanked him for the work, thanked Cuba and evacuated as soon as I could. I was in the ride and out of the lot while people were still coming out of the building we shot in. There was no need to hang around for anything. I have nothing against the people I worked with, they were all really great. I just want to get onto the next thing as soon as I can, whenever I can. The other actors were all together for weeks, I was there on and off for 8 days and had no emotional investment in the thing. It's just work for me. I am glad for it and take it very seriously but I am done with it as soon as I hear that we are wrapped. I am glad to have been in the film and hope that the director will give me some more work. I can always use more of that. 0015 hrs.

17. The War On Christmas Will Be Televised

12-21-07 LAX: 1909 hrs. Sitting in the British Airways lounge. I got up pretty early this morning, went to the office, knocked out some press and then management came by to go over the final dates for the upcoming tours. I will be pretty nonstop through mid-May. June to August, I have no hard plans yet. Hopefully, something will come up. Something usually does although I never count on it.

Tonight's driver is one of my favorites, he's a young Bosnian guy and we always have very interesting conversations about current events. When he dropped me off at the airport there were photographers on the sidewalk who asked to take my picture, so I stood for photos. After that, the TMZ camera guys came up to me and I asked them if I was in some kind of trouble as those guys are never around unless there's trouble. The nice young man told me that I wasn't in trouble. He wanted to know what I thought about Britney Spears' sister getting pregnant. I said that it was too bad that kids are having kids and wondered if statutory rape charges would be brought against the donor of the genetic material. I also added that it's possible to not get pregnant during sex and perhaps the couple had not been briefed on that and then I said goodbye. Getting my boarding passes and dropping my bag off was relatively easy but tonight's security screener was a trip. The line seemed to not move at all. And then I saw him, the man who would be staring at the contents of my backpack. He was an old, large, slow moving mountain of a man. Each article that showed up on his screen seemed to only raise his suspicion and slow him down. I think if he had his way, none of us would have been allowed through. He saw through more than just our possessions, he saw into our very souls and no doubt sensed the security risk that lives within us all. With great regret, he begrudgingly allowed our assorted belongings to pass through to the boarding area, knowing full well he was unleashing hell, one bedraggled, shoeless traveler at a time. From

A Preferred Blur   **353**

there, I came here and have been enduring a woman who came to the quiet part of the lounge, where everyone is reading and launched into a long and loud phone conversation while leafing through the pages of a magazine. It is because of people like this that the iPod, my buddy, was created. Thank you, O iPod for allowing me to sonically bludgeon this woman who should have a fucking spear sticking out of her chest if justice was remotely what it was cracked up to be. Thank you Black Sabbath, for making music to put into an iPod. And then, it was time to go to gate. 1944 hrs.

2046 hrs. I was standing in line and when the lady made the announcement that it was time for first and business class to board, all these people cut to the front of the line. They were really crass, I thought it was funny. A couple went for the front of the line so hard that the female stepped on my feet while cutting me off. Not to be outdone, that actor guy from those Transporter films cut to the front of the entire line and ran on board, as if he was going to get mobbed by us fans if he didn't get the hell out of there and into the safety of the first class cabin. This kind of thing doesn't get to me. In the world of travel, this is a normal occurrence. Eventually, you will get on the plane so it's all fine in the end. Life is short, it's a waste of time to give a fuck about a lot of things.

Now, the whole seating environment for tonight's flight is strange. The window seats are pointed towards the rear of the plane and all the aisle seats are pointed towards the front. Basically, by staring a little to my right, I am looking into the eyes of the passenger sitting next to me. Who comes up with this shit? Luftsthansa can screw up anything from a cup of coffee to making a seat one of the most cramped and expensive of temporary hells. There's a "privacy wall" that can be pulled up to separate us. I wonder which one of us will be the first to this wall of solitude? Well Mr. Gorbechev, I'm waiting!

The first flight is almost 10 hours. I guess I will get into London in the afternoon. I had a couple of hours where I didn't have to do much before the car came today, that was pretty good. I listened to the radio and read news articles online. Bush and his gang seem to want to keep car mpg ratings low and block any states that want to improve upon our poor, poor statistics. It seems that progress really gets to these guys. They had no problem getting a lot of money to fund their fake war on terror, well over a quarter of a billion dollars a day. And the good part of this is... what? Where is the money for all this fun and games going to come from? There's no way America can sustain this. Over a quarter of a billion dollars a day to keep Iraq from invading America. Adults believe this. I can't wait for these motherfuckers to leave.

We are in the air and on the way to London. I am glad to be out of LA and on the move. If I stayed in LA it would have been a bad week of home and office and too much sadness and misery. My anger and basic fucked-upness makes me want to move all the time. For the rest of my life, I am going to travel all over the world alone. At least, that's the plan. I will work and move as much as I can. It's the only way I have found to deal with life. It's how I keep a distance from it. If I stop moving, I don't know what I'll do. Wait it out, I guess. I suppose I am a very negative person. I think life is a flat line fucking bore and I honestly don't know what to do with myself, so I do all this shit. After what I have been through, I have come to the conclusion that I don't give a fuck about anything but the truth and battling my depression. My gut tells me to check out almost daily. I have no more missions to go out on, no more mountains to summit. I just live inside my thoughts with my horror to keep me company. It is my constant companion and keeps me on the straight and narrow. My horror withdraws somewhat when I am alone. It's easier to manage. When I am with people, it makes me feel bad. It's not that I don't like people, it's just hard to be around them. When I am around them, I want to die, when I am alone, I don't feel that way as much. The people I do keep in touch with, I am very careful not to impact their lives by attempting to be too close to them. I see them very infrequently and never mention them by name when I am asked about where I come from. I always say that I sometimes visit some people I grew up with but I always leave their names out, it's not fair to them to mention their names. When I visit my old neighborhood, I see some of these people very briefly and leave them alone to get on with their lives. They impress me with their courage and realness. They are taking chances, they have kids, they are very committed to all that and I admire that duty and responsibility. They are, to me, what it's all about. I don't have any of that stuff but I like to be around it for short periods of time but then I have to get back out into the weather. I am not brave in the least by comparison. It takes a lot of guts to mean something to someone. To be a parent or a husband, the thought of being either makes me want to hang myself. There's no way I have the stamina for that kind of haul. To see the same person day after day for the rest of your life is way too much for me to handle. I would be a complete dud as a parent, husband or boyfriend. Relationships are very confusing to me.

Whenever I think I am feeling lonely, I wonder if that's what I'm really feeling. Lonely for who? Also, I don't understand love. I wonder if I have ever loved anyone or anything or just projected something onto them and called it love. I must love some people because it sure has fucked me up when they have died. Perhaps that's the thing, perhaps I have abandonment issues. It's not as if I am angry at these dead people for leaving me, I just find it impossible to get over them being gone. I make room for it in the backpack but it still hurts pretty bad. It is perhaps one of the reasons I don't invest in friendships much because if something bad happens, the pain is very hard to take. When Ian's mother died, it was hard for everyone who knew her. When I think of her sometimes it hurts so much I forget to breathe. I still talk to her sometimes, thanking her for being so kind to me. I am thankful for all the conversations we had. Now is a virus that I am trying to outrun.

12-22-07 London Heathrow Airport: 1637 hrs. The first flight was late and I am hoping that my bag will be waiting for me on the other end. This flight has been late and slow to board so perhaps I will see my bag again in several hours and not two days. So many times I have had to wrestle my bag back into my possession from the jaws of airports. The hike through Heathrow wasn't all that bad this time. I landed at terminal 1 and took the shuttle here to terminal 4. I don't remember the last time I was in this terminal. It's dark and cold outside. It's a Saturday night in London and part of me really wants to be walking around in the city right now. I didn't like London at first but over the years I really have come to like it and now it's one of my favorite places to be. I like being a world traveler and having all these different cities to look forward to visiting. To be familiar enough with cities all over the world is something you earn by putting in the time. When I am in these places on my own, walking around, I feel like I am really living, like I am free and life is worth showing up for. When I am walking on these streets, I don't want for anything or anyone, I have all I need. I am sitting across from a man who is talking nonstop into his cell phone, mindless bullshit, call after call. Not even my ear plugs can drown him out. It's one of the parts of travel I have never gotten used to. I love it when the announcement comes over the system that all cell phones must be put away. We are several minutes away from that. 1658 hrs.

12-23-07 En Route: It's dark outside. We've been in the air for about 6.5 hours and will be landing soon. I have been reading a very good book by Naomi Klein called <u>The Shock Doctrine</u> and I think it's going to be the best book I have read this year by a mile. I am learning a lot. I know that a fair bit of it is going over my head but there's a lot that's not and thanks to her brilliant writing someone like me can get a handle on the points she's making. This book is connecting the last of the dots for me on the invasion and occupation of Iraq and I'm understanding the whole thing on a completely different level. You learn what has happened to the economies of countries like Bolivia, Chile, Brazil, China, South Africa and Russia and how there always seems to be a Chicago School of Economics crew involved. The outcome always seems to be the same: massive job loss, depression, hunger, homelessness, deadly use of force against the many, and obscene profits for the few. It makes me understand where that douche bag Kudlow is coming from when I watch him on MSNBC. I remember watching one of his broadcasts when one of his guests characterized those who are critical of the state of America's economy as the "hate

America crowd." Nice. I think they are the ones who hate America. They hate Democracy, the New Deal or any government regulation that prevents them from gutting countries and profiting from the blood spill. They are made furious when they are prevented from doing it in America. In the cases of all those countries who got their economy obliterated, Democracy was promised but wasn't anything close to what they really got. What they got was wild and uncontrolled deregulation and privatization. It's ironic that the Milton Friedman school of economics disciples hate Democracy. I see why though. It just gets in the way. Funny when you see the Sean Hannity's with their American flag lapel pins flapping on their chests—there's nothing American about them besides their waistlines and sense of entitlement.

Islamabad Pakistan 0833 hrs. That's right, Islamabad. I figured there was no other place to go. Last year, on 12-31-06, I was in Dubai and ate dinner with members of the American Consulate there. I asked them if there was one place they have lived that they wouldn't go running back to and they all agreed on Pakistan. They said the people were nice but it was a chaotic and unstable place prone to rapid change and they asked me not to go. That sat with me for months and then a couple of weeks ago I came to the conclusion that it was the only place to go. As soon as the idea was in my mind and I couldn't move it, I called management's assistant and asked him to book it. Days later, I had a visa in my passport and was good to go. I am in the breakfast room of the hotel. The coffee isn't bad. Of course, my bag got lost, perhaps I will see it again this week if I am lucky. This hotel is near the airport and doesn't seem to be near much else so I will have to figure out how to get into town. I think I will wait a little while and go out later today and walk around near the hotel and see what, if anything, is happening near by.

The drive in from the airport was great. Cold, sun coming up, a lot of views that reminded me of Afghanistan. A lot of scrub, fairly dry. A lot of people on bikes, people waiting at bus stops. The women here are beautiful in a dangerous sort of way, fragile faces with intense eyes.

I feel a little out of it but ok. I was really looking forward to a good cup of coffee today. Perhaps the coffee in the lounge will do the trick. I am officially gone as far I am concerned. I am tucked away in an obscure corner of the world because I thought it up and did it. This is what it's all about. 0850 hrs.

12-24-07 Islamabad Pakistan: 0024 hrs. Fell into the jet lag sleep. Didn't do much for the last few hours. Read and slept, that's about it. Good internet here so I answered some of the mail that's been piling up at the office. The IFC show is in repeat on Fuse so I am getting letters about shows that are very old like we did them last week. People are mad about the same things that were addressed in the original letters. They like this band, hate Gene Simmons, hate me for not dealing on him, etc. One man was angry because I dared to make fun of the creation museum in Ohio. Please pal, don't defend creationism to me, through the misspellings, poor grammar, and lack of signature, common sense and desire to confront were not on the menu. He did ask me to put him on the show, "if you have the balls!" Oh boy, that sure would be hard to deal with, wouldn't it? Someone sitting across from you telling you how god invented everything. Be still my beating pseudo-intellect! The guy also told me what a great president Huckabee would make. Well, I'm just glad this guy has someone to send mail to, I just wish it was someone else.

Outside is dark and smoky. If I were to walk outside and inhale with my eyes closed, I would swear I was in Afghanistan. The mixture of cold air, car exhaust and whatever it is that always seems to be burning, is exactly the way I remember Kabul.

Outside my window I can see the guards at the gate stopping cars as they approach. Trunks and hoods get opened, everything gets checked and only then does the gate open, allowing the car to come in.

In the dark and cold, thousands of miles away from what I know, I feel a sense of relief. I am alone in this room, living my life, existing in unwitnessed time. Being alone in a room is a state of perfection. 0044 hrs.

0835 hrs. In the breakfast room. Hopefully my bag shows up today but even if it does, it's still hours away. I will wait for a few hours, perhaps get into some clean clothes and get back out into the streets. For the last several hours I have been in and out of sleep, having strange dreams and that's about it. I have a lot of work to do while I am here so I want to get a routine going of getting desk stuff done and checking out the scene. I'll feel better once my bag gets here. I've been in these clothes for a few days now. 0846 hrs.

12-25-07 Islamabad Pakistan: 0702 hrs. This hotel is cheap but very good. They really lay out the breakfast here. I am going into day #03 of no bag. I am ripening by the hour and while it's not the end of the world, it is a drag. Perhaps there will be better news today.

Yesterday, after British Airways confirmed there would be no bag, I went out and walked the streets for quite some time. In the afternoon, it's short pants weather and the air is great. I walked down bird dropping splattered sidewalks and no one paid me any mind besides the scattered soldier/cops who stared at me in that "You're not from around here, are you, boy?" kind of way. I walked up to the Parliament building but it was blocked off by razor wire and many armed men, which I interpreted as a do not trespass kind of thing. I sat in a park for a good while and watched the birds argue. They look like ravens but not nearly as big as ravens I've seen in other places. After walking for quite a long time, I came back here, slept, read, and caught up on e-mail press for the upcoming European dates. The Shock Doctrine continues to be a fascinating read. All the stuff that the radio and TV pundits yell back and forth at each other is, for the most part, just content needed for 24 hour media. It seems to me that the real issues at the center of all the name calling and what all the politicians are dancing around the edges of are the two major schools of thought on the role of government and government spending: The Friedman school versus the Keynes school. Our foreign policy, conflicts, and the aid we dispense are pieces of meat grabbed at by both sides. The Friedman gang wants the government to get the hell out of the way so they can get their business happening without all the paperwork and red tape and the Keynes gang are all about the regulation and that whole "New Deal" thing that was implemented years ago. I've heard Rush Limbaugh say that Roosevelt is dead, his policies live on but they're working on that problem. I think I get it and see where both sides are coming from but I can't say I'm a fan of the deregulate and privatize everything method, seeing how few people benefit and how many people get destroyed. In her book, Klein talks about the rise of homelessness, murder and suicide in Russia after Yeltsin got together with Jeffrey Sachs and put Russia up for sale. I remember walking the streets of Moscow and seeing what looked like whole families out on the street with snow falling on them. I guess what you see in some countries where the few own almost everything is the model that the Friedman gang wants for the rest of the world too. It means less people to talk to and deal with and you don't have to give a damn about anyone but yourself. I bet the whole world will be like that sooner or later. Perhaps Europe will be the last to go but it will eventually fall into the greed pit too.

The creationist wrote me in the early hours to tell me that Darwin admitted to all of his lies upon his death bed. I asked him who would win if Allah, god and Glenn Danzig all got in a fight. This resulted in three return e-mails that I just deleted without opening. We are in the Foghorn Leghorn vs. the Dog phase of our correspondence, the phase I've carefully and patiently been leading him into for the last two days. Now all I have to do is send him one line non sequiturs like "Does Huckabee's semen taste like freedom?" and that will get him all fired up. I will waste 30 seconds a day as he wastes endless minutes straightening me out. It's all in a day's work to bring on the rapture sooner than later.

Speaking of letters, here's one that puts things in perspective:

Dear Henry,

Sorry I missed you while you were at Walter Reed, although its not surprising that I didn't get to see you there. You see I was in that shit-hole of a hospital when it wasn't "in vogue" for people to visit Walter Reed, even the president hid under the guise of "just going in for an MRI" the day he decided to give some of my fellow servicemen and I our Purple Hearts. The news even reported it as if it was an afterthought for him to even visit and give us medals, with statements like "while the president was in for his MRI he decided to pop in to give some soldiers their Purple Heart Awards." Maybe he hides it because he doesn't want the news to see what he sees, the look of disgust in each soldier, airmen, sailors or marines as the president congratulates them on their shiny medals. Congratulations... Like losing a leg or arm or suffering a traumatic brain injury is something to be congratulated on.

So good for you for going to Walter Reed and Bethesda to see the wounded, but let me tell you that the anger you have openly stated that you feel when you are there is nothing compared to the anger I feel as I walk in those doors to see doctors who have told me the same damn thing for three years, told me to take the same medicine for three long years and pretty much just ignored my pain because they were too lazy to do their jobs or just felt that I was just scamming for some narcotics. The anger that boils when dealing with the adminstrative personnel at that place. People that act like I am asking for their firstborn when I am just looking to see a doctor to try to make this pain in my head go away, people that treat me like a second class citizen while they sit on their fat lazy asses behind a desk with no fear for losing their jobs.

You may be wondering, or you may not, how I feel about the war after getting a peice of shrapnel jammed into my skull and being ass fucked by the US Army Medical System. I feel the same way I did the day I got on the plane to go to Kuwait. I think it was/is a bad idea, a clusterfuck of the utmost proportions. Not even 6 months after getting back from Afghanistan we were going to another country to invade? What fucking sense does that make? I am trying to think of a witty analogy but I just cant think of anything that compares. Am I a member of any anti-war groups. Nope, they all are too far from what I feel is the right way to go about trying to fix this monkeybuttfuck of a war that is unfolding before our eyes. Pull our troops out tomorrow, right? Sure...Sorry for coming over and fucking your country up even more than it was before, you have fun with that. How does someone go about fixing the mistakes we made to get us in this crazy shitstorm? Hell if I know, and if I did no one would listen because I am not a pro-life, bible thumping, anti-gay brainless dickless asshole.

You told Anne Coultier to shut the fuck up, well Henry you need to do *the opposite. You need to speak the fuck up. You seem like a smart guy, come out from the underground and let more people hear what you have to say and let them see what you are doing about war, rights and food.*

In the off chance you do actually read this thank you for letting me rant. Sorry for spelling and grammar mistakes... brain injury.

Staff Sergeant _____ (Retired; until the military fucks me out of that too)

Wait, don't tell me, he hates America, right? Lapel pin a little out of place? 0811 hrs.

2149 hrs. Sitting in the back of the hotel at the indoor/outdoor coffee place, taking a break from writing work. I just finished the first draft of the <u>Fanatic! Vol. 3</u> book. Even though I am on "vacation" I still have to keep the work going. I can't leave it for too long. I insist on putting this book out even though I know no one will care! I guess enough people like the series and that's good enough for me. I really like it when I get a letter about the <u>Fanatic!</u> books and that they get the books in the sprit they were made. All it takes is one of those letters and I get very inspired to keep plugging away at it. I know I will still be working on this book all the way into the summer.

I took a cab to a different section of town today and had an interesting experience. I pointed in one direction and asked the man to drive that way for awhile. I think that tripped him out a little. It took me a little while to explain to him that I just wanted to walk around and see what was happening. I like to do this when I can. I get in a cab, go a certain distance and make my way back to the hotel and whatever happens in between the two points is the story. This, for me at least, is what it's all about. There is a certain joy I take in doing this. So much of my life is regimented, scheduled and witnessed, it's great to have no destination be the destination now and then. I am trying to be a traveler and not a tourist. A few minutes into the ride, he pointed to the radio and exclaimed, "Indian music!" to which I replied, "Sounds great!" He smiled and turned it up. Then he asked, "Your father lives?" which I thought was odd. The answer is that I have not a fucking clue but I told the driver that he was living and the man made a wincing/sad expression. Obviously, they have met. Anyway, we stopped at an intersection and I paid and got out. I think

this is where the confusion started. I don't think the driver understood that I wanted him to let me off and go. I started walking and
noticed that he was following me. When he would see me looking, he
would wave. After a few blocks of this, I went up to the taxi and asked
him if I had paid him in full and he said I had. I asked him what he
was doing and he explained in fractured English that he didn't want
to leave me here on my own. I had to convince him that it was ok and
finally, he left. He must have thought I was a maniac.

All the buildings I saw were no higher than three stories and most
of the signs were in English. There were a lot of travel agents and doctor's offices. Two that stood out were The Pakistan Poultry Agency and
an antique store called Butt. The only woman I remember seeing on
her own was a homeless woman, she looked really bad. I walked by
the St. Thomas church. People were lined up and passing though a
metal detector to get in. The men were politely patted down, the
women and children were not. There were not many people in the
street, mostly men walking alone, sometimes walking with other
men. None of them paid much attention to me.

At one point, I found myself on some kind of embassy row, like in
DC. Near the Afghanistan embassy there were some taxis lined up.
One of the men got out of his car and started talking to me in English
about what a great painter he was and how he had studied all over the
world and painted for many famous and important people. He wanted to show me some of his work which, to my good fortune, was
located in his taxi. He told me that if I wanted to buy one of his pieces
that would be fine with him but if not, that would be ok as well. I hate
getting in hustles like this. It reminds me of what happens in places
like Cairo, Turkey, and Lebanon. A man talks non-stop, is very polite
and as politely as you are in your attempts to extricate yourself from
the situation, you invariably have to wait it out as the man pitches
you. When you say no thanks and you really don't want what he's
selling, his display of disappointment is acting of the highest quality.
Anyway, this guy pulls out the most awful stenciled images of women
in the moonlight next to a camel and crap like that. All of it truly
sucked. His rap was amazing, "This is a beauty lady, very attractive for

your wall, sir, yes. I have a smaller one as well, sir, very attractive for you." If only he had added "and they're all awful," then we could have had some laughs. I thanked him for letting me see his work. He thanked me and offered me a discount. Then he asked me where I was from. I told him I was from America. He told all the other drivers and they all became very interested in me. One guy pulled out his cell phone, looked right at me as he dialed and kept staring as he spoke. I thought that was a very good time to evacuate and get down the road. That was a few hours ago. I walked for hours and managed to find my way back here. I washed my only shirt and slept for a little while. So far, no bag from the airport. 2246 hrs.

12-26-07 Islamabad Pakistan: 0819 hrs. Been up for awhile. Made a lot of notes. I can usually wake up fairly depression free. Sometimes depression wakes me up but I can keep a distance from it if I get up early and get to work as quickly as possible. Perhaps this is the big day that I get my bag. It's day #04, this could be the one! I won't be able to get any info on that until 0900 hrs. or later. I was angry about it for awhile but there's nothing I can do and I'll just be happy to get it back at all now. 0824 hrs.

2101 hrs. My bag arrived a few hours ago. I was not overjoyed to see that things had been stolen out of it. That's the breaks of travel. I have been pretty lucky, I have not had much stolen out of my bags over the years but I have definitely lost stuff when the bag gets lost. I don't know why but I put my camera in my bag and of course, it's gone. It's the first time I had ever done that and that's a lesson learned. I deserve that one. It's frustrating to not be able to take any photos here. I don't know if I'll get back here again.

I am sitting on the back patio like last night. I am wearing more clothing this time. It's quite cold and it's hard to write but it's great to be out here. At least the mosquitoes have gone home. Around dusk, I was sitting in a park near here and I noticed a cloud of them around me so I came back here. They fairly swarm at sundown. They come out of nowhere. I got in a good workout and am feeling it now.

There is a major event in this hotel tonight. The lobby is packed with the well-to-do, there's embassy cars in the parking lot and there's armed security all over the place. There's at least one dozen guns between myself and the lobby.

Sarah Pink, the nice lady who handles the affairs of The Ruts, wrote today and asked if she could put the live version of *Babylon's Burning* from the show on iTunes. I told her it was fine with me. So, technically, I am on a Ruts single. That's working for me very well. I managed to hold onto my iPod speakers despite the what-the-fuck-was-I-thinking packing job that I did with my bag. So tonight I listened to some music. I went immediately into a Ruts binge, having to play some of the songs twice. *Give Youth A Chance* was the first song I played as soon as I got the little system going. I know I listen to them too much but it's hard not to.

Believe it or not, I am still thinking about the week with the band and the show and all. It was one of the heaviest experiences of my life. I think there's still some writing to be done about the whole thing. There is one thing I screwed up massively and although it didn't impact the show, I am full of regret about it. I saw Ian in DC a few days after I had signed on for the show. He holds The Ruts in such high esteem and I didn't know if he would think it was a bad idea, treading on sacred ground, or if the whole thing was completely lame. Also, at that point, it was nothing more than this thing I had committed to, I had no real idea as to how it was going to turn out. So, I didn't tell him. Weeks after it was over and I was out of Lebanon back to America, I made a folder on the laptop and started filling it up with the pictures from the event and a long letter explaining the whole thing. When I got back to LA I put it all on a CDR and sent it to him. Days later, I got a phone call from Ian. He had read the files, checked the show on the Youtubes and thought the whole thing was really good. The part that killed me was when said that had he known about the show, he would have come out to London to check it out. Seeing how much of a one time only event it was, I felt really bad that I didn't tell him about it. I explained my reasons and he said he understood but told me that he would never think I was lame and to never think that way again. Well anyway, I felt really bad about it and still do. I should not have cut him out of at least having the option. He would have fuckin' loved that show. I am so alone in my mind that it screws up my thinking sometimes. It's too cold to write out here, my hand is going stiff. 2146 hrs.

2257 hrs. Back in the room. Have been working on 2008 broadcast stuff. I have a lot of pre-tapes to do, I have done a lot but there's still more I have to do. I am sitting in a chair with the notebook and the tunes playing and I am on my own and honestly, that's about all I can handle. I don't feel as bad as when I am alone. Too tired to write 2330 hrs.

12-27-07 Islamabad Pakistan: 1713 hrs. Really good day today. I started out by going to the Islamabad Museum for a couple of hours. There was some amazing stuff in there. Pakistan has been a very interesting place for me so far. So many cultures left their imprint on this place. The placards in the museum go quite a way to explain things where the influences came from, what century, etc. The more I read and saw, the more I wanted to know. One of the first things I read was almost funny so I copied onto the back of my ticket:

Pakistan's location in world geography has always been one of great size. A gaze at the world map will evoke memories of conquerors, invaders and heroic defenders who have shaped history. Some of them were welcomed by the local people while others were not; but this history and the realities of time past can be denied only at the peril of those who do so.

Now there's a warning I can live with. The best part of the museum was the jewelry section. The metal work was so intricate, so well done, it was amazing and so different than anything I have ever seen from western culture. The stuff I saw seemed to be made to be timeless and beautiful in any century, that was the intrinsic value of the pieces, the beauty, not the price.

Walking through the place and considering how much culture a Pakistani person is potentially aware of being a part of made me think about myself and my countrymen and somehow, I went right to the image of a Hooters and what the world must think of us. Pakistan is part of history and so is America of course but more of a brief, bloody, genocidal blip in comparison to other parts of the world. We have a lot of nerve to be telling so many other countries how to run the show. For many Americans still stuck in the Cold War mindset, if another country doesn't have our version Democracy or our military babysitters setting up bases all over their land, they are either vulnerable to the seduction of commie tyranny, Islamofacism or any number of things that are potentially threatening to America. Why so many countries are sick of this bullshit is clear to me. Imagine any foreign military having a presence in America. How many seconds do you think that would last? Why, you wouldn't be able to do an inch of meth of your daughter's tits before all hell broke loose.

Anyway, I sat outside the museum for quite awhile and enjoyed the weather, which was cooler and less humid than yesterday. The sky was clear and the air smelled good. It felt like late September on the east coast.

I got a taxi back to the hotel and got dropped off in front of the gate. I figured there was no need to go back to my room so I struck out again for a different part of the Blue Section and found a great slice of Islamabad. I walked down a long street of markets and kiosks selling all kinds of things. The food smelled great and the sidewalk and stalls were packed with people. I talked to a guy that was from here but lives in Belgium now. He had come back to visit. He was with his cousin and we walked and talked for awhile. I got back to the hotel a little later. I would like to go back to that neighborhood tomorrow.

1919 hrs. Been watching Al Jazeera and listening to the radio. Damn! Benazir Bhutto was assassinated in Rawalpindi, just down the road from here. It went down right about the time I got back here. Apparently, she was at a rally and after she spoke she left the grounds and a bomb went off near her vehicle, a man also shot at her. News reports differ as to which killed her. Early reports say she died of shrapnel wounds but now the news says that the bomber shot her and then blew himself up. On the street outside the hotel, there's been sirens, a lot of beeping and at least one gunshot. Security at the front gate has been beefed up. There's a lot of VIPs at the hotel right now. I think they are here for safety purposes. The EU Election Observation

Team is on my floor but I don't know who all these other people are. The news says that Ms. Bhutto expired at 1816 hrs. and they will return the body to her home town. 1941 hrs.

2211 hrs. Outside in the back of the hotel. Many of the people in the lobby are on their phones. Some serious private security types in the lobby and standing next to cars outside. I have been in the room watching the Al Jazeera. That's a great station. It should take the place of CNN in America immediately.

It should be interesting on the street tomorrow. I have no idea as to what the temperature will be amongst people around here but I am interested to find out. Bush issued a statement from his "ranch" in Texas but seemed annoyed to have to be speaking at the time and looked like he couldn't wait to leave the camera frame. Do a little research on how fake that ranch is and see how long he stays there after his term is over. He's not a Texan, not a cowboy, not a leader. He never misses an opportunity to make America look bad.

It's amazing to me what people derive from the information they have in front of them. People defend Bush, the invasion of Iraq and will tell you that WMDs were found in Iraq. I am sure there are people who think JFK shot himself or that his wife did it in a jealous rage because of his dalliances with Marilyn Monroe and that's why she was trying to get out of the car. People defend Enron executives.

Musharraf has put the army on red alert and they will be rolling out all over cities in Pakistan. I am around the corner from the Parliament building, apparently you can't get near that place now. The next couple of days should be interesting to say the least. 2235 hrs.

12-28-07 Islamabad Pakistan: 0039 hrs. One of the assignments I had for myself on this trip was to look over all the tour dates and other work I have planned for 2008. I have been able to devote some time to it and so far, it's looking good. It's not there yet but it's getting there. If the schedule is too lax, the work will suffer. It is only when I have bitten off more than I can chew and the schedule has attained a certain velocity and density that I can deliver. When I look at the itinerary and wonder how I am going to get through it, that's when I know it's good. I need to keep distracted from myself and suitably blurred, otherwise, life is unendurable. 0054 hrs.

2105 hrs. Today was eventful. Around 1330 hrs. I walked down Khayaban-E-Suhrawardy, the same street I was walking on yesterday. I noticed immediately that things were different. The road was almost empty of vehicles. I saw two boys walking towards me, each one had a metal pipe in his hand. I imagined how I was going to die. I was going to see my own brains leaving my head as I was beaten to death Clockwork Orange style. They looked at me and I looked back at them. They turned their attention from me to a light pole in the middle of the road, climbed up and started demolishing a large banner of some man's face. After they had mutilated that, one climbed up slightly higher and smashed out the light. I watched them for a little while and then moved on. Ahead of me, I saw columns of smoke. I was very interested to see what was happening up there. I figured it was perhaps not the wisest choice to walk towards the smoke but there was no way I wasn't going to go.

When I got to the intersection of Khaya Ban-E-Suhrawardy and Municipal Rd., I saw the source of the smoke, several tires had been set on fire. A light pole had been pulled down and was lying diagonally across the intersection. Several police dressed in protective gear were sitting casually and seemed unconcerned as boys lit tires on fire. I looked around and saw no women or girls at all, men and boys only. Many of the adult men were weeping very loudly. When one would see another he recognized, they would embrace and both of them would weep more intensely. The sun was out and it was a very nice day with lots of smoke and fire and the sound of men weeping and chanting.

I saw a car pull up and a white man and what looked like two Pakistani men get out and set up a camera on a tripod. I heard the white man speak, he sounded British. He was going to do a news drop. He lined up the shot so he had smoke, fire and chanting men in the background. He counted himself in and immediately went into an almost perfect imitation of a John Cleese character from a Monty Python routine, he was hilarious. The smoke shifted and screwed up the shot and they did another take, the smoke moved again and they did another take, the camera man kept requesting more takes for one reason or another. On one of the takes, he almost got through it and suddenly the afternoon prayer came booming out of the mosque located across the road. The audio of the prayer was killing their shot but for some reason the reporter thought he could yell over it and get by. When he started yelling over the word of Allah, all the locals standing around gave the guy such a look that he just stopped. He eventually got the shot after the prayer had finished. After he was done, I walked back down to the intersection to see what was happening. From a block away, I saw a large group of men walking towards the intersection, many of them had lengths of pipe or pieces of wood in their hands and they were chanting loudly. The camera crew saw the group of men coming, got in their car and sped off. I reckoned they knew something I didn't but I stuck around anyway. It was at this time I noticed that there were no women around, only men and boys.

Eventually, the men arrived at the intersection and joined in with the other men who were already gathered. The two groups seemed to energize each other and they started marching down the street towards the mosque. I figured the best way not to stand out was to join in so I walked into the back of the group and worked my way in. No one seemed to notice or care that I was there. The several policemen who were stationed at the intersection didn't seem to be concerned at all at the group's size or movement. Never once did I notice any violence or aggression towards me. The mood seemed to be sadness and frustration more than anything.

When the group of men got in front of the mosque, they all stopped and immediately formed shoulder-to-shoulder lines across the street. I saw that it was prayer time and I was in the middle of it. I was now going to be standing out so I started to get out of the way. I managed to get out of the line of men but had nowhere to stand except in the rolls of barbed wire in front of the mosque which snared me up very quickly. There was one moment when I thought I was going to fall over as I had to hold this stress position for the duration of the prayer. Luckily for me, it wasn't long and soon we were marching back to the intersection.

When we got to the intersection, a small part of the group split off and marched, chanting, back towards the mosque and everyone else stopped. Men hugged and shook hands and after a few minutes there were hardly any of them left at the intersection at all. The tires were now out and only ashes and the steel belts remained. The police were still sitting there and I found myself more distracted by the beautiful sunset than by what had just occurred in front of me.

As I stood on the corner, taking it all in, two men came up to me and asked me what I was doing in Islamabad. I told them I was here on vacation and they both laughed. They said there was no doubt that Musharraf was responsible for Bhutto's death. They said that under him, food prices had started to go up and people were getting very angry. They also said that he didn't listen to the people. I asked them what they thought the future of Pakistan was and when there would be elections. None of them had any idea. They thanked me for coming to Pakistan and left. Another man walked up and asked me if I was from the embassy. When I told him I was here on vacation he asked me why I came here and I told him I came all the way out just to met him and he laughed. The man told me to tell Bush not to be friends with Musharraf. "Mr. Musharraf is a terrorist!" I told him that the president didn't listen to me but I would try. He said that we must never stop trying and we shook hands on that and he walked away.

I reckoned there was nothing more to see and so I headed back towards the hotel. As I walked, I thought about the idea of not knowing where your country was going and how destabilizing that would be and then it occurred to me that was the exact situation America was in and that any speculation could only lead to dire predictions.

Now I am back at the hotel. I have the window open and I can smell the rubber burning outside so something's happening out there tonight. The experience of today is so packed into the moment, it's like time on speed or enhanced time. There was a moment when the men were walking towards the intersection chanting and pumping their sticks and pipes in the air where I could feel my heart pounding

Henry Rollins

in my throat, I felt so alive in that moment that it snapped me out of it for a second and forced me to think about it. It was like running on a treadmill that was going a little faster than I thought I could go and then seeing that I could, I acclimated. Now, I am bored. This is why I overwork and when possible, travel to places like this so I am at a good level of stress a lot of the time. Being in environments like this somewhat neutralizes the urge to check out, which I feel constantly. I do not love life. I fuckin' hate it. I think of the deaths of D. Boon and Joe Cole, that both happened in December, and everything seems without purpose. The only way I can cope is to have a constantly challenging schedule so it becomes an entity in and of itself that is trying to break me. That's always how it has been. Tours are mountains to climb, marathons to run. It becomes the thing I need to survive. This is the way I go at pretty much everything I do. I have to be in conflict with something, confronting something, going up an incline or against a current or else I don't feel life is worth it. Struggle keeps me honest. If things get too slack, all I want to do is break shit. It's why I came here. Why? Fuck it, that's why. 2223 hrs.

12-29-07 Islamabad Pakistan: 0009 hrs. Tonight I walked in the cold and thought of my hometown. I do that on nights in distant cities. I feel closer to the place when I am out here than when I am actually there. Not being there allows the imagination and the memories to run, not bound by reality or actual landmark.

When I think of where I grew up and my past, I imagine living there in a small apartment that I can't put much in and what I would do with myself every day and I come to the conclusion that I couldn't do it and then I miss my past terribly.

When I had a small space, I had few things. When my space got bigger, I put more things in it. I fill space and then look for a bigger space once I run out of room. As I have gotten older, my sadness has grown with me and takes up more space. When I was young, the city I lived in was big enough to hold the sadness and depression but now it's too small. Now, I need a place about the size of the world to live in. I need miles and miles of escape route and I know that I can never stop. Soon, I will be back in Los Angeles and I will feel like death warmed over.

Sometimes when I am back in the neighborhood I grew up in, I walk by the apartment building I lived in and look into the window of my old room and wonder what it would be like to be back in there again. It's a small room. It was a small world for me in those days. Now the world is my neighborhood and sometimes I feel that even that is not enough room. Best thing to do is keep moving and stay to myself as much as I can. 0031 hrs.

12-30-07 Rawalpindi Pakistan: 0720 hrs. At the airport. This particular airport requires a great deal of patience. The lines are long and slow. I don't know how security procedures are normally conducted here but at the moment it is very serious but only in a thorough and methodical manner. Two pat-downs before getting to the boarding area but the laptop was allowed to stay in the backpack and I didn't have to take off my shoes. I left for the airport around 0420 hrs. The streets were empty and I saw no signs that there had been anything happening on them. I am waiting for the boarding announcement so I am a little distracted.

0755 hrs.: On the plane now. More security checks just to get onboard, they're not messing around. If all goes according to plan, I will get back to LA with enough time to go to the grocery store before it closes on the 31st and will have a few days to get myself together before everything gets up and running again later in the week. I still have a lot to do to get the radio show ready for Tuesday night. I think the office opens on Wednesday and the grind resumes. Once we take off, I can get the laptop fired up and start working on all this stuff. I am starting to get that feeling of agitation that always happens when I am heading back to LA. It's like I know I am going into a trap but I'm going anyway. I don't like it but here I go. Here in Pakistan, I wasn't connected to anything or anyone and I felt like myself but knowing I am going back to LA where I plug back in and resume standard operating procedure nerves me up and makes me feel like I am failing. I will be gone again in a week and a half for quite a long time and I have much to do in the time back so I better get it all outlined. I don't want to think about it though. 0812 hrs.

1244 hrs. London Heathrow Airport: The first leg of the flight was relatively painless. I worked on the new years broadcast and I think it's going to be a great one. I worked on <u>Fanatic! Vol. 3</u> for a long time but mostly I read <u>The Shock Doctrine</u>, which gets more interesting as it goes. I am reading a section that deals with Iraq and it has connected the remaining dots and now I think I have a much better understanding of the real motivations for America going there. Put the spotlight on Paul Bremer and learn all you can. 1248 hrs.

18. How It Ends

12-31-07 LA CA: 2032 hrs. I worked on radio stuff today here at the house and at the office, unpacked, laundry, workout, that kind of thing. I didn't get much sleep and had really strange dreams. I fell out for about an hour a few hours ago and had one of the most vivid dreams I have ever had. In the dream, I was sitting where I'm sitting now, looking out the window into the backyard. I see a massive bird that looks like an owl but many times larger. Then a woman dressed in khaki, pith helmet, the whole jungle outfit, walks by the bird, looks at me and puts her finger in front of her lips like "keep quiet" and disappears. After that, the backyard fills with brightly colored birds and monkeys. It woke me up and I have not a clue what the hell it was about.

So, it's the last night of the year and I am here with nothing going on. I was out in the backyard a moment ago getting some cold air and it hit me how different the air smells at night in Islamabad than it does here. Then I came to the conclusion that I wished I was still there. I have been here for about 30 hours and I am ready to bolt. If I could fly back there tonight I would.

The IFC show is still in re-run on the Fuse Channel so I keep getting those letters. Letters about Gene Simmons more than anything, he really gets them going. I don't care. He's not killing kids in Iraq so he's really not a fish I am interested in frying. I must have said something about Christians in one of the shows because I am getting letters from individuals who got their feelings hurt about whatever it was I said. I don't care about this and cheerfully answer their letters and tell them so. They always write back, over and over. It's like they're on a crusade to make me see it their way. Can't do it. I like those kind of letters though. I like disagreement and opposing points of view. I like confrontation and argument. I like disharmony and discord. I don't like war, especially the heist happening in Iraq, but I like when someone gets all irate and explains to me how I hate America or some bullshit. It's not really anything to lose sleep over but it's good to keep the blood thin.

The older I get, the less people are part of my life. I like audiences and I like meeting those people after the show is over but I don't feel the need to be with people on a day to day basis. I really do like those small pockets of time, like the last few days in Pakistan where I knew no one and only had a room and an unfamiliar city to live in for a few days. I like the dislocation of the whole thing. A lot of it has to do with being outside of America. In a way, America is the world to me and being out of it is like being on another planet. I bet that sentiment is not unique and that many Americans feel the same way. I am not saying that America is the only place in the world, obviously it's not but if I were in the middle of nowhere in America, I would still be in America and I wouldn't be able to get that reference out of my thinking. I have been through America so many times for so many years that the entire country feels more like a state or a massive neighborhood to me. Only when I leave America do I feel I am really somewhere. It's in the somewhere that I feel like I am alive.

With whatever time I have left, I want to live in hotels here and there all over the world and just walk around and be no one in a city. In a few days I go back out on tour and am leaving a couple of days early so I can have some extra time in a city with nowhere I have to be. There will be enough work to do on those days but at least I won't have to run around. There will be a ton of that next year anyway.

I am pretty run down and depressed but I can't wait to get out there and hit stage and get working again. It's when I am working and moving and under pressure that I move at the speed of life and don't have to think about the bad stuff as much. It's times like these, when there's nothing happening, that are difficult for me.

2156 hrs. I have been sitting here, listening to music, trying to wrap up this year and get my head around what happens next. There's enough work scheduled for next year for it to feel uphill enough to make it real and keep me honest and reaching for it. I wish I had some music happening but when those feelings come around, I try to ignore them. It's frustrating to do that but I think of the reality of going out into the world with a band and it seems like it would be a waste of time and effort. When I think of that 2006 tour all I get is mad. Now and then, I get letters from one or two of the old band members and I get madder. One of them wrote me the other day when I was in Pakistan and I had to report to the gym afterwards and workout hard for over an hour to wear myself out I was so mad. That's the one thing I have going for me I reckon. I am still mad. Fuck it.